SEXUALITY AND THE U.S. CATHOLIC CHURCH

The Boston College Church in the 21st Century Series

Patricia De Leeuw and James F. Keenan, S.J.,
General Editors

Titles in this series include:

Handing On the Faith: The Church's Mission and Challenge

Priests for the 21st Century

Inculturation and the Church in North America

Take Heart: Catholic Writers on Hope in Our Time

The Church in the 21st Century Center at Boston College seeks to be a catalyst and resource for the renewal of the Catholic Church in the United States by engaging critical issues facing the Catholic community. Drawing from both the Boston College community and others, its activities currently are focused on four challenges: handing on and sharing the Catholic faith, especially with younger Catholics; fostering relationships built on mutual trust and support among lay men and women, vowed religious, deacons, priests, and bishops; developing an approach to sexuality mindful of human experience and reflective of Catholic tradition; and advancing contemporary reflection on the Catholic intellectual tradition.

SEXUALITY AND THE U.S. CATHOLIC CHURCH

Crisis and Renewal

LISA SOWLE CAHILL,
JOHN GARVEY, AND
T. FRANK KENNEDY, S.J., EDITORS

A Herder & Herder Book
The Crossroad Publishing Company
New York

The Crossroad Publishing Company
www.CrossroadPublishing.com

Printed in the United States of America

The text of this book is set in 10.5/14 Sabon.

Library of Congress Cataloging-in-Publication Data

Sexuality and the U.S. Catholic Church : crisis and renewal / edited by Lisa Cahill, T. Frank Kennedy, and John Garvey.
p. cm. – (Church in the 21st century ; v. 2)
Includes bibliographical references and index.
ISBN-13: 978-0-8245-2408-1 (alk. paper)
ISBN-10: 0-8245-2408-X (alk. paper)
1. Sex – Religious aspects – Catholic Church. 2. Catholic Church – Doctrines.
I. Cahill, Lisa Sowle. II. Kennedy, Thomas Frank. III. Garvey, John, 1944-
BX1795.S48S52 2006
241′.66088282 – dc22

2006021806

1 2 3 4 5 6 7 8 9 10 12 11 10 09 08 07 06

Contents

Introduction

In 2002, the Roman Catholic Church experienced a trauma of unprecedented proportions when a series of investigative reports in the *Boston Globe* unraveled a long string of incidents of sexual abuse of minors by priests. The Archdiocese of Boston became the epicenter of a national crisis in which hundreds of priests and several bishops were accused either of molesting minors or of enabling such activities by neglecting to report them to civil authorities, remove suspected priests from ministries providing access to children, or, in many cases, even acknowledge that abuses had occurred. Notorious Boston perpetrators were Paul Shanley and John Geoghan, both of whom eventually received lengthy jail sentences; Geoghan was murdered in prison by another offender. Before long, many cases of abuse were exposed nationally and even internationally. In 2003, after many months of resistance, Bernard Law resigned as Cardinal Archbishop of Boston, and was given a new post in Rome by the Vatican.

Many of the laity were more disappointed in or angry with episcopal leaders and Vatican spokespersons who were perceived to have denied or "covered up" such crimes than with the abusers themselves. Calls for honesty, apologies, future transparency, and reforms were frequent and loud. Many Catholics withheld financial support from dioceses and called for a more active and participatory role in the Church. Many also called for a married priesthood or the ordination of women, citing celibacy and an all-male ecclesial elite as important contributing factors to the crisis.

In fact, reports of priest sex abuse dated back to at least the 1980s, and in 1993 the national bishops' conference had begun to address the situation in earnest by establishing guidelines for every diocese in the nation. However, these guidelines were implemented unevenly, according to the preferences of local bishops. The events of 2002–3 instigated a renewed episcopal process of policy making intended to make precautionary measures more uniform, sanctions on offending priests more stringent, and the involvement of the laity in review of policy and cases more extensive.

These measures have been met with varying levels of approval and criticism. While certainly an improvement over the circumstances leading up to the sex abuse revelations, they still depend on the compliance of individual bishops for implementation. Some critics see the new policies as penalizing priests too readily or too severely in some cases, while exempting bishops from any serious consequences of their own abuses of authority.

Another line of criticism focuses on the Catholic Church's approach to sexuality. Here opinions divide between those who think a repressive attitude toward sex and women contributed to secretive and distorted sexual expressions on the part of some clergy, and others who think the Church has not been aggressive enough in enforcing authoritative sexual norms keeping all sex in marriage. The former type of critic advocates for more open discussion of human sexuality, better formation of those entering a celibate religious or priestly vocation, and the inclusion of women and gay persons in the reformulation of norms. The latter critics hold up the fact that most of the priests accused or found guilty were not true "pedophiles," but abusers of adolescent boys. They maintain that the "sexual liberation" of the 1960s and 1970s infected the Catholic mentality in ways that were later to prove disastrous, including permissiveness toward gay priests. In their view, the bishops and hierarchy should be castigated, not for insisting on an all-male priesthood isolated from cultural experiences, but for not being adamant enough in holding all Catholics and especially priests to traditional sexual expectations. The exchanges between these opposite approaches became at some points quite rancorous in the turmoil following the disclosure of so many tragic violations of children and young people. In their hurt and dismay, many Catholics looked for a simple explanation, a clear answer, and a direct road to a reformed Church of the future.

In 2002, Boston College, under the leadership of its president, William J. Leahy, S.J., began a project called "The Church in the 21st Century." The purpose of this initiative was to begin to heal the wounds in the Catholic community and build up hope for a renewed Church. The project, its executive committee, its advisory board, and its events brought together more traditional and more reformist Catholics to identify common values and goals for their Church, while encouraging respectful exchanges about points of disagreement. Expressing the role of Boston College as both Catholic and a university, "C21," as it came to be called, sponsored dozens of lectures, panels, conferences, and workshops over the next three years, bringing together different points of view, interpretations of the crisis, and agendas for the future. These events focused around the three themes of roles and authority in the Church, sexuality, and the faith of the next generation. Several events or series of events produced published volumes, of which the current book is one.

The majority of the papers here included originated at events on the Boston College campus under the aegis of the C21 Sexuality Committee in 2002–3. The co-chairs of that committee were John Garvey, Dean of the Law School; T. Frank Kennedy, S.J., Director of the Jesuit Institute; and Lisa Sowle Cahill, the J. Donald Monan Professor of Theology. Though we did not and do not see eye-to-eye on every issue, we worked together collegially and in friendship, and strove to produce a published product that might draw others into the kinds of interaction that enhance mutual understanding and clarify important aspects of disputed questions.

Our aim is not to dwell on the causes of the crisis, but to help other Catholics rethink and reclaim some wisdom from our tradition in remedying its effects. Two framing essays, by Naomi Meara and Stephen Pope, set the sex abuse crisis in the larger context of Church governance and lay involvement. Meara and Pope both offer recommendations for rebuilding trust and mutual responsibility within the Church. (These papers were originally given on one occasion, together with the paper of John Witte on celibacy.)

Two essays by young theologians, David Cloutier and William Mattison (married, with children), examine the "theology of the body" promoted by the late John Paul II. They acknowledge its wide cultural appeal, yet question whether some of its popularizers have really done justice to the hard work that marriage requires, and the limitations of sex as a way to experience the divine. Nevertheless, they suggest, any viable sexual ethic for tomorrow will have to offer young people the idealism and high standards for which they yearn. Christopher Kaczor, a philosopher (also, married, a parent, and at the beginning of his career), offers some reflections on how Catholic teachings about sex might illumine for young adults what is best and most fulfilling about marriage and parenthood. Cristina Traina, a feminist theologian, reminds readers that the relations of power operative in sexual relationships can distort what is considered moral and right, and can especially affect the agency and roles of women.

Several authors in this volume address celibacy, which came so frequently under attack in responses to the sex abuse crisis. Three of our authors are themselves religiously committed celibates, while one is a Protestant historian of law and culture. John O'Malley, S.J., offers a history of celibacy in the Catholic Church; Columba Stewart, O.S.B., a Benedictine monk, describes the challenges and rewards of monastic life; and Margaret Farley, R.S.M., takes a hard look as a feminist theologian at the opportunities and constraints celibacy offers for Catholic women. John Witte sets contemporary Catholic experiences in the context of Reformation critiques of celibacy and the reaffirmation of marriage as a Christian vocation.

Our two essays on homosexuality represent two sides of an issue that is one of the most contentious and emotionally laden in Catholic sexual ethics today. It is an issue in which many are personally invested, and on which they are politically committed. Gay marriage and the legal protection of gay unions were highly inflammatory topics during the 2004 national elections, and continue to be so, among Catholics and others. Christopher Wolfe, a professor of political science, presents what he believes to be the cogency and persuasiveness of the Catholic teaching that those with a homosexual orientation do not sin as long as they take up the challenge to live a chaste and celibate life. James Alison, a priest and theologian who has authored books on his experiences as a gay Catholic, contends to the contrary that respect for homosexual people and their personal identity demands that those in committed gay relationships be accepted by the Church and society.

The role of this book is not to settle debates, to give a hearing to every perspective on Catholics, sex, sexual morality, or clergy sexual behavior, or even to cover all the fundamental points that should go into a Catholic theology and ethics of sex. Rather, our purpose is to give voice to our continuing struggles with the human meaning of sexuality and its place in the Christian life and in society, while holding out hope for a self-critical, creative, and faithful reappropriation of Catholic values for tomorrow.

Chapter 1

Rebuilding Community

Credibility, Sensitivity, and Hope

NAOMI M. MEARA

IN THESE VERY TROUBLED TIMES for our church I believe that it is critical to engage the wisdom, fruits, and expertise of the Catholic intellectual tradition in order to focus on the multiple problems, conflicts, possibilities, and hopes of Roman Catholicism. Thus, I begin my remarks by quoting the late Richard A. McCormick, S.J., as fine a priest, scholar, theologian, and ethicist that the twentieth century or any century has known. In Chapter 3 of his book, *The Critical Calling: Reflections on Moral Dilemmas since Vatican II*, Father McCormick explicates aspects of the nature of moral argument in Christian ethics. He presents a list of "Cultural Factors Affecting the Understanding of Moral Argument in the Catholic Tradition." In this section he says: "Certainly in our time the enormous sensitivity to lived experience and the relevance of the cognate disciplines make moral argument much more complicated."[1]

These complications are ones that have been often ignored in recent years, and this neglect accounts in part, I believe, for the current crises and highlights the need for competent, scholarly conversation to be rekindled in our church and in our world. The scandal of course is sexual abuse, but the crises and its causes (and they are plural in my judgment) focus on loss of faith and hope in the institution and the hierarchy. These losses are occasioned by (a) misunderstanding of the nature and uses of authority, power, and privilege particularly on the part of the bishops and those who have appointed them, (b) unwillingness to engage intellectually with the modern world and its scholarly disciplines, particularly the natural and social sciences, and (c) lack of emotional closeness, basic empathy, or a generous and compassionate spirit in relating to the ordinary experiences of human beings. These human beings are the people of God who look to the church for sanity and hope, and whom the church is pledged to serve. This loss of faith and hope in the institutional church and its hierarchy can be characterized as failures of community at the professional, intellectual, and emotional levels.

Stripped of its ecclesiastical trappings and institutional structures our church could be described as Sacrament, Word, and Community. I leave it to the theologians to assume leadership in debate, explication, and interaction with the magisterium and the faithful on matters of Sacrament and Word, matters that need to be addressed. In matters of Community, however, psychologists and social scientists have something to offer. For instance, I believe in-depth awareness of the (a) proper exercise of the responsibilities of professional life, (b) contributions of natural sciences, social sciences, and other disciplines (maybe especially psychology) to greater understanding of the human condition, and (c) emotional tenor of lived experiences of everyday life have much to offer the church in creating, re-creating, and understanding the dynamics of professionally sound, intellectually vigorous, and affectively sensitive communities. Such awareness could help us to restore a community of believers that is credible and sensitive and that is sustained by and inspires (in each other and in all whom they meet) hope, holiness, kindness, and care.

Professional Community

It seems safe to say that the institutional Roman Catholic Church is built on a hierarchical model; and, despite documents on collegiality from Vatican II, power, privilege, and authority are centralized. The further one rises in the hierarchy, the more power one has. As one rises in such a system (e.g., in the church as priest, pastor, bishop or in the academy as department chair, dean, provost), there is a temptation to exercise authority with less and less consultation. One has the "legitimate" power to do so, and it can also be more efficient. Thus professionals have to be vigilant in such a structure to ensure they properly exercise their fiduciary responsibilities. I am not arguing here for a structural change (although I am not precluding discussion of that or anything that would help us), but rather for now I am arguing for a proper exercise of professional responsibilities (of one's vocation if you will) within this structure, an exercise of responsibilities informed by professional ethics, canons of academic or intellectual discourse, data from the social sciences about individual and group behaviors, and a recognition of the moral significance of the emotional experiences of ordinary persons in everyday life.

Most professionals and those they serve believe that the "language of ethics not just the logic of commerce"[2] or the ambitions of self ultimately guides or should guide the professional and personal interactions of those who bear such titles as priest, lawyer, physician, or professor. Church leaders are professionals and can be aided in fulfilling these ethical responsibilities to the community more credibly and sensitively by conversing with and studying how professionals in other callings (e.g., professors, physicians, or lawyers) see their obligations, and are enjoined to treat others by their codes of ethics.[3]

As an example of how the experiences of other professions might be helpful to the church, I suggest that we could begin with some thoughts about how recent commentators have viewed the role of virtue ethics in enriching our understanding of applied professional ethics. Several (e.g., Drane, Bennett, Meara, and Day) have maintained that the purposes, practices, and roles of a profession determine its needed virtues.[4] For example, Drane states that the primary role of physicians is to heal; therefore their primary virtue should be compassion. Bennett views the primary goal of the academy as advancing learning and knowledge through discourse. From his perspective essential virtues to reach this goal are hospitality and thoughtfulness, which he describes as both intellectual and ethical in nature. Hospitality "is the willingness to consider, acknowledge and attend to the strange and the new as well as to reassess the old and the familiar." Hospitality implies generosity and goodwill. Thoughtfulness, the other virtue he identifies as essential to realizing the goals of the academy, embodies judicious evaluation and sensitivity to others. That is, a thoughtful person is both reflective with respect to ideas and considerate with respect to others.

Elsewhere I have stated that I believe that the situations of church leaders are analogous to those of other trusted professions.[5] In fact, the expectations and implied community contracts that attend authority, power, and privilege are especially pronounced for women and men of the church who claim to serve the Will of God among us, and to proscribe for us mores of conduct that encompass every aspect of our human existence. Thus, I argued that the primary mission of church leadership includes inspiring us (i.e., the community of all of us,[6] i.e., episcopal leaders, clerics, religious, and laity) to be a spiritual, holy, and hopeful people, and guiding us to care for one another by enabling us to bring love and kindness to our personal relationships, and to work for peace and justice in the world. In short, the primary mission of the hierarchy is to inspire holiness and to foster care. To pursue this mission the church needs persons of integrity, who understand authority as a relational construct, focused on "authoring" spiritual growth or other goods.[7] Finally, I asserted that the episcopacy and the institutional church needed to be marked by virtues of prudence, respectfulness, compassion, and humility.

These arguments are meant to invoke (inspirational and substantive) conversation about the links between mission and professional or vocational conduct. Besides their understanding of professional ethics, psychologists and other social scientists can bring empirical data to the conversations about such things as the damaging effects of violations of professional boundaries,[8] overidentification with or excessive internalization of assigned roles, and the positive effects of appropriate and encouraging role models with whom others can identify.[9] For example, thirty years ago Phillip Zimbardo and his colleagues conducted what came to be known as the Stanford Prison Experiment.[10] The general proposition being investigated in this work was how an immediate situation (role internalization) can override personality traits or dispositions generally considered to be determinants of behavior. The researchers (and the psychological world) were totally unprepared for how much support this "situational hypothesis" garnered. College students, who volunteered for the project and who knew what it entailed, completed a battery of psychological tests to verify (as best as we can measure it) that they were psychologically healthy. Then they were randomly assigned as a prisoner or a guard for a two-week period to Stanford Prison (basement of the psychology building). Within six days the researchers had to terminate the project; the prisoners either suffered "acute psychological traumas or breakdowns" or became blindly obedient to the demands of the guards. Many of the guards broke the rules and began mistreating the prisoners, and were indifferent to the harm they caused; guards who did not participate in the mistreatment did nothing to stop it. The significance and ethics of this study have been much discussed among psychologists and policymakers.[11] Issues of power are part of abuse; and yet, society and church have been slow to recognize the dynamics and devastation of child abuse. Now, however, many are trying to remedy these deficits. Psychology can help because it has expertise and data the church needs about: (a) mature and healthy sexuality, (b) those who abuse, (c) their victims, and (d) lasting damages that can result from sexual violation of professional boundaries.[12]

Intellectual Community

The Roman Catholic Church has a rich intellectual tradition, has been a leader in education in the early years of our Republic, and has prided itself on the integration of faith and reason. We need to recapture this legacy, as in recent times conversations between hierarchy and academy (including distinguished academic theologians) have not been characterized as much as they might have been by thoughtful, spirited debate or heuristic dialogue about the integration of faith, reason, the contemporary world, and the Catholic tradition. In addition, there is not much acknowledgment of how scholars from the social and biological sciences or other disciplines might contribute to the revitalization of the church's moral and intellectual discourse. I worry that this seeming unwillingness to engage intellectually with the sciences is part of a broader uneasiness between church and academy, or the church and the life of the mind. Although these issues have been raised before,[13] such uneasiness still seems ironic since for many years the church has often been the protector of the intellectual life.[14] In addition, the church has appropriately criticized many aspects of our modern culture, but seems to be in danger of joining in with one of its greatest deficits: anti-intellectualism. One example suffices. Not only is the reserving of priestly ordination to men alone "to be definitively held by all the Church's faithful,"[15] it has been declared by the Congregation for the Doctrine of the Faith "to have been set forth infallibly by the ordinary and universal magisterium,"[16] and is not to be considered "open to debate."[17]

I think the models from the academy and academic psychology can assist the church in rejuvenating the intellectual vibrancy of thought and conversation among its community of believers, and in restoring to prominence its intellectual traditions. I start by reiterating a motto of the Dominicans: *contemplare et contemplata aliis tradere,* to contemplate and to share the fruits of that contemplation with others. This can be construed in part at least as a call to serious conversation, and is consonant with Bennett's view (presented above) that the major goal of the academy is to advance learning and knowledge through discourse.[18] In the same vein Meara and Day have asserted that the particular charge of the academy is to generate and interpret knowledge; and they go on to point out that this responsibility creates an uncertain, yet intellectually exciting ambience that underscores the importance of credibility and sensitivity for professor-scholars.[19] Meara and Day also note some unique features of psychology and special ethical commitments of psychologists. Two of these features of the discipline seem relevant to what we are about here: (a) the personal and uncertain nature of psychological knowledge, and (b) the interpretative and schematic aspects of psychological research, instruction, application, and advocacy. The ethical commitments for psychologists include (a) increasing "peoples' understanding of themselves," and (b) using psychological knowledge "to improve the condition of individuals, organizations, and society."[20]

What non-psychologists or non-social scientists might see as weaknesses or indeterminate science (uncertainty, individual differences, or variability in the data) can be strengths and can be of assistance in restoring and fortifying an intellectually rigorous Roman Catholic community. Uncertainty invites conversation, conversation that is interpretative, and open to multiple perspectives and possibilities, or in Bennett's terms, hospitable.[21] Faith, a conviction of the heart, is at root an intellectual commitment, built upon uncertainty and in need of Community (as well as Sacrament and Word) to sustain it. For most, this Community needs to make intellectual sense in addition to providing emotional support and social cohesion.

In recent years the discipline of psychology has thrived on (and made important contributions to society by) researching, "reconciling," developing, and interpreting ideas from different theoretical perspectives. For example, principles of behaviorism have enabled the development of reward structures that have been used to teach developmentally disabled children important life skills;[22] meta-cognitive strategies have facilitated the teaching of how to learn;[23] and psychoanalytic conceptualizations have assisted therapists in understanding personality development, internal motivations, and potentially self-destructive or self-enhancing behaviors of their clients.[24]

Of the many perspectives and contributions that psychology may have to offer the conversations of the Roman Catholic Community, I focus here on the perspectives and alternate worldviews developed by feminists. Although there is coherence, feminism is not one viewpoint, nor is feminism from psychology's perspective one voice.[25] Rather psychologists who are feminists examine the psychological consequences of taken-for-granted structures about how the world "ought" to work, its distribution of power and its allocations of other burdens and benefits. They also imagine, research, and advocate alternative patterns of societal organization and interpersonal interaction that promote psychological health, emotional well-being, social justice, and constructive opportunities for individuals, organizations, and the society. Feminist analyses have had profound effects on all of psychological knowledge, its applications, and in its public policy initiatives. Feminist researchers, thinkers, and commentators engage in these activities to seek justice and care for all of whatever gender, race, ethnicity, class, sexual orientation, religion, national origin, or the like. For example, in reexamining private and public roles for women and men, feminist researchers and advocates have increased opportunities for both sexes in work and family life. One example seems particularly salient: the research and scholarly inquiry on fatherhood.[26] This rich and growing literature is complex (as race, culture, socioeconomic status, individual differences, and methodological challenges temper broad generalizations); nonetheless, it has presented us with many images of constructive fatherhood,[27] clear evidence of the positive effects on children of psychologically and emotionally mature and satisfying relationships between father and mother.[28] Further it has demonstrated that following divorce single resident fathers are as competent as single resident mothers in child-rearing.[29] And it has established that pre-school children of accessible and substantially positively engaged fathers exhibit more cognitive competence, internal locus of control and empathy, and less gender role stereotyping.[30] These qualities would seem constructive in later life for building close relationships, raising children, participating in church life, succeeding in the world of work, and exercising responsible citizenship in a democracy.

Emotional Community

A community can develop close emotional bonds and empathy among members if they share common experiences and goals. Such bonds can lead to compassion in understanding the lived experiences of everyday life. Those one is attracted to or identifies with are a source of emotional closeness, support, and influence.[31]

Psychologists have studied myriad aspects of bonding (e.g., intimacy, commitment, and passion in romantic relationships, attachment styles and their effects on parent-child and later adult relationships; qualities and procedures for building therapeutic alliances). One of the themes that could encompass much of this research (and other research like it) is the psychological powerfulness and personal meaningfulness of the affective security (and general sense of well-being) that emotional closeness (including that which accompanies healthy sexual intimacy) provides; and the devastating effects that acts (perceived and actual) of betrayal, disrespect, or disloyalty have on that security, well-being, and individual feelings of self-worth. Structural change, improved professional behavior, and intellectual understanding can be helpful in explaining and perhaps preventing future community estrangement or alienation. However, emotional injuries can only be repaired (forgiveness and compassion offered and understood) if the parties involved have the affective competence and empathy to acknowledge not only how their actions can be construed, but also how much anger and hurt a betrayal causes particularly in those who have been loyal and faithful to the relationship.

Research related to perceived control and vulnerable populations (e.g., those with less power such as children, elderly, medical patients, low-status employees) indicates that those who perceive they have more control have better emotional health and better coping strategies.[32] Young children often do not have control, but they can often identify with or become attached to attractive role models who are very influential[33] and thus by definition more powerful. Certainly in Western culture, roles and various representations of father are extremely powerful voices, influences, and images in everyday experience as well as in art, literature, psychology, and religion. Thus the psychodynamic complications that have ensued from this scandal of our church and that will linger long after the headlines fade cannot be overestimated because those who have committed so many acts of betrayal (i.e., both direct acts of abuse and apparent lack of commitment to stop them) came to vulnerable individuals ("their daughters and sons") in the protective garments of beloved, powerful, protective, and responsible father. As Henry Abramovitch notes, "the reconciliation between father and child is one of the fundamental projects in a person's life."[34] As we rebuild the Roman Catholic community, psychological research that is conducted in the field (as opposed to the laboratory) can provide all of us with a more sophisticated understanding of the complexities and relationships of power, attraction, affective bonds, and psychosexual maturity. Applying this knowledge as we live with and listen to the voices of countless faithful who live ordinary lives can enable all of us (particularly those of us who have power) to understand better the consequences of what we do (and who we are) in relationship with others. Such living and listening can also allow us to be more compassionate and generous of spirit in our moral judgments and interpersonal interactions.

Common Ground

I have suggested that psychology and the social sciences have much to offer in re-creating and enhancing (professionally, intellectually, and emotionally) a credible, sensitive, and hopeful Roman Catholic community. I have further suggested that assistance can come from (a) modeling how other professions (e.g., professors and physicians) enact their ethical professional-vocational responsibilities, (b) engaging with other disciplines in thoughtful, intellectual conversations to rekindle moral discourse, and (c) developing a generous, emphatic, compassionate spirit in understanding the significance of the lived experiences and emotional lives of ordinary individuals.

Before he died, Joseph Cardinal Bernardin (1928–96), Archbishop of Chicago, began the Catholic Common Ground Initiative to encourage dialogue among all members of the church (episcopacy, clergy, religious, laity) on issues confronting it.[35] These issues included such things as changing roles of women, Eucharistic liturgy, sexuality, responsibility to the poor, cultural diversity, and church governance. These are precisely the matters, referring to Richard McCormick's point with which we began this discussion, that "make moral argument much more complicated"[36] and whose neglect brought us to this scandal. Although the cardinal's initiative was rebuffed in public by his fellow bishops,[37] I propose, in the spirit of what this good and holy man had hoped for our church, that there already is common ground between what psychology can offer, and what theologians and other church leaders have advocated over the last thirty years. We should build upon this common ground. Father McCormick of course supports inclusive continuing moral analysis and discourse with all its complications, and the theologian Stephen Pope has engaged the natural and social sciences in intellectual discourse; note, for example, his recent work on human evolution and moral responsibility.[38] The theologian Catherine Mowry LaCugna in her seminal work on the Trinity expresses the importance of right relationships (to others, God, ourselves) and the fullness of humanity in glorifying God.[39] Community is the responsibility of all of us; the hierarchy does not need to bear the burden themselves. If they are open to right relationships with the rest of us, they can find the presence of the Spirit as well as intellectual meaning, emotional support, and social cohesion in the companionship of ordinary members of the faithful.

Historically, it has not simply been academic theologians who can find common ground with the ideas presented here. For example, in the early 1970s the Catholic Bishops Conference supported psychological investigations of the priesthood by psychologists.[40] The underlying theoretical orientation used to study these men was Erikson's stages of psychosocial development, and a number of the conclusions from the report of these investigations seem as salient today as they were then. Briefly, the priests they studied were seen as ordinary men: intelligent, able, and dedicated, but who were not fully developed as persons. The remedy suggested for this lack of development was to encourage the priests in more meaningful participation in life itself, and to become more fully responsible for themselves and their vocations.

Significantly, common ground is also easy to find in the work of the Dominican feminist theologian Mary Catherine Hilkert. Her extraordinary treatise on the life, work, and charisms of Catherine of Siena parallels the arguments being made here.[41] She suggests that like Catherine we are all gifted by the spirit to speak with authority by virtue of (a) our vocations as baptized persons, (b) wisdom that comes from contemplation and dialog, and (c) compassion born of our own trials that puts us in communion with those who care and those who weep. Finally, there is no community without flaws; we must discern them, and we must find ways to go beyond them. I am optimistic about our possibilities for we are a Resurrection community whose faith and love are built on hope.

Chapter 2

Heaven Is a Place on Earth?

Analyzing the Popularity of Pope John Paul II's Theology of the Body

DAVID CLOUTIER

SEXUALITY IN OUR CULTURE raises more questions than answers. Each episode of the cultural flashpoint TV series *Sex and the City* is built around a question that main character, journalist Carrie Bradshaw, types into her stylish laptop. Far from reflecting certainty, Carrie's character embodies the uncertainty that pervades the lives of twenty- and thirty-somethings as they attempt to negotiate the multiple options, directions, and experiences of their sexual lives. While the questions vary, most of them reflect an underlying question: "I couldn't help but wonder.... Do the central sexual myths of our culture match up to reality, particularly the reality of our true desires?" That is to say, the questions are posed not simply to cultural narratives, but also more deeply to our own internal desires, the question of what we really want. The series is not a simple paean to sexual liberation and freedom, but instead captures the tension between the undeniable pleasures of this freedom and the wondering about (and the occasional experience of) something more meaningful, real, and authentic.

The cultural success of John Paul II's Theology of the Body, while certainly more modest, is nevertheless striking, and raises real and important questions for Catholic theologians thinking about the topic of sex. Any item given coverage by the *New York Times* officially qualifies as a cultural phenomenon, right?[1] I want to argue in this paper that the success of the Theology of the Body has a great deal to do with the way it responds to the same plausibility structure — the same naming of experience — which makes *Sex and the City* successful. I will contrast this structure with some other theological attempts to generate a positive sexual ethic. The Theology of the Body recognizes and effectively narrates the central problem in the "relationship marketplace" of today: the way in which we instrumentalize others, rather than loving them.

Whereas other sexual ethics appeal to justice and reciprocity in relationships as the key for sexual behavior, the Theology of the Body appeals to authenticity. Expanding on an idea developed by Charles Taylor, I will suggest that authenticity is a hallmark of contemporary culture's ethical discernment about sex, and the Theology of the Body offers a renarration of what authentic relationships mean. On the other hand, the Theology of the Body's extraordinarily romanticized view of self-giving, a central part of its appeal, also raises certain questions which it will have to confront, and these questions may prove fruitful ground for continued theological development of a Catholic sexual ethic.

Some of the raw material for this study is found in a series of interviews I conducted with undergraduates and young adults who have encountered and been attracted to the Theology of the Body.[2] The study should be considered nothing more than anecdotal — a theological reading of a series of conversations, which offer some insight into how the Theology of the Body is viewed and where its appeal lies. I need to contexualize this commentary before I begin. There is substantial controversy in the literature over whether "younger Catholics" are in fact becoming "more conservative."[3] This debate can't be settled here; I am merely positioning the people who are talking about theology of the body. By and large, these young adults are quite ordinary, normal, social people, who are just as much at ease criticizing "old men in Rome" and talking about sex as everyone else around them. Yet they all obviously bring a very intentional (and intellect-driven) desire to embrace their Catholic faith and really make it defining of their identity. They are certainly not the majority of my Catholic students, but they do tend to be the ones who lead

Catholic student groups, do campus ministry, go on alternative spring break trips, and end up as theology majors.

The Appeal: Contrasting Narratives of Experience

An initial point cited by *all* my Lake Wobegon area interviewees provides a place to start. The Theology of the Body, interviewees said, presented sexual ethics not as a set of "fear-based prohibitions," but rather as an inviting call to sexual fulfillment. One young female student said she found the theology so "liberating," because it was "not rules, but instead this beautiful plan God has for you." Another said that the "rules" always came across as "a bunch of prudish prohibitions from celibate white males," but the Theology of the Body looks at how sexuality is "liberating" and "appealing."[4] Certainly a crucial characteristic of the Theology of the Body is its almost astonishingly positive reading of the potential of human sexuality. The Theology of the Body agrees with several generations of Catholic moral theologians who have critiqued the tradition for its legalism, and, by contrast, seek to offer a more positive way.

Anyone who has taught young people today knows that simple prohibitions, based on appeals to authority, can no longer work. As I have argued elsewhere, this phenomenon of questioning church teachings is not properly read as an embrace of the "dictatorship of relativism," but rather a good desire to understand why certain actions are good and others not good.[5] Students show a desire (shared by my own generation) to understand, or even be convinced, rather than blindly following.

Yet, when all of the traditional norms of sexual ethics come through this new story intact, the whole package remains appealing. Why? I want to argue initially that the Theology of the Body remains attractive because its appeal to *experience* is particularly effective for members of the under-forty generation. Several writers have commented on the importance of personal experience for younger people, particularly in their understanding of religion and of sexuality.[6] Because younger people have grown up and matured in a world where pluralism is taken for granted, and where there is no dominant religious or moral consensus, experience "is treated as a straightforward and universal category and is used frequently without any attempt to discern its structures, its history or its potential."[7] When wondering about who to believe or which way to go, personal experience seems like the most unassailable guide.

However, as we are aware in our postmodern era, all experience needs narration; no experience comes without attempts, before and after, to fit it into available stories or categories.[8] Thus, when ethics consists of storytelling, rather than mere deductive argument, we cannot understand it simply in terms of dissecting the arguments. Rather, we have to look at *why* the story is perceived as truthfully narrating the world and one's own experience. A story is not simply logical or illogical; instead, it needs to be *compelling*.

In order to illustrate what makes a story compelling, it is helpful to contrast it with other stories, which attempt to narrate similar kinds of experience. In particular, the Theology of the Body is usefully compared to revisionist sexual ethics of the previous generation, since it is consonant with their attempts to develop a more positive picture of human sexuality, but is contextualized in quite a different way. A number of books might be used; I will draw on Joan Timmerman's *The Mardi Gras Syndrome*, which I think lucidly and accessibly reflects much revisionist sexual ethics in the 1970s and 1980s that sought to develop a positive view of human sexuality.

Timmerman's basic starting point is the concept of sacramentality. As she puts it, "Human sexuality participates in the sacred; it is capable of revealing God and God's action in human life, and of transforming human existence from an isolated and disconnected experience to one of unity and ecstasy."[9] While this idea of sacramentality is central to Catholic tradition, the tradition's thinking on sex has been clouded by a dualistic view of reality, in which the avoidance of the body is seen as the way to the sacred. Timmerman decries the resulting "impoverishment of the spiritual life of the laity" when sex and married life are disconnected from "the life of union with God."[10]

The Theology of the Body argues the same. If anything, it is even more enthusiastic in its intentions to connect sex to the sacred. Peppered throughout Theology of the Body Web sites and talks is the fundamental insight: "the human body reveals God."[11] Or as Christopher West, the primary American popularizer of the pope's theology, puts it in rejecting dualism, "Christianity says, 'The body is so good you can't even fathom it.' "[12] Sex and marriage are not simply connected to "the life of union with God," but rather are the "least inadequate analogy" for reflecting God's own inner life and God's communion with the world. Says West, "God wants to marry us."[13]

This sort of thickly theological narration of sexuality is a major aspect of the Theology of the Body's appeal. It was noted by nearly all of my interviewees. One indicated that "it all made sense" because of the Theology of the Body—and by this, she did not simply mean the traditional sexual teachings, but rather "everything," beliefs about God and Christ and the Trinity and God's love. Another student noted how she now saw birth control not as an issue of individual acts, but part of a "bigger picture" in which she now could see "how it all fits."[14] For young people, the recognition that their beliefs have this kind of "cash value" in practice is always striking, especially in light of chronic reports of poor or nonexistent formation in the church today.[15]

However, one of the most common critiques of the Theology of the Body is exactly this theological abstractness.[16] While this is partially overcome by West's very engaging and concrete presentation, is this sufficient to counter the criticism that the Theology of the Body does not in fact mesh with the experience of real people?

But *whose* experience? Here I think we come to the crucial point. Appeals to experience are not common in the history of Catholic sexual ethics, and the problem of starting to make them is that people inevitably differ. However, we can make sense of *their* making sense of experience by recognizing the "plausibility structures" set up by these two works, the ways in which they rely on certain head-nodding explanations of common experiences in order to draw listeners into the whole picture.[17] Attending to the plausibility structures constructed in support of appeals to experience helps to make sense of why such appeals work or do not work.

Timmerman's plausibility structure is exemplified in her title, which draws from references in medieval handbooks advising against sex on most days of the week, for various theological reasons — for example, no sex on Saturday so as to honor Mary. She jokes that their "Thank God It's Tuesday" celebrations must have been greater than any Friday night revelry we now have! For generations of Catholics raised in the pre-Vatican II church (not to mention in the middle-class mores of the 1950s and before), these medieval handbooks resonated with their experience of the church as an institution which built elaborate hedges around anything sexual.[18] The images are particularly resonant for women. Timmerman mines this perspective of fear and loathing quite deeply into the tradition, even beyond the standard explanation of "Greek" contamination, right back into the New Testament and later Old Testament writings, such that little if any of the tradition can be regarded as a plausible source for wisdom.[19]

Catholics raised after Vatican II, by contrast, are not likely to read the medieval prohibitions as reflective of their own experience. Indeed, they are likely to read them as they would strange cultural taboos from a very foreign place and time. The vast majority have experienced the church's teachings (if presented at all) as offered in a slightly embarrassed and apologetic tone, and they have subsequently looked around at the adults in their church, including their own parents, and concluded that no one in fact takes these matters seriously. Thus, many dismiss them easily as a quaint archaism — for us, dissent comes easily — or perhaps (as some students put it) as analogous to speed limits: you don't have to follow them *exactly,* but they keep things from getting out of hand. Thus, they will not relate to the medieval handbooks or to the *Baltimore Catechism.*

Without this plausibility structure, Timmerman's constructive and liberatory case threatens to become no big deal, saying nothing that common cultural narratives don't already say. Sex as involving personal awakening and individual empowerment is not a struggle most young Catholics face today. While she several times criticizes sexual hedonism as a false and profaning understanding of the sacred reality of sex, her references are passing, as if to say to her readers, "well, all of us know that I don't mean *that,* we don't even find that attractive," and they move on. Her audience is not persons tempted by sexual hedonism, but those suffocated by the traditional teachings, leaving them hurt, confused, and lost. The "threat" against which the book is written is the suffocating tradition, not the hedonistic elements of the culture.

The Theology of the Body does an interesting flip of this picture. Its *passing* critique is of the "thou shalt nots" we grew up with (as if to say, "none of us bought that legalistic stuff, did we?"), and its much more *sustained* critique is of the larger culture. What does this reflect? Unlike the previous generation, the strongest narrative influencing the formation of younger people's asexual sensibilities was not the church, but rather the many and various stories of the culture. Hence, the success of the critique will not hang on assailing (yet ultimately saving) the plausibility structures of the Catholic tradition, but rather those of the dominant culture.

In this sense, the pope's theology needed someone like Christopher West. West, in his presentation, trades heavily on confessions of his own past, and the way he narrates that past (and through it, the cultural reality) is one of the most interesting aspects of the Theology of the Body-as-public-phenomenon. West is no Augustine, making sonorous and painful laments over his sins, but rather a truth-teller who explains how we have been *duped* by the culture. Hence, it is a complex sort of critique — explicitly anti-culture at times, but yet with a constant sense that the cultural narrative is groping toward a certain reality. It is, of course, a critique that understands the uncertainty of *Sex in the City* perfectly. West often uses the image of the counterfeit $100 bill in referring to the culture: it's not wrong to find it appealing, but it is necessary to recognize that it is *not* the real thing. Such a critique is not only very plausible to those who have in fact been trading in counterfeit sexual currency, left with a feeling not of guilt but of emptiness, but also to those who have not been but want to understand all the people around them who are. As one student put it, the Theology of the Body "also makes me realize that the people here who live unchastely aren't bad people; they've just bought into the 'dumpster' of today's society. I'm in no way worthy of judging them, but I am called to help them see the goods they are disregarding."

The Theology of the Body is easy to misread in this regard. It is not simply a trashing of a hedonistic culture. If it were, it would not mark any sort of decisive development in Catholic teaching! Indeed, West's own "exploits" do not exactly qualify for much of a steamy movie; on the contrary, his stories are not really about *promiscuity.* Rather, the problem in the culture is selfishness, an *instrumentalization* of relationships — a problem that might be seen in a one-night stand *or* a long-term college relationship. In either case, "the dumpster" involves looking at another person as something for your own use, pleasure, and manipulation — looking at a given relationship primarily or exclusively in terms of benefits to self.[20] A young woman indicated that the Theology of the Body had instant appeal because it portrayed genuine relations as "NOT about 'what can you do for me?'" Another student encountered her roommate in tears about a fight with her boyfriend, and she was able to say, "This is what JP2's logic says about your boyfriend." The problem of the culture is revealed not as hedonism as much as an inability to love in a truly self-giving way.

Other writings confirm this narrative. In her study of a sampling of young Catholics who are embracing the faith, Colleen Carroll explains that, in sexuality, these young Catholics are not fighting for "sexual liberation," but for "stability" and "respect."[21] Both in the world around them and in their own experiences, young people, particularly in college and beyond, will have already had experience with intense, interpersonal relationships — and often enough, their loss. William Sneck refers to this phenomenon as "premarital divorce," and the term is not inappropriate, since many of these relationships function as quasi-marriages — they involve daily sexual intimacy (even if not actual intercourse), they involve doing a variety of daily activities together very regularly (eating, shopping, etc.), and they ordinarily advertise an emotional intimacy and availability that is thought to be higher and more sacred than friendships.[22] When these relationships fail, there is often the same sense of confusion, loss, and hurt that is virtually inevitable in divorce. Young people who avoid quasi-marriages, on the other hand, live in a world where people are quite up-front about the instrumental character of the relationships going on. And, sadly, quasi-marriages often involve unequal levels of commitment and unspoken motivations which result in a great deal of hurt. In any of these scenarios, young people are inevitably going to be exposed to a sort of violence (for want of a better word), the experience of the destruction and loss of a relationship which (at least for a while) likely seemed very "real." At some level, all nonmarital romantic relationships (and likely many marital ones!) involve a greater or lesser degree of instrumentalization, since there is a necessary level of noncommitment and ambiguity built in. While most would agree that these relationships involve much that is good, even beautiful, the fact that they end is seldom a happy experience.[23]

Thus, the Theology of the Body comes across as far less naïve than Timmerman and many other works by Catholic authors of that era. In these texts, it is rather easily assumed that we can sort out what constitutes a "loving" context for sexual acts from one that is destructive. Timmerman herself cites masturbation, loving homosexual relationships, regular contraceptive use, long-term relationships between twenty-somethings, and second marriages as potentially good, indicating that these are readily distinguishable from rape, bestiality, incest, teenage sex, and pornography.[24] But selfishness — in sexual terms, the Theology of the Body almost always uses "lust" — can pervade any sort of sexual relationship, including a marriage, but perhaps especially apparently successful and mutually beneficial "long-term relationships," the hallmark of the twenty-something culture of today. The problem with these contractual, "reasonable" relationships, according to the Theology of the Body, is not that they are entirely bad, but that they are counterfeit goods, and that they ultimately lead to emptiness, not real communion.

The Ideal: Authenticity

We can see here that the ethical categories of the Theology of the Body differ from those of other sexual ethics. Instead of a good/bad dichotomy, sustained either by laws or (as in Timmerman) by appeals to justice and reciprocity, the Theology of the Body trades on the categories of real/counterfeit.[25] What the Theology of the Body offers is a theology that contrasts the authentic meanings of human sexuality with the tempting-but-empty counterfeit forms offered by the wider culture (and by the church's past). The notion of authenticity is, as Charles Taylor has argued, a very compelling ethical foothold in a culture where other, more classic forms of moral argument are in doubt. Taylor criticizes various aspects of contemporary culture, including "the primacy of instrumental reason,"[26] but then separates himself from social critics such as Christopher Lasch and Allan Bloom, who go on to paint the entire culture in terms of narcissism and selfishness. Rather, the modern desire for self-fulfillment contains a kernel of a "moral ideal"—namely the ideal of authenticity—and if people can be made to reflect on this ideal in a more disciplined way, there is some hope for resisting instrumental reason and individualism. In the aforementioned *New York Times* article, one of West's quotes is: "It's an invitation to the joy of authentic love."[27] As one of my interviewees put it, "who would not want to love and be loved as he describes?"

Another example, a sort of countervoice to Joan Timmerman, might flesh this out a bit. Lauren Winner, a hip young Episcopalian evangelical in a doctoral program whose spiritual autobiography, *Girl Meets God,* attracted a good deal of attention, has a new book on sex which exemplifies this generational focus on authenticity. In contrast to Timmerman's title, which focuses on recovering the joy and pleasure of sexual love from the fences of the tradition, Winner titles her book *Real Sex: The Naked Truth about Chastity.* At one point early on, she makes a key comparison: "Indeed, one can say that in Christianity's vocabulary the only real sex is the sex that happens in a marriage; the faux sex that goes on outside marriage is not really sex at all. The physical coming together that happens between two people who are not married is only a distorted imitation of sex, as Walt Disney's Wilderness Lodge Resort is only a simulation of real wilderness. The danger is that when we spend too much time in the simulations, we lose the capacity to distinguish between the ersatz and the real."[28] Winner, no fresh-faced evangelical virgin herself, is not naïve about the real pleasure and even goodness that is felt in nonmarital sex. She harshly criticizes Christians who scare young people off from sex by telling them they will feel badly. Rather, she says, "premarital sex is bad for us, even if it happens to feel great." Why? Not because sex is bad, but because "we are, after a fashion, sleepwalkers going through our routines, eyes closed to reality as it really is."[29]

It is notable how these claims work analogically like claims about food. No one here, I hope, would claim that we live in a culture that glorifies real, authentic food. Surely we do not. Yet I confess that whenever yellow cake with chocolate frosting arrives on the scene, the experience of eating it is great. Is yellow cake going to make me immediately unhealthy? No. Will it taste bad? Definitely not. But is it real food? Well, no, not really. The constant consumption of highly processed foods shapes us to come to prefer the processed food to real food; analogously, a preference for sex stripped of the context of total interpersonal commitment, community responsibilities, and procreation may very well be a tasty treat, but it can easily come to seem more enjoyable than the "full meal" of marital sex. After all, processed food (like nonmarital sex) is so much easier and more convenient.

In summary, the plausibility structures for claims about sex have changed for those under forty. The sexual ethics of the immediate post-Vatican II generation were (rightly) concerned about problems of access. But for this new generation, *access* to sex, or a sort of liberation to discover and explore one's sexuality, is simply not a concern.[30] The problem is instead, in the bewildering variety of sexual practices available to us, which ones are truly human, genuine, authentic, "the real thing"?

The Challenge: Loving Broken Bodies

By effectively narrating the experience of the world today, particularly the instrumentalization of human relationships and the longing for authenticity, I think the Theology of the Body provides clear cues for theologians working in Catholic sexual ethics. However, on these very terms, the Theology of the Body's widespread use in the church faces a crucial challenge.

One might call this challenge the *Titanic* problem. West uses, and one interviewee cited, a study of young girls who went to see the movie *Titanic* nine to ten times, because they found the overwhelming beauty of the love story so compelling. But none of us are naïve about the problem with "movie love." Donna Freitas and Jason King recently wrote, "The thing is, though, and you have heard this before of course, movie love is pretty misleading. Fairy tales are rare."[31] We have heard this before. We know love is not like in the movies.

Or do we? Barbara Dafoe Whitehead and David Popenoe, of the National Marriage Project at Rutgers University, reported in a large-scale survey a few years ago that 94 percent of American young people seek to marry someone who is a "soul mate."[32] The report cautions that the cultural view of marriage may be evolving from the two-century-old companionate model into a model of "an exalted and spiritual union of souls." Moreover, despite widespread pessimism about the cultural state of marriage expressed in the same survey, most respondents showed surprising confidence that, *in their own case*, they would undoubtedly find this soul mate. The soul mate would be a person where both could be entirely comfortable with the other person, and it was not a matter of economic, religious, or familial commonality. Rather, it was a simple idealism that "someone" was out there who fit.

Furthermore, David McCarthy, citing the work of cultural critic Eva Illouz, notes the inconsistency between our practical-minded rejection of movie love in the abstract and our desire to narrate our own experiences according to such a script. Illouz's work shows that "the romantic story is recognized as flawed when set in the abstract or experienced by someone else; yet, romance is preferred when the respondents are asked to take the question of love personally."[33]

Clearly, the Theology of the Body, with its exaltation of the spiritual significance of these bodily relationships, is going to appeal to this cultural impulse which accords (from a Christian perspective) a problematic "ultimacy" to sexuality.[34] The importance of realizing the power of truly mutual self-giving love is a beautiful and necessary thing for Christian lives. But it is precisely the purity of the pope's vision, a purity which is part of the appeal of the Theology of

the Body, which also threatens it. Mutual self-giving love over a lifetime is a messy thing. As Richard Gaillardetz elegantly explains it, it involves a participation in the paschal mystery, not just once in making the marriage commitment, but every day.[35] The pope's vision is not very engaged in this messiness, and this is especially so in popular presentations.

This lack of nuance may be partially rooted in the fact that the Theology of the Body does a poor job of sustaining a distinction between the character of marriage and the character of sexual acts. West offers up a story of his late father-in-law who, after his wedding night, went to daily Mass the next morning and said, "For the first time in my life, I understood Christ's words, 'This is my body, given for you.' "[36] But surely the key passage from Ephesians 5, as well as the constant use of the metaphor of marriage to describe the relationship between God and His people, is about marriage, not about individual sexual acts. I don't want to be misunderstood here: the Theology of the Body is working against theologies and a culture which all too easily neglect the intrinsic *connections* between sexual acts and the ongoing "act" of marriage. However, maintaining this intrinsic connection becomes deceptive when the goods of the marital relationship are supposed to be completely encapsulated in sexual acts. It may be the case that students are not always buying the whole package that the Theology of the Body is selling.[37]

Another way to understand this problem of romanticization is to confront the Theology of the Body with the actual Gospel stories. The Theology of the Body, like all of John Paul's work, is intensely scriptural. Yet, in its focus on the bookends of Scripture, the Theology of the Body may neglect the central narratives of the Gospels, perhaps because this scriptural reflection is so deeply tied to the project of justifying traditional natural law claims. Besides Jesus' oft-noted dim view of the biological family, the Gospels tell repeated stories about how real love is messy, unclean, and most often involves interacting with social outcasts. Educating his disciples on the importance of the marriage relationship does not seem to be high on Christ's list of priorities. Rather, a much more compelling case can be made that the works of mercy (Mt 25:31–46), the suffering encounter of broken bodies embracing one another in compassion, are the true "theology of the body."

Nevertheless, a vision of authentic love in a world of imitation, of a mutual love that images God, is not one that Christian theologians should easily give up. I chose the title of this paper from a no. 1 hit from Belinda Carlisle from 1987, when I was a young and idealistic fifteen-year-old, a breezy '80s classic that anthematically reflects the kind of hope one might put into a relationship. The refrain ends, "They say in heaven, love comes first, we'll make heaven a place on earth." Though perhaps lacking John Paul's subtlety, this lyric is the nerve center of the Theology of the Body's message: that God is love; that God made us for true love; that true love is bodily; and that our participation in "heaven" (i.e., God's love) begins on earth in the sacrament of marriage and in sex. Beyond my small survey, my (much larger and less self-selected) sexual ethics classes this past semester clearly have the same sort of hunger for real meaning in relationships. Whatever directions Catholic sexual ethics takes in the future, it must develop plausibility structures to address this felt need for a story that lifts up authentic love amidst the allures and confusions of the present mega-mall of available sexual experiences.

Chapter 3

"When they rise from the dead, they neither marry nor are given to marriage"

Marriage and Sexuality, Eschatology, and the Nuptial Meaning of the Body in Pope John Paul II's Theology of the Body

William Mattison

No paper on the "theology of the body" should fail to mention George Weigel's much-trumpeted claim that the late Pope John Paul II's writing on this subject is a "theological time bomb set to go off, with dramatic consequences, sometime in the third millennium of the Church."[1] Given the popularity of the theology of the body among a vocal and active population of young Catholics — recognized even in a *New York Times* article[2] — it seems the countdown to Weigel's prognostication is on.

The reasons for the "explosive" popularity of the theology of the body are beginning to be the subject of academic scrutiny.[3] That endeavor is not the purpose of this essay.[4] The growing popularity of the theology of the body is both granted and welcomed here. For the reasons outlined by authors such as Cloutier and Riley, many young Catholics are hungry for an account of relationships, sexuality, and marriage that is narrated from a faith perspective and issues a challenge to live a disciplined life of chastity. The theology of the body effectively responds to this hunger.

However, the vision of marriage and sexuality presented in the theology of the body should not be endorsed uncritically. In fact, the purpose of this essay is to examine certain shortcomings of that vision for the ultimate purpose of responding most truthfully to the aforementioned hunger among young Catholics. After all, the goal of Catholic educators, parents, and mentors ought not to be simply satiating a readily apparent hunger for guidance among young people on matters pertaining to sexuality. Rather, our goal should be responding to that hunger most truthfully, so that the bread which is offered does not perish, but gives eternal life.

What prompted this examination of the theology of the body was a *prima facie* tension evident in John Paul's thought. On the one hand, one of the most foundational claims of his theology of the body is that the human person is marked by what he calls the "nuptial meaning of the body." However, how can John Paul label the body inherently "nuptial" if Christ himself claimed (in the title quotation of this essay) that there is no marriage in heaven?[5] A central tenet of Christian faith is bodily resurrection, which is marked by continuity — though obviously not sameness — with one's body in this earthly life. Thus if, as John Paul claims, our bodies are essentially nuptial, and if there is no marriage in heaven, then it would seem that John Paul is committed to the view that the resurrected body is not simply a transformed and perfected earthly body, but is radically discontinuous with our earthly bodies. Does this *prima facie* criticism of John Paul II's theology of the body stand?

Fortunately, the pope devoted extensive attention to the synoptic passage driving this criticism. The first task of this paper is an exploration of John Paul's conception of the nuptial meaning of the body, particularly as it is related to this synoptic passage. This inquiry will reveal that John Paul has a more nuanced understanding of the "nuptial meaning of the body" than that presupposed by this initial critique. He has an explanation for how the nuptial meaning of the body can be fulfilled for both celibates in this life, and the blessed in the next. Nevertheless, though his overall analysis is adequately qualified to ward off this *prima facie* critique, John Paul may rightly be criticized for his use of the term "nuptial" in describing the fundamental meaning of human existence. Doing so leads some of the more popular proponents of his thought to describe marriage and sexuality as more foundational to the Christian life than is warranted by the Christian eschatological tradition.

Thus, the second part of this essay explores how some misleading thrusts in Pope John Paul II's thought led to a problematic view of marriage and sexuality in certain popular presentations of the theology of the body. Though other proponents of the pope's thought will be mentioned, the focus will be on the work of Christopher West, by far the most popular advocate of the theology of the body. True, proponents such as West do not claim that the human person's "nuptial meaning of the body" is fulfilled only in marriage and sexuality. Nonetheless, they do depict a vision of marriage that is inadequately shaped by Christian eschatology. In this section, attention will also be given to the extent to which these problems are nascent in the pope's thought, or rather impositions on that thought.

From this critical examination of the theology of the body from an eschatological perspective, other shortcomings of the theology of the body's portrait of redeemed marriage and sexuality also become clear. The third section of this essay identifies a myopic fixation on the extraordinary acts in married life. The theology of the body does offer an account of how God's grace transforms married life, but the account is limited to a rather exclusive set of actions. As argued below, what makes this charge an eschatological critique is the vision of grace implicit in the myopia.

The fourth section examines a charge made by previous critics of the theology of the body, namely, that its vision of marriage and sexuality is more accurately understood as a return to the state of original innocence than it is redemption of wounded, sinful sexuality. In order to determine whether or not this charge holds, the task here is to distinguish these two graced states of salvation history, and identify how an ethic of marriage and sexuality would look different for each. It is argued here that this charge is indeed accurate, and suggestions are offered for how the theology of the body might be amended to ward off this critique.

The last section offers more speculative reflections on why the theology of the body is marked by these inadequacies. It turns out that some of the very features driving the popular appeal of the theology of the body, giving it its "sex appeal," may also provide its Achilles heel when examined from the perspective of Christian eschatology.

John Paul II on the "Nuptial Meaning of the Body" and Christian Eschatology

The purpose of John Paul's theology of the body is to better ground Catholic teaching on marriage and sexuality in the larger Christian story of creation, sin, and redemption. In fact, this triptych governs the series of 129 or so Wednesday papal audience addresses[6] that make up what is commonly called the "theology of the body."[7] John Paul starts with Matthew 19:3–12 where Christ responds to his Pharisee interrogators on divorce by twice referring to "the beginning." The pope thus springboards off of Matthew 19 to examine what the first two chapters of Genesis say about creation, the human body, marriage, and sexuality. Moving on to the second stage in salvation history, he then analyzes Matthew 5:27–28 (on adultery and lust), along with several Pauline passages, to examine human embodiedness, marriage, and sexuality as marred by sin.[8] Finally, he explores redemption as it concerns the body, marriage, and sexuality by beginning with the synoptic passage on marriage in heaven, continuing with Matthew 19:10–12 and 1 Corinthians 7 on celibacy, and concluding with extensive examination of Ephesians 5:21–33 on the sacramentality of marriage.[9]

Defining the Nuptial Meaning of the Body

The theology of the body quotes Scripture extensively, and is shaped by the Christian story of salvation history. Yet John Paul places an original term — the "nuptial meaning of the body" — at the very heart of this vision. In fact, John Paul claims that the "awareness of the meaning of the human body that is derived from [the first pages of Genesis] — in particular its nuptial meaning — is the fundamental element of human existence in the world."[10] This is a strong claim, indeed. But what exactly is the nuptial meaning of the body?[11] Nowhere does John Paul offer a precise definition. But three aspects of the "nuptial meaning" are mentioned repeatedly throughout his work.

First, and most centrally, the "nuptial attribute" of the human body is the "capacity of expressing love, that love in which a person becomes a gift and — by means of that gift — fulfills the meaning of his being and existence."[12] Since humanity finds its origin in the Author of Life, who created all from nothingness out of love, it is unsurprising that John Paul affirms that the human person finds himself only in the "disinterested giving of himself."[13] Second, "the body has a nuptial meaning because the human person, as the Council says, is a creature that God willed for his own sake."[14] With this reference to Vatican II's *Gaudium et spes,* John Paul goes on to say that just as the Creator wills the human person for his or her own sake, the nuptial meaning of the human person's body is the "capacity of living the fact that the other — the woman for the man and the man for the woman — is, by means of the body, someone willed by the Creator for his or her own sake."[15] Third and finally, the original gift of the human body and sexuality is marked by a two-fold freedom. It is freedom *from* constraint by sin, and freedom *for* self-gift. John Paul claims "this freedom lies at the basis of the nuptial meaning of the body."[16] Thus the nuptial meaning of the body is the person's call to and capacity for self-giving love, in a manner that is truly free and acknowledges the other (and the self) as someone willed and loved by God for one's own sake.

Nuptial Meaning Fulfilled Non-Nuptially

Given this definition, it is unsurprising that John Paul claims the nuptial meaning of the body can be fulfilled without marriage. The pope explains this in his exegesis of the synoptic passage on the absence of marriage in the resurrection. Clearly the eschaton constitutes a "definitive fulfillment of the nuptial meaning of the body,"[17] a fulfillment that is "totally manifested" in "virginity."[18] Thus marriage and procreation "do not constitute the eschatological fulfillment of man,"[19] since in the eschatological state "men 'neither marry nor are given to marriage.' "[20] In fact, this is why celibacy is such an important practice for the church in this stage of history, before the eschaton. Today's celibate for the kingdom "indicates the virginity of the eschatological man," in whom exists the "absolute and eternal nuptial meaning of the glorified body in union with God himself."[21]

Yet how can John Paul delineate a nuptial meaning of the body and claim it may be fulfilled without the practice of marriage? John Paul details the relationship between marriage/ sex to the nuptial meaning of the body in this extended quotation:

> [In the beginning,] in the unity of the couple man becomes male and female, discovering the nuptial meaning of the body as a personal subject. Subsequently, the meaning of the body, and in particular, being male and female in the body, is connected with marriage and procreation. . . . However, the original and fundamental significance of being a body, as well as being, by reason of the body, male and female — that is, precisely the nuptial significance — is united with the fact that man is created as person and called to life in *communione personarum. Marriage and procreation in itself* [*sic*] *do not determine definitively the original and fundamental meaning of being a body or of being, as a body, male and female.* Marriage and procreation merely give concrete reality to that meaning in the dimensions of history.[22]

The nuptial meaning is therefore primarily an orientation toward (free, self-giving) communion of persons. This happens in a "special way" in marriage.[23] Marriage and procreation "give concrete reality" to the nuptial meaning, but do not themselves constitute that meaning.[24]

So Why Call It "Nuptial"?

Such more nuanced treatments of the body's nuptial meaning, and in particular its relationship to marriage and sex, reveal that John Paul is not susceptible to the *prima facie* criticism that the human person is depicted as having a meaning that is radically discontinuous with human fulfillment at the eschaton as indicated by Christ's own words. Nonetheless, this does raise the question of why John Paul chose to label the body's meaning "nuptial."

John Paul constantly mentions masculinity and femininity while describing the nuptial meaning of the body. The human person is called to self-giving love as an embodied creature. And embodied persons are male or female. Hence John Paul says, "in his body as male or female, man feels he is a subject of holiness."[25] Yet as reflected in this quotation, a person experiences holiness as a woman or a man, but gender is not determinative of the particular type or form of holiness. Rather, masculinity or femininity is simply a feature of the embodied person who is called to self-giving love.

Yet in other quotations, masculinity and femininity do not merely appear to be features of bodies, which are visible signs of the meaning of the human person; rather, gender appears constitutive to that call to self-donation. As one such quotation states, a person lives the fact that the other is willed by the Creator for their own sake — "*the woman for the man and the man for the woman.*"[26]

There appear to be three levels of analysis of the nuptial meaning of the body. First, the essence of this meaning is clearly the human person's call to self-giving love found in a communion of persons. Second, persons are embodied as male or female. Thus that call will always be experienced by a person as an embodied man or woman.[27] Third, as male and female, human persons are oriented toward each other to enflesh self-giving love in marriage and sex. Clearly John Paul's nuptial meaning of the body refers to the first two levels of meaning. But though it seems natural to move right to the third level, the Christian must be cautious in doing so for the same reasons John Paul refuses in the above extended quotations to map fulfillment of the nuptial meaning of the body directly on to marriage and sex. While surely important, marriage and sex are relativized in the Christian tradition by Christ's teaching on the resurrection and the practice of celibacy. And surely other relationships — friendships, family ties, etc. — can be vehicles for expressing the nuptial meaning of the body to which all are called.

Yet while insisting at key points that the third level of analysis, marriage and sex, is not essential for the nuptial meaning of the body, John Paul does move rather cavalierly between appeals to levels two and three. Certainly the use of the term "nuptial" seems to tie human fulfillment directly to marriage and procreation. He also claims that the self-giving communion of persons toward which humanity is oriented, and indeed through which the person images the triune God, is "bound up" in the theology of the body, which is "also the theology of sex, or rather the theology of masculinity and femininity."[28] "Man became the 'image of God . . .' through the communion of persons which man and woman form right from the beginning."[29] These quotations, along with the above "the woman for the man and the man for the woman,"[30] specify marriage and sex as the fulfillment of the nuptial meaning. Despite the more nuanced treatments found in John Paul's work, quotations such as these unsurprisingly prompt popular proponents of the theology of the body to graft the body's nuptial meaning more directly onto fulfillment in marriage and sexuality than is warranted in a Christian tradition shaped by eschatological belief in the resurrection of the body.

Why, then, does John Paul repeatedly label human fulfillment "nuptial"? One possible solution involves switching what are commonly taken to be the referent and analogue in scriptural passages on marriage. What if the primary referent for the "nuptiality" in which the human person is fulfilled is not the marriage of husband and wife of Genesis 1–2 and Matthew 19, but the union of Christ and the Church of Ephesians 5? John Paul seems to indicate as much when he states:

> The union of Christ with the Church permits us to understand in what way the spousal significance of the body is completed with the redemptive significance, and this in the diverse ways of life and in diverse situations.[31]

In this way of thinking, the relationship between Christ and the Church, described as marital in Ephesians 5, is that to which all are called and in which all find true fulfillment. This seems to be the only way to make sense out of John Paul's speaking of "the human body in its perennial masculinity and femininity, in its *perennial destiny in marriage*."[32] He must be speaking of marriage in terms of Christ's union with the Church; how else to make sense of these claims when there is no marriage in heaven? Marriage in this life is therefore only a participation in that ultimate nuptial fulfillment.

Surely this last claim is affirmed by all. But that does not render heavenly union the only true marriage any more than speaking of the heavenly banquet renders eating only genuinely present in heaven. This approach turns an analogy on its head. The epistle writer tries to make the invisible relationship between Christ and the Church more comprehensible through an analogy to the visible relationship of husband and wife in earthly marriage. The passage only works if earthly marriage is the referent, the primary understanding of nuptial. Eschatological two-in-one flesh union with Christ may indeed be that for which earthly sacramental marriage prepares one. Yet the terms "marriage" and "nuptial" must refer primarily to the earthly relationship for the analogy to work. Furthermore, consider the "cost" if heavenly marriage is actually the primary referent. Marital exclusivity and orientation toward procreation, both absent in heaven, would both be rendered accidental to the notion of marriage. Surely this is not what proponents of the theology of the body intend.

Rather, what actually appears to be at work in John Paul's theology of the body is at times nuanced and at times careless interplay between eschatological fulfillment of the nuptial meaning of the body and the specific earthly form of fulfillment in marriage and procreation. Two reasons are suggested for this vacillation between what is termed here the second and third levels of the nuptial meaning of the body. First, the more male/female union in marriage and procreative sex can be tied to the very meaning of the human person, the more weight the body's nuptial meaning can bear in normative discussions of nonmarital sex, homosexuality, and contraception, all clear concerns of those promoting the theology of the body.[33] Second, a vision of the human person tightly tied to fulfillment in marriage and sexuality affords the theology of the body an instant credibility in a modern Western society preoccupied with sexuality. The problem with this, as is seen in the following section, is that it affords marriage and sexuality a centrality in the Christian life that the tradition has consistently displaced.

Granting Marriage and Sexuality Undue Ultimacy in Popular Presentations of the Theology of the Body

Though the first section demonstrated that John Paul is not susceptible to the *prima facie* criticism that he neglects Christ's words on the resurrection by positing a nuptial meaning of the body, the pope's thought can be misleading, at times grafting the body's nuptial meaning more directly onto fulfillment in marriage and sexuality than is warranted by Christian eschatology. This second section examines how popular presentations of John Paul's theology of the body — particularly that of Christopher West, who is by far the most popular[34] — springboard off these thrusts in the pope's thought and portray marriage and sex as too central in the Christian life. No Christian would contest that virtuous marriage and sexuality are important components of Christianity, and that one's practices in this realm should reveal one's Christian faith. Nonetheless, popularizers like West make sex and marriage unduly "ultimate"[35] in the Christian life. Three ways of doing this are identified here.

First, West overemphasizes the importance of marriage and sexuality by presenting marriage as the fullest expression of the Christian life. "Marriage is the most fundamental expression of that call to communion [with others], the paradigm or model in some sense of all human communion and self-giving."[36] Immediately after making a beautiful connection between the two-in-one flesh union of marriage and Eucharist, West claims, "Of all the ways that God chooses to reveal his life and love in the created world, John Paul II is saying marriage — enacted and consummated by sexual union — is most fundamental."[37]

No citation is given here to John Paul's work, and on this claim West does not echo John Paul.[38] Yet nor is he alone. The normally more academically precise John Grabowski makes similar claims by saying marriage is the "most fundamental and intense form of human community," and again that "the self-giving love of marriage is a paradigm for all human community and indeed the whole of reality."[39] On these claims both West and Grabowski extend beyond John Paul's work, and grant marriage and sexuality an undue ultimacy in the Christian life.

Second, West repeatedly claims that understanding the truth about marriage and sexuality is the way to fully understand Christianity. It offers a sort of privileged avenue of access to the Christian story. "We cannot understand Christianity if we cannot understand the truth and meaning of our sexuality."[40] Note the claim here is not that understanding the truth about marriage and family is a helpful way to better understand Christianity, or that one's Christian faith leads to a truthful grasp of marriage and sexuality. No Christian would contest these statements. Rather, the claim is that "we cannot understand the inner 'logic' of the Christian mystery without understanding its primordial revelation in the nuptial meaning of our bodies and that Biblical vocation to become 'one flesh.'"[41] Marriage and sexuality are wonderful facets of human life, but asserting that the truth of human existence can only be grasped through them grants them an undue ultimacy. Interestingly enough, West does accurately cite Pope John Paul II's 1994 "Letter to Families" to support this claim.[42]

Third and finally, besides the source of knowing and fullest expression of Christian life, West also portrays marriage and sexuality as the very crux and content of the Christian meaning of life. Consider these quotations:

> Everything that God wants to tell us on earth about who he is, who we are, the meaning of life, the reason he created us, how we are to live, and even our ultimate destiny is contained somehow in the truth and meaning of sexuality and marriage.[43]

> God gave us sexual desire itself to be the power to love as he loves, so that we can participate in divine life and fulfill the very meaning of our being and existence.[44]

These quotations make sex the point of the Christian story, and sexual desire the *imago Dei*. Here (and in the above quotations) the essence of the body's nuptial meaning — its orientation toward self-gift — is mapped directly onto marriage and sexuality. Marriage and sexuality in effect become the meaning of life.[45] "This is why John Paul can say that if we live according to the truth of our sexuality, we fulfill the very meaning of our being and existence."[46] Or finally, "disputes about sexuality are disputes about the very meaning of life."[47] Such disputes may indeed *reveal* competing accounts of the meaning of life, but surely it is not the case that the meaning of one's life is constituted by one's sexual morality. In this third example of undue ultimacy on marriage and sexuality, West does not accurately represent John Paul's theology of the body. The only time John Paul says something close to the contents of this paragraph is his reference to the nuptial meaning of the body as the "fundamental element of human existence."[48]

This academic scrutiny of popular works such as those of West may seem unfair. First, it seems it simply cannot be the case that West thinks marriage and sexuality are the very center of the Christian life. Though this is likely true, and indeed certain quotations can be marshaled from his work in support of this claim,[49] the preponderance of quotations to the contrary as listed above reveals the thrust of his work as it is presented to his audience. Second, why bother with this methodical analysis of writing directed toward a more popular audience? As noted above, the overall project of those promoting the theology of the body is affirmed here. But it is crucial, for the sake of those receiving this teaching, that it be presented as accurately, or as true to the Christian tradition, as possible. This section demonstrates that popular presentations of the theology of the body, such as that of West, do a disservice to their audience to the extent that they present marriage and sexuality as unduly ultimate in the Christian life. Though attractive to young Catholics who are understandably preoccupied with the subject due to their age and the culture in which we live, claims such as those analyzed above violate the Christian tradition's affirmation of, but simultaneous relativization of, marriage and sex in the Christian life understood from an eschatological perspective.

A Myopic Fixation on the Extraordinary

This paper was conceived as an analysis of the eschatological adequacy of John Paul's concept of the nuptial meaning of the body, with attention to how central to the Christian life marriage and sexuality are portrayed in popular presentations of the theology of the body. Thus the first two sections of this essay explain why an eschatological perspective precludes the Christian from tying human fulfillment too directly to marriage and sexuality. This and the following section continue the critical examination of the theology of the body from an eschatological perspective. However, the question now at hand is not the relative importance of marriage and sexuality in the Christian life, but rather how this facet of Christian living is redeemed by God's grace. After all, eschatology concerns God's definitive presence in the "already" as well as the "not yet."

The theology of the body certainly offers an account of how God's grace transforms Christian marriage and sexuality. In fact, the largest section of papal audiences concerns the third stage of salvation history: redemption. However, though proponents of the theology of the body are clear *that* grace transforms marriage and sexuality, there are two problems with *how* that transformation is depicted. This section explores the first: a myopic fixation on the extraordinary. The theology of the body is characterized by an overemphasis on a small set of extraordinary acts — in particular, acts of sexual intercourse — as "completely encapsulating" the goods of the marital relationship.[50]

Surely is it one of the great attractions of the theology of the body that sex is regarded as meaningful, and an arena where one can express the self-giving love that is indeed the fundamental element of human existence. West typifies this in his claim that "sex is meant to express wedding vows," or even more strongly, that "sex is so beautiful, so wonderful, so glorious that it is meant to express God's free, total, faithful, and fruitful love."[51] West even claims that "sexual intercourse is meant to participate in the very life and love of God."[52] West's basic inclination to see sex as a physical expression with deeper meaning is wholeheartedly affirmed here.

However, just how is it that sex is an expression of such deeper meaning? In his *Sex and Love in the Home,* David McCarthy critiques a group of contemporary Catholic theologians whom he labels "transcendent personalists," a category into which West would surely fit.[53] These theologians portray sex as a *sui generis* physical sign of total self-giving, an expression of the whole person. They thus view sexual intercourse as a liminal act, transcending time and lifting the couple out of ordinary life to express and experience full self-gift in two-in-one flesh union. Yet McCarthy claims:

> This ritual context suits a honeymoon or anniversary day consummation, but I dare to say that our everyday bodily presence is far more subtle and patient. Those who believe sex is earth shattering will put it out of marriage.[54]

As indicated by this quotation, the claim that proponents of the theology of the body overemphasize acts of sexual intercourse and thus myopically fixate on the extraordinary is not a claim regarding the quality of a couple's sexual experience. Rather, it is a concern that individual acts of marital sex bear the burden of "represent[ing] a lifetime of friendship between husband and wife."[55] McCarthy claims, to the contrary, that for sex to have fully marital meaning, it must be contextualized in "extended bodily communion over time."[56]

Perhaps this is what one recent critic of the theology of the body had in mind when he called this approach ironically "disembodied."[57] Sex is certainly a bodily act. But to assign it such liminal significance ironically disembodies marriage. As McCarthy claims: "Each act of sexual intercourse is assumed to have immense meaning, but a single act carries the meaning of the whole so that continuing embodiment adds nothing."[58]

Such a view of sex is far less "embodied" than a depiction of sex marked by what McCarthy calls "enduring bodily belonging," a "day-to-day bodily presence" between spouses exemplified in intercourse but also in such acts as "sleeping in the same bed, caring for each other in times of illness, trusting, and desiring each other's non-erotic touch."[59]

This liminality, or myopic fixation on extraordinary (and primarily sexual) acts, of the theology of the body is evident in West's work as well as those shaped by it. Consider the common West anecdote about his grandfather claiming, at Mass the day after his wedding and its presumed consummation, that he finally understands the meaning of the phrase "This is my body given up for you."[60] It is also seen in a recent graduate student who told the man she was dating that she longed for her wedding night so that she could finally experience the full union of Christ with the Church. Or finally, it is reflected in the story relayed by a youth minister who was told by one young theology of the body enthusiast that the bedroom is the altar of marriage.

It is beautiful that we have gotten to the point in Catholic morality that sexuality is understood and experienced as reflecting Christian faith.[61] Yet as McCarthy says, "the problem in this . . . account of sex is, not that it goes wrong, but that it says too much to be right."[62] It is inaccurate to make the wedding consummation bedroom, or even subsequent acts of marital sex, the focal point of how our lives image God's love. David Cloutier is surely right when he says the "great mystery" of Ephesians, which refers to Christ and the Church, is best understood not as sexual intercourse, but rather as an enduring faithful marriage, made up of countless sacramentalized acts including — but far from limited to or even focused upon — sexual intercourse. One can maintain the distinct status of sexual intercourse as a particularly important marital act without affording these acts such unique significance that they are no longer embedded in other acts of love and the marriage relationship as a whole.[63]

Note that this is an eschatological critique, and not simply one of moral action theory. The latent assumption in an emphasis on liminal acts fully encapsulating a marriage relationship is that God's grace works only in the extraordinary, in acts that seem to transcend time and space. In addition to presenting an idealistic view of marital sexuality, this approach neglects the fact that sex acts are importantly embedded in the everyday ordinary acts that constitute a marriage whose bodily two-in-one flesh union is expressed outside the bedroom as well as inside. Surely West and John Paul would agree with this claim. Yet by presenting a vision of marriage and sex that focuses disproportionately on liminal acts, they at least implicitly say otherwise.

Chaste Marriage and Sex in the Theology of the Body: Originally Innocent or Redeemed?

The next problem in the theology of the body from an eschatological perspective concerns the distinction between original innocence and the state of redemption. Both John Paul II and West speak extensively about marriage as a human state of life where God's redemption may be found. They have eschatological understandings of marriage in the sense that through marriage God's grace restores fallen humanity so that marriage can become an occasion where spouses experience the self-giving love of communion of persons that is tasted now and completed in the eschaton. Thus to say that the theology of the body offers a view of marriage that is untransformed by the grace of Christ would be inaccurate.[64]

Yet how does this transformation play out? In an earlier article on this topic David Cloutier claims that the approach to marriage and sexuality in the theology of the body constitutes a case of a "restoring Eden."[65] M. Cathleen Kaveny similarly argues that theologians of the body like West make the mistake of "eliding the original state of grace with the state of redemption."[66] Of course, since it is the one and same God at work in the "first grace" of creation[67] and the grace of redemption, West can accurately claim that the grace of redemption "enables us to gradually reclaim God's original plan for men and women."[68] Is there any significant difference on this point between West on the one hand and Cloutier/Kaveny on the other?

What would make Kaveny's and Cloutier's charges "stick" would be identifying how the state of original grace differs from that of redemption, and demonstrating that the theology of the body presents a vision of marriage and sexuality corresponding more to the former than the latter. This can be done. Both states of creation and redemption share in common an absence of sin. But they are importantly different in their freedom from sin.

Perhaps a scriptural image will help demonstrate this best. The risen Christ, foretaste of embodied eschatological life, is spiritual and glorified, but his risen body still bears the wounds of the passion. His glorified body is healed, but the evidence of former brokenness remains. The glory achieved is not one that erases the risen Lord's historical suffering and passion, but rather transforms it. Though the analogy fails in that Christ's brokenness was not sinful and our redemption in this life is not complete, the analogy applies to our experience in that we people who are redeemed by grace in our lives, which includes our sexual lives, experience that redemption not as one of original innocence but rather as one of healed sinfulness. Life in grace, tasted here and complete at the resurrection, will always retain the "wounds" of past sinfulness, including sexual sinfulness. This means that though life in grace is in accordance with the self-giving nuptial meaning of the body that characterizes prelapsarian humanity, it also bears remembrances of the sin from which one has been healed. Lest one think that this renders eschatological life somehow more imperfect than the original state, one need only recall St. Paul's claim that "where sin abounds, grace abounds even more," or the Good Friday exaltation of "O Happy Fault!"

The Christian story is not one of a purity untainted by sin. There is nothing inherently wrong with purity — were there no sin, this would indeed be the Christian ideal. But where sin and brokenness are present, the Christian is called to participate in the often uncomfortable and messy healing work of redemption.[69] A theology of marriage and sexuality that does not reflect the importance of this healing can accurately be criticized for "eliding the original state of grace with the state of redemption" or espousing a return to Eden rather than a journey to the New Jerusalem.

How might redeemed Christian love look different from originally innocent love? One excellent place to start would be the seven corporeal and seven spiritual works of mercy.[70] These fourteen acts all constitute Christian responses to sin and brokenness in the world. Be they the corporal acts of feeding the hungry and tending to the sick, or the spiritual ones of comforting the afflicted or forgiving wrongs willingly, the real healing presence of redeeming grace in marriage is particularly evident in these sets of acts.[71] And they certainly constitute redemption rather than a return to innocence. They are messy, but where sin abounds, grace abounds more.

Cloutier and Kaveny rightly question whether the sort of Christian marriage depicted by the theology of the body is truly eschatological. It is argued here that what distinguishes redemption from original innocence is not just an absence of, but a healing from, sin. But nowhere does either John Paul or West provide guidance on how marriage is a source of grace understood as healed sinfulness rather than restored innocence. Others in society do offer such guidance. Consider Stanley Hauerwas's typically outlandish claim that "you always marry the wrong person."[72] Or Rick Gaillardetz's discussion of the difference between his youthful idealization of marriage and the reality of the graced marriage he now experiences.[73] I think of my own students' quizzical yet fascinated looks when I tell them that nothing in life has made me more aware of my sinfulness than my marriage; and that this is actually God's grace at work in our marriage.

But for theologians of the body marriage is idealized and romanticized.[74] West admits "we must certainly avoid all false hopes of restoring paradise on earth."[75] But he seems to fear that setting a "low bar" for young people on matters of marriage and sexuality denies the power of God's grace (2 Tim 3:5). He prefers to have confidence that young people will be given the help of Christ needed to "receive" and "live" the "original meaning of marriage."[76] West should be commended for this faith in God's grace. Too often it is assumed that young people cannot live the challenges of Christian chastity. West refuses to do young people such a disservice, and thus presents the "high bar" of Christian chastity.

However, West fails to grasp how grace functions among sinful humanity. Grace not only prevents further sin, but heals that sin which is already present.[77] Describing redeeming grace solely in the language of purity, and not in the language of healed sinfulness, ignores a crucial function of God's grace. West apparently takes Kaveny's charge that it is "deceptive and cruel" to encourage young people that "they too can have a relationship like the one between prelapsarian Adam and Eve" to mean that she does not think all things are possible with God's grace.[78] But this is not at all her point. Rather, Kaveny fears that: "Transfixed by the illusory promises of a return to the purity of creation, they may be blind to the possibilities for a gritty but real redemption in their own lives."[79] In other words, Kaveny does not doubt the possibility of graced life, but rather wants to ensure that young people are offered not a cheap salvation that ignores human sin but a thoroughgoing redemption that transforms and heals the sinful human heart.

Why These Particular Blemishes on the Theology of the Body?

Given these criticisms of the theology of the body, examined here from an eschatological perspective,[80] one question that remains is "why?" Why does this approach afford marriage and sex an undue ultimacy in the life of the Christian? Why is the saving character of marriage foisted onto punctuated acts — particularly sex acts — that are forced to bear the burden of embodying an entire marriage relationship, to the ironic disembodiment of marriage as it concerns other ordinary acts of self-giving love? Finally, why do theologians of the body depict the graced transformation of human sexuality in this world primarily as a return to the state of original innocence rather as redemption in which human sinfulness is not simply prevented but also healed?

In his *De doctrina christiana* (On Teaching Christianity) St. Augustine explains why it is important to employ tools of "the world" in teaching and spreading the Christian faith.[81] He is talking about the pagan art of rhetoric, but his analogy applies here as well. He recalls the Exodus story of the harried Israelites departing Egypt, and how they "despoiled the Egyptians," taking from their former captors precious metals to be melted down and transformed for use in service to the People of God.[82] Similarly, Augustine encourages his reader to use the fruits of the pagan art of rhetoric in service to the gospel. Once melted down, these tools can be put to proper use in service to God.

It seems that John Paul II and especially Christopher West provide modern examples of despoiling the Egyptians. The "Egyptians" in this case is a reference to contemporary Western society, and the available resource is that society's fascination with human sexuality. John Paul and West laudably seek to use this fascination in service to the gospel. In doing so they stand within the great tradition of the prophets, St. Paul, and the author of Revelation by using the analogy of marriage to depict God's faithful, fruitful, and indissoluble relationship with humanity. After all, marriage and sexuality are readily accessible to human experience, and so using these realities to illuminate facets of God's relationship with humanity is an effective catechetical tool. This is all the more true today in Western society since so many of these experiences are marked by painful brokenness, leaving people longing for a richly fulfilling understanding and practice of marriage and sexuality.

John Paul and West rely on this fascination with sexuality, and this longing for fulfillment in that arena, to provide access to and interest in the gospel. However, in despoiling our society's fascination with sexuality, they must be sure it is adequately melted down so as to be placed in genuine service to the gospel. This paper has identified aspects of the theology of the body that are adulterated by problematic characteristics of contemporary Western culture's fascination with sexuality. In the "world" today sexuality is commonly regarded and sought with an ultimacy that has always been rejected by the Christian tradition. Secular society's vision of romantic love and sexuality too often leaves behind the graced ordinary facets of faithful relationship by focusing on passionate love and sexual intercourse. Finally, in broader cultural parlance, romantic sexual relationships offer a sort of salvation marked by the "happily ever after" of innocence rather than the messy self-giving healing love of Christian redemption. Thus the three problems with the theology of the body identified here may render it more palatable to contemporary Western culture, but they also render it in tension with the Christian tradition. John Paul and West laudably seek to use societal fascination with sex in service to the gospel. This is part of the theology of the body's "sex appeal." But this appeal becomes an Achilles heel to the extent that the theology of the body feeds the hunger of young Catholics today with a vision of marriage and sexuality inadequately shaped by Christian eschatology.

Chapter 4

Being in Love and Begetting a Child

A Greek Myth of Eros *and the Christian Mystery of Marriage*

CHRISTOPHER KACZOR

> Marriage and conjugal love are by their nature ordained toward the begetting and educating of children. Children are really the supreme gift of marriage and contribute very substantially to the welfare of their parents. (*Gaudium et spes,* 50)

TO MANY CONTEMPORARY EARS, these words are shocking. It may come as a surprise to learn that they come from the Second Vatican Council, and not Augustine of Hippo, Thomas Aquinas, or another teacher of centuries ago. As a culture, we do not tend to view children as the "supreme gift of marriage." Although good parents contribute very substantially to the welfare of their children, we do not instinctively think that children contribute "very substantially to the welfare of their parents." Perhaps in an agricultural society, children might contribute to the welfare of their parents, or perhaps when the parents need care in advanced old age, but normally we tend to think of the benefit traveling one way from mother and father to offspring. The parents provide; the children receive. And although it is the norm for married couples to have children, the links between love, sexual activity, children, and the welfare of their parents are not always easy to see.[1]

Of course, "love" is a multifaceted concept that includes what the Greeks would distinguish as *eros* and *philia,* erotic love and friendly love. A good marriage enjoys both kinds of love, as well as a healthy dose of *storge* or affection and *agape* or self-giving love. In an ideal situation, husband and wife are lovers and best friends and give of themselves in service to each other. Here, I would like to focus especially on erotic love and its relationship to the procreation and education of children.

It is important to consider erotic love as an aspect of the flourishing of spouses, in part because it can be especially difficult to see the link between erotic love and the procreation and education of children. It might seem at first glance that the education and procreation of children are an afterthought to the cozy arrangement of lover and beloved, an unwanted intrusion on the intimacy of the marital couple. Children are an option, an option one may not want to exercise.

In some traditions, erotic longing and procreation appear closely linked. In Genesis, for example, we can perhaps see an account of love that would provide a close link between erotic longing and procreation. Adam finds no partner among the beasts, and his yearning for union is completed only in Eve. This yearning and its completion "at last this is flesh of my flesh and bone of my bone" (Gn 2:23) take place before the fall. The blessing and commission "Be fruitful and multiply" also occur before the fall (Gn 1:28). In Genesis, the *eros* between Adam and Eve is part of the divine plan from the beginning and is in no way connected with punishment. Nothing satisfies the erotic longing of Adam until the creation of Eve. Following the fall, this relationship is tarnished. Adam, who failed to confront the threatening serpent with Eve, blames Eve for their situation and implicitly also blames God: "The woman you [God] put here with me — she gave me some fruit from the tree" (Gn 3:12).[2] Marital relations become martial for the first time. The first man fails to see his wife as a blessing from God. However, the erotic love of man and woman is a part of the original blessing of creation, an original blessing damaged but not removed by original sin, a blessing linked from the beginning with a (partial) re-creation of the original unity of man and woman in their sexual acts and the fruit of these acts, their offspring.

For an apparent contrast to this account, I would like to focus in particular on the nature of *eros* by turning to Plato's *Symposium,* a dialogue in which friends and lovers at a drinking party give speeches in praise of love. The comic playwright Aristophanes delivers the most memorable oration, a speech about the genesis of *eros.* This mythic account of *eros* has drawn high praise from a wide variety of contemporary critics as capturing essential insights about the nature of erotic love. After surveying the literature, James Rhodes notes: "[N]early everyone . . . becomes lyrical about the superior truth and beauty of Aristophanes' account of *eros.*"[3] What then is Aristophanes' account of *eros?*

Originally, Aristophanes says, there were three kinds of human beings in circular shape, pure males arising from the sun, pure females from the earth, and a mixed creature half-female and half-male from the moon.[4] These primordial human beings roughly resembled cylindrically shaped conjoined twins. Joined at the back, these elemental humans had four arms, four legs, and two faces. Their round shape enabled them to travel with great speed by rolling around like tires in a manner akin to acrobats or gymnasts cart-wheeling. Although their appearance may seem bizarre to us, they were powerful creatures whose pride led them to rebel against the gods. As punishment, in order to weaken and disorder these creatures making them less of a threat and more useful to the gods, Zeus split them in two. The scene is both comical and sad:

> Now, when the work of bisection was complete it left each half with a desperate yearning for the other, and they ran together and flung their arms around each other's necks, and asked for nothing better than to be rolled into one. So much so, that they began to die of hunger and general inertia, for neither would do anything without the other. And whenever one half was left alone by the death of its mate, it wandered about questing and clasping in the hope of finding a spare half-woman — or a whole woman, as we should call her nowadays — or half a man. And so the race was dying out.[5]

As a result, erotic desire of three kinds arose as each creature yearned to find its lost half. The split of the original male/male humans brought about individual males with erotic yearning for a lost male half. The split of the original female/female humans brought about individual females with erotic longing for a lost female half. The split of the original male/female humans brought about individual females with erotic yearning for males and males with erotic longing for females. *Eros* in all its forms is a hunger to be reunited with our lost half — to find our "soul mate," one could say. When we fall in love, we find the one who completes us. But this arrangement could not continue since the newly created race of humans was dying, leaving the gods bereft of their sacrifices and service:

> Zeus felt so sorry for them that he devised another scheme. He moved their privates round to the front, for of course they had originally been on the outside — which was now the back — and they had begotten and conceived not upon each other, but, like the grasshoppers, upon the earth. So now, as I say, he moved their members round to the front and made them propagate among themselves, the male begetting upon the female — the idea being that if, in all these clippings and claspings, a man should chance upon a woman, conception would take place and the race would be continued, while if man should conjugate with man, he might at least obtain such satisfaction as would allow him to turn his attention and his energies to the everyday affairs of life. So you see, gentlemen, how far back we can trace our innate love for one another, and how this love is always trying to reintegrate our former nature, to make two into one, and to bridge the gulf between one human being and another.[6]

The longing for union is given a specific outlet in this new arrangement, sexual intercourse. The craving to be united leads erotic lovers to ardently desire to be together, within each other's sight, and to enjoy sexual intercourse with one another. If this coupling takes place between members of the opposite sex, procreation may result.

Aristophanes' account of *eros* differs significantly from the account of Adam and Eve present in Genesis though both accounts share a sense of love as yearning for completion. In Genesis, *eros* is part of the original blessing of creation. For Aristophanes, by contrast, *eros* arose as a result of a divine punishment for wrongdoing. Before rebellion, and before punishment by the gods, there was no *eros* and indeed no procreation. God enjoins Adam and Eve to be fruitful and multiply. By contrast in Aristophanes' account, "*eros,* in its aspiration to heal our dividedness, is therefore a force in opposition to the rule of Zeus (i.e., to civilizing law and custom)."[7] Indeed, as another scholar notes, "sexual generation is thus the mark of imperfection in man's current nature."[8]

Aristophanes also differs from the Genesis account in giving an explanation of the origin of erotic love between members of the same sex. Indeed, the comic orders various kinds of erotic love (gay, straight, and lesbian) as better or worse, explicitly and implicitly. The Platonic Aristophanes suggests that erotic love between men (or more precisely between a grown man and a youth) is superior, for the male yearning for the male is "the most hopeful of the nation's youth, for theirs [the males'] is the most virile constitution."[9] Men attracted to men are the "only men who show any real manliness in public life."[10] By contrast, those desiring heterosexual unions, Aristophanes characterizes as unfaithful and adulterous.[11] Implicitly, the Platonic Aristophanes indicates the superiority of male homosexuality over heterosexuality by suggesting that the origin of the male-male primordial humans is the most noble of heavenly bodies — the sun — while those desiring heterosexual unions arose from the moon, an inferior heavenly body. *Eros,* in its most exulted form, excludes procreation.

What does the tale of Aristophanes teach? The popularity of Platonic Aristophanes has certainly not led to uniformity of interpretation. According to Bloom:

> Plato makes Aristophanes the expositor of the truest and most satisfying account of *eros* we find in the *Symposium.* There has probably never been a speech or poem about love that so captures what men and women actually feel when they embrace each other. To say, "I feel so powerfully attracted and believe I want to hold on forever because this is my lost other half,"

> gives word to what we actually feel and seems to be sufficient. It does not go beyond our experience to some higher principle, which has the effect of diluting our connection to another human being, nor does it take us down beneath our experience to certain animal impulses or physical processes of which our feelings are only an illusory superstructure.[12]

For Bloom, the speech of Aristophanes both captures our lived experience of erotic love as well as saves us from two mistakes in conceptualizing this experience.

The first mistake is to so elevate *eros* that it becomes divine (as the previous speakers in the *Symposium* had contended). In this view, the deeply *human* character of erotic love becomes obscured, and it turns out that we are not so much in love with the beloved as such, rather we love the divine transcendent in which the beloved somehow participates. Love and sex can become on this view utterly serious, the closest link to the divine possible. Sex and love may be viewed as a sort of savior that, when enjoyed, satisfies the deepest longing of the human heart and leads to perfect human fulfillment.[13]

The other mistake reduces erotic love to animal instincts, physical processes, and biological chemistry. The human experience of being in love is nothing more than a mistaken apprehension of physical, animal desire with no more real significance than any other desire shared with animals — such as being hungry. In this view, the distinctly human character of erotic love again disappears from view, for *eros* is nothing else than the desire animals have for one another. The first mistake errs by considering those in love as under the divine power of an erotic god, the second mistake errs by reducing lovers (qua lovers) to nothing more than beasts in heat.

Martha Nussbaum corrects the first type of error, treating love and *eros* with a divine solemnity, by highlighting the comedic aspect of *eros*. "As we hear Aristophanes' distant myth of this passionate groping and grasping, we are invited to think how odd, after all, it is that bodies should have these holes and projections in them, odd that the insertion of a projection into an opening should be thought, by ambitious and intelligent beings, a matter of the deepest concern. . . . From the outside we cannot help laughing. They want to be gods — and here they are, running around anxiously trying to thrust a piece of themselves inside a hole; or perhaps more comical still, waiting in the hope that some hole of theirs will have something thrust into it."[14]

It *is* funny to rethink sexuality and *eros* in these terms. The comedian Aristophanes plies his trade in depicting a side of *eros* that thus far had been underappreciated by the earlier speeches in the *Symposium* that solemnly divinized *eros*. The seriousness with which we take *eros* and its distinctive act, the thrusting of a piece of ourselves in a hole or the receiving of a piece of another into ourselves, would be utterly ridiculous were we to substitute for the coupling of sexual organs putting one's ear lobe into another's outer ear canal. It is hard to imagine intense jealousy, devastating betrayals, or soaring feelings of unity resulting from the intercourse of ear lobe and ear canal. Indeed, the unity of ears utterly lacks even the intimacy and excitement of kissing. Great drama can hinge on unity between some human organs, but not all.

However, this indicates that in love and sex, something else is going on besides simply the unity of holes and projections as comic as it is to consider (and sometimes to perform). Without denying a comedic aspect to *eros* and its acts, to see *only* comedy is also to fail to capture much of human experience. There is a power and drive to *eros* not easily captured by an understanding of *eros* as comedic alone. In emphasizing this aspect of *eros,* it might be concluded that *eros* is nothing else than the primordial urge of animal attraction.

This characterization of *eros* (the second "mistake" described above) is perhaps more common today than thinking *eros* to be a kind of god. Erotic love, being "in love," can be reduced to a mere kind of animal magnetism, a physical attraction. In connection with the question with which the essay began, it must be immediately admitted that children do not contribute much, if anything, to erotic love if it is understood in this sense. Sexual attraction arises between the couple and never extends to children, save among the most perverse. Although sexual attraction has a biological basis in signs of fertility,[15] procreation and sexual attraction are not necessarily related; indeed sometimes they are inversely related. Bearing children often renders a woman less physically attractive, at least according to the standards set by flashy magazines, both those catering to the adolescent male as well as those aimed at young women. And, if the procreation of children does not undermine the "zing" a couple once shared, there is a good chance that the education of children will constrain the joys of the marital bed. The education of children, understood in its broadest sense of properly caring for them and raising them, very often stands in the way of enjoying bodily pleasures. Indeed, the cost and attention required to raise a child properly channels energy and attention away from devotion to seeking bodily pleasures. Those who follow their pleasures and devote themselves wholeheartedly to bodily attractions — be they of food, drink, drugs, or sex — will find it difficult if not impossible to provide the good moral example to his or her children that is certainly an element of "education" in its proper and fullest sense. Physical attraction and the procreation and education of children stand in no small tension.

It is easy to understand the confusion of *eros* and physical attraction because the two have much in common. Both are intense, passionate, and deeply sexual. Both can intoxicate, addict, and spur to valiant action. Both can begin with a glance and can be entirely spent in nine and a half weeks. Each aspect of this commonality merits its own attention.

Eros and sexual attraction share intensity. By intensity, I mean, that both *eros* and sexual attraction can fully grip our attention. We are drawn, as if by tractor beam, to the beautiful person. When an extremely gorgeous person or our beloved enters the room, we watch and everyone else disappears from view. This passion is the polar opposite of a casual indifference and is linked in important ways to sexuality. *Eros* and sexual attraction are for the beautiful, and we desire to possess, enjoy, and have intercourse with the beautiful.

Eros and physical attraction can intoxicate the mind, warping a normal sense of time and judgment. To be with the beautiful or the beloved is a goal the achievement of which can seem worth virtually any price. A face can launch a thousand ships. And as anyone who has asked out a person of doubtful reply will tell, beauty and *eros* are worth risking humiliation. Love dares all.

Eros and physical attraction can also both share immediacy. One knows, generally immediately and almost always after a few minutes of conversation, whether one finds another person sexually attractive. *Eros* can be similarly immediate. Although some couples fall in love over time, it is also true that we speak of "love at first sight." How often have we heard people say that they knew right away that their beloved was "the one."[16]

But the alacrity of the genesis of *eros* and physical attraction is sometimes matched by the brevity of their duration. Although *eros* and physical attraction can begin immediately, they can also both run their course in a very short time. We can fall in love in a flash, but we can also fall out of love before we know it. Physical beauty alone, even among the most beautiful, hardly ensures a long-lasting or satisfying relationship, as a host of super-beautiful, short-lived celebrity couples makes clear.

Although *eros* and physical attraction have much in common, it is important not to overlook the *differences* between mere sexual magnetism and erotic love. Erotic love yearns for expression in sexual acts; mere attraction is exhausted in sexual acts. Erotic love focuses on one particular beautiful person; mere attraction is for any number of beautiful people. Erotic love is a preoccupation with the whole person of the beloved — the way he or she laughs, writes letters, and cares for friends. Mere sexual attraction focuses on a reduced conception of the person as an actual or potential sexual partner. This kind of desire is akin to other animal desires, such as hunger for food. It is precisely here that we can find the difference between mere sexual desire and love. We hunger for any kind of food, but love only one particular person. If I want nachos, any given plate of nachos will do. If I love Jennifer Turner Kaczor, only Jennifer Turner Kaczor will do. Mere sexual desire seeks any given attractive partner; erotic love seeks the beloved and the beloved alone. A final way to consider the difference between erotic love and mere sexual attraction is in terms of the *desired duration of relationship*. Although both sexual attraction and erotic love are notoriously short-lived in duration, erotic love *wishes* to be with the beloved *forever*. Mere sexual attraction, on the other hand, wants its object of affection *right now. Eros* seeks eternity; mere sexual attraction seeks rapidity. So although mere sexual attraction and the procreation and education of children have no necessary relationship, we might still find some link between the procreation of children and erotic love.

Of course it is also possible to artificially sever the links of *eros* and physical attraction. In correction of Freudian interpretations, C. S. Lewis, for example, sometimes obscures the links among *eros,* beauty, and sexuality. In laudable efforts to combat a reductionism of *eros* to animal sexuality, Lewis overstates his case when he writes: "A man in this state [of *eros*] hasn't the leisure to think of sex. He is too busy thinking of a person.... He is full of desire but the desire may not be sexually toned."[17]

However, erotic love, unless the term is used in an idiosyncratic sense, cannot be removed from the context of sexuality. *Eros* is *more than* mere sexual desire, but it is certainly not *unrelated* to sexual desire. Can we really imagine a person deeply in love who was indifferent about having sexual intercourse with his or her beloved? Lewis notes the erotic lover desires to "go on thinking about" the beloved, but this thinking cannot be entirely separated from the beauty of the beloved — a beauty hardly unrelated to sexuality (though, as he rightly notes, is *more* than mere sexuality).

Indeed, the Platonic Aristophanes provides an erotic account of *eros* in which, according to Bloom, sexual acts are at the very core of "what *eros* is about and are splendid as ends in themselves."[18] This sexual activity has no connection to procreation. Since according to Aristophanes, *eros* in its purest and best form is between males, the most divine form of erotic love entirely forecloses the possibility of procreation. The "best sort" of people have no inclination to procreate.

> I know there are some people who call them shameless, but they are wrong. It is not immodesty that leads them to such pleasures, but daring, fortitude, and masculinity — the very virtues that they recognize and welcome in their lovers — which is proved by the fact that... they are the only men who show any real manliness in public life. And so, when they themselves have come

> to manhood, their love in turn is lavished on boys. They have no natural inclination to marry and beget children. Indeed, they only do so in deference to the usage of society, for they would just as soon renounce marriage altogether and spend their lives with one another.[19]

The best kind of *eros* excludes procreation, but even between a man and woman under the spell of *eros,* there is no *necessary* link between *eros* and procreation drawn by Aristophanes. Indeed, Bloom contrasts the biblical conception of love, tied so closely to procreation and family, with the Greek conception.[20] If Aristophanes is right about *eros,* then the procreation and education of children would not be expected to contribute substantially to the welfare of spouses, at least in terms of their erotic love. And this view is often believed today — which may partially explain the ongoing popularity of the account of *eros* given by the Platonic Aristophanes.

And yet, perhaps the relationship of *eros* and procreation is not as straightforward as this reading of the text might suggest.[21] Aristophanes claims that the couple touched by *eros* wishes for nothing less than complete unity — to be together forever, forged into one. Near the conclusion of his speech, Aristophanes says:

> Now, supposing Hephaestus [the god of the blacksmith's fire] were to come and stand over [the lovers] with his tool bag as they lay there side by side, and suppose he were to ask, Tell me, my dear creatures, what do you really want with one another. And suppose they didn't know what to say, and he went on, How would you like to be rolled into one, so that you could always be together day and night, and never be parted again? Because if that's what you want, I can easily weld you together, and then you can live your two lives in one, and, when the time comes, you can die a common death and still be two-in-one in the lower world. Now, what do you say? Is that what you'd like me to do? And would you be happy if I did? We may be sure, gentlemen, that no lover on earth would dream of refusing such an offer, for not one of them could imagine a happier fate. Indeed, they would be convinced that this was just what they'd

> been waiting for — to be merged, that is, into an utter oneness with the beloved.[22]

So *eros,* according to Aristophanes, is most fundamentally the desire for unity with the beloved. For this reason, those under the spell of *eros* desire sexual relations, for in the sexual act bodies become intimately joined and during orgasm even the psychic distinction between lover and beloved becomes blurred. Sexual relations aim at and partially achieve the goal of *eros* — unity with the beloved — but it is this desire for union that is at the core of *eros,* and not merely a desire for sexual relations.

Taken at face value, Aristophanes' view of erotic love is ultimately tragic, for complete and lasting unity of lovers can, in fact, never be achieved. *Eros* drives a couple together, but that which they seek to achieve through sexual intercourse can never be obtained. Fractional, fleeting unity of body in sexual intercourse can by itself never overcome its partiality or its brevity. If Aristophanes is right, sexual acts cannot fully satisfy the yearnings of *eros.* As James Rhodes notes:

> Aristophanes does not say that the coitus actually makes two lovers one, even for a moment. Perhaps we should assume that it temporarily alleviates their pain by affording them a pleasurable illusion of wholeness. The illusion, however, is fleeting, the yearning resumes and the delusive wholeness looks more like another of the tortures inflicted on human beings by Zeus than a genuine cure of our ailments.[23]

Erotic love forever pursues what it can never grasp — unending unity with the other. *Eros* dooms us to the tragic unhappiness of compulsively seeking what can never be found. Bloom himself recognizes that even soaring *eros* leaves something left unsatisfied:

> Aristophanes' loves are pointed toward each other horizontally, with no upwardness or transcendence implied in them. Socrates' loves, as we shall see, are vertical, pointing upward and beyond. Aristophanes allows us to take our beloveds with the utmost seriousness, and this is what we seem to want in love. But, for

> those who have really plumbed the depth of the erotic experience, there is a haunting awareness that one wants something beyond, something that can poison our embraces. . . . Socrates' entering wedge against Aristophanes is made here, at the point where our consciousnesses tell that our loves are enchanting, but. . . . [24]

Here Bloom leaves the reader to complete the thought that *eros* as unconnected to anything beyond the two lovers is, *on erotic grounds*, not completely satisfying.

Even if we could have unending unity with the beloved, the kind talked about by Hephaestus, it is unclear that this fusion is what we really want. If we accept that *eros* is a yearning for unity with the beloved,[25] must we also accept that the lovers most deeply desire to be united, merged into one? In other words, do couples in love really desire to be fused together? Would the offer of Hephaestus satisfy erotic lovers?

At best, literal unity with the beloved would be a comical solution to the desire for union as illustrated by Steve Martin and Lily Tomlin in *All of Me*. Two psyches sharing one body is not bliss but schizophrenia. Couples under the spell of *eros* do not wish to become conjoined twins. Indeed, to be fused into one would probably be more penitential than comedic.

Thus, perhaps the real point of Aristophanes' tale is to highlight the "dark side" of *eros*. *Eros,* and its act of sex, has been considered in various times and places (especially those dominated by Manicheans of various kinds) as a demonic force that leads to pain, suffering, and ultimately death. William F. May notes that our Victorian forebears held this view,[26] but the movie genre of "erotic thriller" (*Fatal Attraction, Basic Instinct, Dangerous Liaisons*) indicates that at the very least our imaginations are still much taken by *eros* considered as a powerful malevolent force.

Considering the original context of the *Symposium,* the reference to Hephaestus by Aristophanes may be meant to move the consideration of *eros* in this direction. Original readers of the *Symposium* would be intimately familiar with the works of Homer. In Homer's

Odyssey, Hephaestus comes upon his wife Aphrodite in an adulterous union with the god Ares. Using his blacksmith talents, Hephaestus makes the marriage bed a trap from which Aphrodite and Ares cannot leave nor move apart from one another. When the adulterous pair gets caught in the trap, unable to move from each other, Hephaestus remarks, "I think they may not care to lie much longer, pressing on one another, passionate lovers; they'll have enough of bed together soon."[27] Echoing this scene, Dante in the *Divine Comedy* places a couple, Francesca and Paulo, in an eternal sexual embrace. But their permanent merger into one takes place not in Heaven, but rather in the second circle of Hell as a punishment for their adultery.[28] And justly so. To be partially united with the beloved for a time can be heavenly. But to be completely united with the beloved for all time would not be self-fulfillment, but rather self-extinction.

So *eros* may turn out to be something of a curse. As Stanley Rosen notes, "Man is perpetually restrained within the self-contradictory dimension of desire and satisfaction: self-contradictory because perpetually cyclic."[29] In other words, "Man is perpetually at war with self, gods, and cosmos."[30] Rosen continues, "If *eros* were to succeed in making one from two, he would not heal human nature but destroy it. Aristophanes' real teaching is that cure and ailment constitute a perpetual cycle wherein human genesis gives birth to disease in the act of quenching it. *Eros* is not merely man's friend, but his enemy as well."[31] An *eros* that does not transcend itself can become a kind of death wish, for in desiring to become one with the other, one wishes for self-destruction. Orgasm has been called *le petit mort,* the little death, and *eros* is perhaps ultimately on this view linked to war and self-destruction.

But perhaps this is too dark a reading of *eros* and Aristophanes. Can these difficulties and tensions be eased? How can self-identity be retained, and yet deep and lasting unity of lover and beloved be achieved? Is *eros* a tragic desire for what cannot ever be attained and for what, if attained, would lead to death?

Perhaps *eros* leads to life. The desire to be one with the beloved and yet retain self-identity can be fulfilled at least in part through procreation. Every child of a couple creates a unique unity between them, a unity that not only preserves the individuality of husband and wife but manifests that individuality in a new way. Each child is an enduring expression of a unique union of the couple. In their offspring, a couple realizes the dream offered by Hephaestus to be "rolled into one," "fused together," and "never to be parted." So long as the child shall live, he or she, every one of us, is a living sign, a sacrament if you will, of the union of man and woman — a realization of the dream of eternal unity of lover and beloved. They become one flesh and dwell among us.

The unity achieved by a married couple in procreation includes but also transcends a merely physical unity of various DNA strands. Each child creates in the parents a new unity, for man and woman together become parents to this child. A new and shared dimension is added to them both. She makes him a father; he makes her a mother. They share a lifelong unity as parents of their child. By begetting a child, they will forever be related to one another in a bond that remains as long as the child lives.

In addition to the physical unity achieved in the child, and the familial unity of becoming parents to this child, characteristically a unity of affection and desire also arises between the parents ordered to the care of their child. Among happily married couples, this is most obvious as both mother and father busy themselves in direct and indirect collaboration in raising children. They coordinate plans and cooperate in the running of a home. But even among those who are unhappily married or divorced, characteristically there remains a unity of affection and desire for the well-being of their children. A divorced mother and father may positively hate one another, but with an equal ferocity both parents love and desire the well-being of their children. Indeed, the unity of love and affection for children is sometimes enough to overcome or at least check marital hatred, as when a divorced pair both act "on their best behavior" so as not to spoil a special event for a child or when a couple in crisis gives yet another chance to their marriage so as to save the offspring from a broken home. Even turbulent marital strife characteristically does not shatter the unity of affection and desire achieved through procreation. The procreation and education of children realizes in its own way the deepest desires of *eros* for enduring unity, even after *eros* itself has long since departed.

United physically in the body of the child, united by parenthood in the begetting of the child, united by affection in the care of the child, the procreation and education of offspring realizes, in a certain way, the dream of Aristophanes — that the two shall become one. The procreation and education of children should not be understood therefore in opposition to *eros* but rather as a fulfillment of the deepest aspirations of *eros*.

Vatican II captures the fundamental insights of Aristophanes about *eros* as a drive for unity more than twenty centuries later in teaching that conjugal love is by nature ordained towards the begetting and educating of children who are the supreme gift of marriage. When the Council in *Gaudium et spes* speaks of children contributing substantially to the welfare of the parents, this contribution can be understood to include achieving the goals of *eros*. Now if we understand marital love to include *philia* and *agape,* the procreation and education of children make an even more profound contribution to enhancing love and achieving love's aims, but that is a topic for another occasion.

Chapter 5

Under Pressure

Sexual Discipleship in the Real World

Cristina L. H. Traina

Pope John Paul II's greatest contribution to the Christian world may have been his call to radical discipleship. Reflecting on Jesus' response to the query of the rich young man, John Paul II noted that the Christian life calls for more than simply observing the commandments. It involves accepting the invitation to follow Christ by imitating his complete self-gift:

> The invitation, "go, sell your possessions and give the money to the poor," and the promise "you will have treasure in heaven," are meant for everyone, because they bring out the full meaning of the commandment of love for neighbor, just as the invitation which follows, "Come, follow me," is the new, specific form of the commandment of love of God. Both the commandments and Jesus' invitation to the rich young man stand at the service of a single and indivisible charity, which spontaneously tends towards that perfection whose measure is God alone: "You, therefore, must be perfect, as your heavenly Father is perfect" (Matthew 5:48).[1]

But if the call to radical discipleship is for everyone, in whatever circumstance, that should not imply that it is has only one shape. The traditional Roman Catholic division of vocation between the married and vowed celibate acknowledges this variety in a very basic way. The shape of radical discipleship depends on vocation: the mode and emphasis one has chosen for one's life, cognizant of the intersection of one's gifts with the needs of one's community, often in response to a sense of having been called or elected, within the limits that one's place and time have imposed.[2] "Sell everything and give it to the poor" can apply literally only to people whose vocation does not involve the daily care of dependents, for instance. The first challenge of radical discipleship, then, is defining what radical discipleship means for people in other circumstances.

Second, as John Paul II himself argued, radical discipleship does not apply from the moment of birth, even though it is a universal calling. Discipleship is a developmental commitment. "What can I  do to be perfect?" is a question that "requires mature human freedom." It is the "something more" to which people must come on their own. It is the prompt for an invitation, not the fulfillment of a command. It can be asked only by a person who already loves and respects and has exhausted the commandments that are the platform for Christian life, and it is a question that must be answered by grace.[3]

Where vocation — what is God calling *me* to do? — meets social ethics — what needs to be done? — a third challenge arises: to recognize which of the tasks spread out before me run counter to discipleship and which, although they may be compromised by all sorts of human errors and failings, current and future, I must still undertake from within my vocation. In the real world, radical discipleship can mean lovingly shouldering the least imperfect of a number of inadequate responses to sin and brokenness, if the alternative is doing nothing at all. Some would count Dietrich Bonhoeffer's participation in a plot to assassinate Adolf Hitler in this category. At a more pedestrian level I have the decision to buy organic produce trucked in from a hundred miles away rather than conventionally grown vegetables that are produced locally. The first protects land and workers but spends petroleum and probably more of my budget; the second compromises land and workers but conserves gasoline and my financial resources. Neither is perfect. The question is which, in the circumstances of my calling and the needs of my community, is more faithful?

The fourth challenge of discipleship is even more ordinary: to decide how many of the tasks before me to pursue, and when to pursue them, within the limits of my life and abilities. Radicality cannot mean limitless responsibility, for a person who is responsible for everything cannot truly love any of it. This is the inspiration behind the *ordo caritatis,* which creates rings of decreasing responsibility for the people to whom I am connected. A dullingly familiar example of this sort of priority-setting is the pile of requests for donations that accumulates in nearly every American mailbox. Even if I sell everything and give the proceeds to the poor, to which poor shall I give it? In addition, supporting even a few worthy people and programs can easily erode my ability to meet the other obligations of my vocation. I must choose. This is a limit created by finitude rather than sinfulness, a limit that we must embrace and call good. Radical discipleship may have transcendent significance, but its requirements cannot exceed the practical exigencies of time, place, and embodiment.

Finally, the content of discipleship's foundation — respect for the commandments — is not self-evident. The commandments must be interpreted: "do not kill" becomes "do not murder"; "do not steal" becomes "do not take another's possession unless it is necessary to your survival"; "do not commit adultery" does not condemn rape victims. The meanings of the act protected and of the transgressions proscribed also develop over time; for instance, "do not steal" used to forbid interest charges on loans, but it now forbids only exorbitant interest. According to John Paul II, only charity, a gift of grace, makes it possible truly to fulfill the commandments,[4] implying that only charity makes it possible truly to interpret them as well.

The contemporary American discussion about sexuality has not focused on sex in the context of radical discipleship but has tended to frame itself around the question, "What is commanded or permitted?" Even when the question, "What does radical discipleship mean for sexuality?" is asked, the answer usually consists mainly of prohibited and permitted acts. Yet, as we have seen, the question of radical discipleship is the question of vocation and of real circumstances. What does it mean for us to live our sexuality as disciples in our relationships with spouses, friends, partners, coworkers, and children? How do we account for the fact than some (or many?) Christians are not yet ready for radical discipleship, and what does that mean for the theology and spirituality that underlie our sexual norms? What are the social circumstances — for instance, injustice or coercion — that might mold my sexual behavior, and in what way should I respond to them for the sake of love and justice? Given the limitations of my humanity, how much physical affection will I spend, on whom, and in what way? How many children can I raise? How do I find the appropriate balance between sexual affection, with the responsibilities it entails, and the other good calls on me? Finally, have we exhausted the meaning of adultery and sexual covetousness? Have we in charity fully comprehended the goods the commandments protect? Have we finished interpreting them?

It may appear at this point that the purpose of this essay is to whittle the "radical" in discipleship down to nothing. It is not. The purpose instead is to meditate on the distinction between the profound freedom of inner assent on one hand, and the severe restrictions on external freedom of action on the other. Where should the inner freedom of discipleship take a poor, young Latin American mother with several children who has nearly died in childbirth and whose husband and only economic support has declared that he will abandon her and their children if she refuses sex or if he learns she has had a tubal ligation?[5] Where should it take a thirteen-year-old from a struggling family unknowingly lured into sex slavery in Thailand? Where should it take an unemployed twenty-year-old South African woman supporting her AIDS-orphan siblings who is promised housing and spending money by an older married man in exchange for sex?

In sexual ethics as in all areas of Roman Catholic social ethics — even in the stance of radical discipleship — the question is not how to create perfection, but how to follow perfectly in situations that, because of bad luck, human finitude, or other people's sinfulness, are imperfect. Sexual ethics is no exception; it too needs to take account of the fact that our partners and contexts will rarely fulfill the ideals for relationship and that we are often coerced in ways that threaten our own survival or the survival of those for whom we must care. In addition, in sexual ethics as in all areas of Roman

Catholic ethics, we must be careful to preserve the tradition's wisdom, noting its deepening, increasingly nuanced understanding of the commandments and the goods they protect.

In what follows, the task will be to appreciate the tradition's teaching on sexuality not from the perspective of acts but through the lenses of our deepening sense of the goods that the teaching has protected and of the meaning and demands of vocation in an imperfect and finite world.

Traditional Anthropological Contentions

We can begin with the goods embedded in the tradition. Placing Church teachings against the background of cultural trends highlights the tradition's distinctiveness. Contemporary tendencies in sexual behavior and attitudes are likely no worse than at any other stage of history,[6] but they are still problematic, and they subtly color popular Christian views of sex. Among affluent Westerners, for whom desire no longer centers on basic needs, an individualistic ethic of self-development easily combines with a focus on pleasure to become a drive for self-gratification. High school and college students have sex out of boredom. In less affluent communities and in more patriarchal cultures, men of means take advantage of women's and younger men's poverty to exploit them sexually. In all dysfunctional situations — military occupation, prison, addiction — sex becomes currency. Depending upon where one lives and who one is, sex may be reduced to a thrill, an exercise of power, a means of survival, or an amusing pastime.

Roman Catholicism has some prophetic words to speak in this world. One of these is its double claim about *embodiment*. First, the person is a unity of body and soul.[7] As St. Augustine says, "A man's body is not mere adornment, or external convenience; it belongs to his very nature as a man."[8] The social justice tradition of the last century weighs in heavily here, announcing that dignity demands that bodily integrity must be respected and bodily needs, met. In addition, we believe that God constructs us so that meeting basic bodily needs is by and large pleasurable.[9] Moreover, community is fleshly; at the most basic level, justice and communion entail the negotiation of concrete goods.

But, second, bodily goods are not ultimate goods. Our good in God transcends a good meal, a comforting hug, warm clothes, and all those other physical things that we both need and enjoy. This care to protect, delight in, and celebrate the body without idolizing its goods is one of the keys to Christian ethics of sexuality.[10] Creation, incarnation, and resurrection together mark the channel for all varieties of vocation, warning that faithfulness forbids both rejecting bodily pleasure on one hand and pursuing it single-mindedly on the other.[11] The developed tradition in ethics adds an additional caution: true psychological, physical, and spiritual health is, in any walk of life, a matter of integration and moderation.

In addition, it is only in and through the body that we experience grace; therefore the body also has *sacramental significance*.[12] We wash, and we are baptized. We eat, and we partake of Eucharist. We touch to heal, transfer power, and comfort, and we absolve, confirm, ordain, and anoint the sick. In each of these six sacraments the body is sign and symbol of a sacred reality, a mystery. Our tradition teaches that in marriage the union of bodies is also a sign and symbol of grace that is really present. Recent teaching has emphasized that the self-giving love of each partner for the other, epitomized in the spiritual, emotional, and physical ecstasy of intercourse,[13] is an "efficacious sign" of Christ's love for the Church.[14] This point will be developed further below, but it also has significance far beyond either ecclesiology or theology of sexuality. Contemporary writings on social justice and the environment have also recommended the spiritual, vocational discipline of running sacramental symbolism backward to remind us of the sacredness of all created things: use water reverently, in honor of our baptism; eat reverently, in honor of the Eucharist; fast, but also feast.[15] In marital sexual union, as in other sacramental acts, the elements — here our bodies themselves — must be revered and  honored as the icons of transforming grace. Likewise, the desire for touch and its satisfaction must be reverent, both inside and outside the sacrament of marriage.[16]

At the same time, we must be cautious about overextending the metaphor, thereby missing something profoundly important about the human reality on which the sacrament depends. Short-circuiting the full character of sexuality by moving immediately to theology of marriage is something like reducing a discussion of the meaning of eating to theology of Eucharist. Although this strategy exposes much that is good, true, and essential to sexuality, it does not reveal everything that is good, true, and essential to it. In particular, there is much to learn about appropriate and holy uses of sensuality and noncoital sexuality from sources beyond theology of marriage: the psychology of touch, non-Christian cultures, and gay and lesbian Christians.[17]

Further, for Roman Catholic Christians the decision about how to live one's good sexuality has always been one of *vocation,* not mere lifestyle choice. Although in generations past, monogamous, heterosexual marriage (partly because of skepticism about sexual activity, and partly because of its discouragement of contemplation) was not always revered as highly as vowed celibacy, both marriage and celibacy have always been seen as callings that involve particular social and ecclesial roles; the development of very similar virtues, including chastity; and thoughtful support and encouragement from both the Church and wider society. We can expect that any additions we might want to make to the vocational list — for instance, indefinite or provisional singleness, or gay and lesbian marriage — would pursue the same virtues and require the same kind of support. Such a vision of sexual vocation contrasts starkly with contemporary Western secular culture, which sees decisions about the structure of sexual life as lifestyle choices that, although almost unlimited, do not involve any responsibilities beyond those one chooses to embrace; nor, sadly, are they seen as deserving or needing any material or communal support.[18] In sum, a theology of vocation sees the sexual self before God and in community — "What is God through others inviting and enabling me, in my embodiment, to be and to do?" — rather than in isolation — "What do I want to be? How do I organize my life in order to fulfill my desire for pleasure and make myself happy?"[19]

Traditionally in Roman Catholicism, the vocation of active sexuality is also the vocation of married *procreativity.* One way of putting this is that coitus is appropriate only when intentional, loving procreation is appropriate, and procreation is appropriate only when a couple is vowed to each other and is (at least implicitly) open to cooperating with God's creative power. Ideally, they are also supported by church and community in these commitments, not to mention aided by the sanctifying grace of the sacrament of marriage.[20] This is not just a matter of honoring the awesome and holy power of procreation. It is also a matter of justice on both the microscopic and macroscopic levels. Children created carelessly by parents who are not committed to a household, who do not see their children as divine gifts, and who do not see the raising of them as a holy task will suffer.[21] This is why the Church condemns narcissistic procreation.[22] On the societal level, children who lack the social and legal protections that most societies give to marriage typically suffer economic, social, and political marginalization, as do their mothers.

A further argument for the link between marriage, procreation, and intercourse has developed since the Vatican's recognition of the romantic, companionate marriage in the mid-twentieth century: married love that does not turn outward in mutual vulnerability to nurture and possibly also to create life is fundamentally selfish. Married love must expand to support the community (by bearing and raising new members of church and society, by practicing hospitality in the community, or both) or it becomes insular and festers.[23] It ceases to be a vocation and is reduced to a lifestyle. This deepened vision of marriage's character and goods is one of the most profound developments in Church teaching on marriage and sexuality.

The same respect for the holiness of procreation and parenthood as a vocation lies behind Roman Catholicism's *condemnation of a contraceptive mentality:* an attitude that, by removing parenthood completely from the meaning of marital heterosexual intercourse, sees sex purely as power, play, or mutual pleasure, with no transcendent dimension. If the vision behind this attitude is purely immediate — if it is missing a divine referent, a sense of calling — marriage has ceased to be a vocation. Pope Paul VI was at least partly right when he said that wide availability of contraceptives could lead us, especially men, to exploit our sexual partners and could lead governments to intercede in the process of couples' vocational decisions about parenthood.[24] But this same reminder that marriage is a vocation, deepened and enriched in recent restatements, also opens the door to the possibility that neither contraception, nor even regulation of intercourse so as to prevent all future conception, necessarily involves a contraceptive mentality. For example, in the case of hospitality to an ill child or aging parent, a couple might opt against conception indefinitely, precisely out of their sense of marital vocation. In couples for whom decisions about intercourse lie mainly with the husband, decisions about when to conceive children will not be fully mutual; in these cases a woman's use of contraception actually increases the likelihood that a couple will put off conception until both partners are truly prepared to conceive and care well for a (or another) child.

Finally, despite Thomas Aquinas's classification of sexuality, reproduction, and education of children as characteristics we share with animals,[25] twentieth-century Church teaching was very clear that sex does not have the inevitability of blind instinct. Like all passions, sexual desire is good in itself, because it directs us to a genuine good. But it is not yet moral; we can easily fasten it on an object or a situation that would pervert its purposes. It must be humanized by being made *subject to reason,* reflected upon, channeled, and controlled, directed to an appropriate purpose. This claim is what makes sex a matter of vocation, of spiritual growth, and of moral debate rather than something that merely "happens" to us. This claim, too, will be developed further below. It is essential to note for now merely that Roman Catholics across the spectrum, regardless of their position on homosexual unions, oppose the reduction of sexual desire to an itch that must be scratched. All affirm that sexual desire in itself indicates a good-for-us, a good so sacred and so strongly connected with vocation that it must be channeled rationally and reverently. This is a prophetic reminder in a culture that often encourages abdication of responsibility by suggesting that romantic urges are only irresistible, insignificant impulses.

Classical and contemporary teaching, then, bring us to at least the following affirmations:

- The body, its desires, and its pleasures are good creations integral to human nature.

- The goods to which desires point must be pursued rationally, within the limits set by vocation. In particular, vocational choices about the sexual use of our bodies are a recognized matter of spiritual vocation, and they demand and deserve the support of the community.

- Embodied relations honor their inherent vocational and sacramental significance by pointing beyond themselves to transcendence (rather than being caught up merely in the physical) and by opening generously toward others (rather than being caught up in themselves).

- Of all dimensions of sensuality and sexuality, vaginal intercourse must be especially carefully protected, supported, and revered, because it participates in God's creative power and can entail a lifelong vocation of parenting, recognized and supported in the sacrament of matrimony.

Refining the Focus: Sexual Vocation and Theological Method

Addressing the body and vocation in a general way provides a platform for thinking about sex and real-world discipleship, but the unique richness of Roman Catholic discourse on sexuality also flows from its careful development of three distinct but presumably coherent levels of discourse: discussions of individual virtue, or chastity; discussions of couple relationships; and discussions of communal relations, or justice. It also entails negotiations about the power of new insights to alter specific moral conclusions reached in earlier times. Unfolding and relating these overlapping conversations are the keys to bridging the apparent gap between the invitation to radical discipleship and enacting love and justice in a finite, imperfect world. Their mutual implications have not been fully developed.

The Individual

On one level, Roman Catholic ethics of sexuality is about the moral and spiritual growth of the individual. Two kinds of questions traditionally arise for individual sexual virtue: vocation (discussed above) and chastity. Chastity is one of two sexual virtues that fall under temperance, which has to do with the pleasures of touch.[26] In the past, discussions of chastity have been underdeveloped: they focused almost exclusively on intercourse, and consequently chastity's connection to its root virtue was often incompletely explored.[27] Yet in recent Church writings chastity and sexuality seem to be undergoing an expansion of meaning that could increase their usefulness not only for sexual ethics but also for an ethic of sensuality generally, emphasizing sex, from the perspective of individual experience, as a special case of touch. Such a development considerably enlarges and nuances Roman Catholic notions of the purposes of sexuality in ways that have not been acknowledged fully, promising us tools for thinking about the significance of physical affection in the complex jumble of relationships that make up a real life.

Chastity is rooted in temperance, the habit that moderates desires for pleasures of touch; traditionally, food, drink, and sex.[28] Hagiography, manuals of moral theology, and even *The Da Vinci Code*[29] create the impression that temperance is a form of self-denial that cultivates hatred for these desires and pleasures. As contemporary American experience with food, alcohol, and sexuality confirm, this sort of self-denial and hatred is destructive, leading either to illness and death (as in anorexia) or to obsession and bingeing. True temperance, on the other hand, entails learning rational enjoyment of food, drink, and sex, things God has created for our good. The point is to calm and channel the impulses of the passions in a way that promotes physical and spiritual flourishing.[30] Temperate desires and pleasures preserve the body's health, are appropriate to the social and cultural situation, and preserve time, attention, and resources adequate to our other obligations.[31]

However, Thomas Aquinas and the subsequent tradition do not treat touch in precisely the same way as eating and drinking. For example, the temperate person avoids not only overeating and obsession over food, but also undernourishment and revulsion toward food.[32] This suggests that a discussion of chastity would begin with touch, discuss the dangers of excessive and inadequate touch, and then treat intercourse as a special case. Rather, in the tradition, chastity by definition is about intercourse, which in turn entails observing the absolute limits set by theology of marriage. As a result, Thomas's schema reduces the ethics of touch to the ethics of intercourse, including a perfunctory treatment of looking, kissing, and erotic touching under purity and lust, and ignoring general touching altogether.[33] Unlike food and drink, for Thomas sexual touch is not essential to every individual's health; its purpose is to serve humanity generally through procreation in the vocation of marriage. Virginity is not a frustration of sexuality but a choice not to use it. Therefore excessive sex is any use of intercourse that does not at least potentially benefit humanity through marital procreation. Deficiency can exist only in marriage: refusal to pay the marital debt, or total avoidance of procreation.

The possibility that physical affection might be as important as food is to individual flourishing, or as sex is to the human race, does not occur to Thomas. This lacuna, repeated in subsequent discussions of temperance, has led to a culture that has (sometimes simultaneously) treated touching as at least incipiently sexual and therefore as forbidden outside marriage on the one hand, and as irrelevant to chastity and purity and therefore as morally uninteresting on the other. This seems inadequate to all we know about the necessity of touch for human flourishing and about the potential abusiveness of "friendly" touch. It is as possible and as wrong to touch too little as too much.[34] Reading chastity against temperance, it seems appropriate to extend the traditional formulation a bit, using the plans created for food and drink to build an addition to the house called "touch."

Such an expansion of temperance may be in the offing. The *Catechism* now contains language that seems to extend sexuality to encompass sensuality. According to the *Catechism,* although sexuality's purpose (finality) is procreation,[35] sexuality permeates our whole existence and grounds all our relationships: "*sexuality* affects all aspects of the human person in the unity of his body and soul. It especially concerns affectivity, the capacity to love and to procreate, and in a more general way the aptitude for forming bonds of communion with others."[36] Over forty years ago, Pope John Paul II wrote that "an exuberant and readily roused sensuality is the stuff from which a rich — if difficult — personal life may be made. It may help the individual to respond more readily and completely to the decisive elements in personal love. [When sublimated,] primitive sensual excitability (provided it is not of morbid origin) can become a factor making for a fuller and more ardent love."[37] The heavy lines between love, sex, touch, and friendship have blurred; it becomes impossible to think of even virginity or abstinence as "not using" sexuality. Second, the *Catechism* affirms the social character of chastity, taking it far beyond the "delectations of touch" and into conversations about justice and community; the point of chastity is love, the capacity to give our whole selves, generously and undistractedly, in loving friendship and spiritual communion.[38] Combining these two developments, we begin to piece together a vision of touch and of sexuality that has a "finality" that is not exhausted by procreative marital unity.[39] Such a development can connect temperance (my virtue with respect to what is good for me, physically and spiritually) with justice and hospitality (my virtue with respect to what is due others). This expansion of vision makes temperance an ideal and welcome resource for dealing with the whole range of physical affection.

In harmony with contemporary developmental psychology, recent Vatican statements have also reemphasized that although everyone is called to chastity,[40] chastity — like any virtue — is not a habit that anyone should be expected to possess instantaneously: "chastity has *laws of growth* which progress through stages."[41] Developing healthy, balanced desires and a reliable habit of appropriate responses to them takes practice. We should anticipate that we will develop chastity with great effort, over a lifetime, with some slips and mistakes; we should never consider chastity to have been acquired once and for all. A language of absolute sexual norms is not adequate to this developmental vision, a fact acknowledged by recent cautions to tread gently in many cases of masturbation and homosexual sex, for example.[42] Yet the *Catechism* also warns that the stages through which chastity progresses are "marked by imperfection and too often by sin"[43] and that difficult external circumstances never justify transgression of (for example) proscriptions of cohabitation and remarriage.[44] This combination of claims raises an important complex of questions that has not been addressed adequately: what are the relationships among developmental stages, virtue, imperfection, and sin? What would sinless development or growth in virtue look like? What is the distinction between imperfection and sin? Is "developmentally appropriate" behavior "right" even if it is "unperfected"? A passage from *Love and Responsibility* exemplifies some dimensions of this complexity:

> A man and a woman whose love has not begun to mature, has not established itself as a genuine union of persons, should not marry, for they are not ready to undergo the test to which married life will subject them. This does not, however, mean that their love must have reached full maturity at the moment of marriage, but only that it must be ripe enough for its continued ripening in and through marriage to be ensured.[45]

This claim makes eminent pastoral sense, but its meaning for moral theology is unclear. If love — and presumably chastity — are not complete at marriage, is this a matter of incomplete development, of sin and virtue, or of both? This is the gap that we have not filled: what shape does a good life take *on the way* to sexual virtue and maturity, and *on the way* to mature acceptance of radical discipleship?

Finally, the Church teaches that chastity's acts are shaped by cultural and relational circumstances: chastity requires the "practice of an ascesis adapted to the situations that confront [us]."[46] For instance, St. Paul's nuanced instructions about eating meat offered to idols indicate that what temperance requires in a given setting is governed by what witnessing to Christ demands, then and there. We still lack similar concrete applications of chastity for situations in which, for example, little or no "cultural effort"[47] is being made to support it, or in which customs for betrothal and marriage do not follow the Western model.

The Couple

Perhaps the most heralded recent development in Church teaching on sexuality was *Casti connubii*'s recognition of the unitive meaning of procreative intercourse, followed closely by *Humanae vitae*'s declaration of unity's equal status with procreativity. It is impossible to exaggerate the significance of this development for a tradition that not long ago considered intercourse so destructive to human rationality that it merely tolerated sex, and then only for the sake of the rational end of procreation.[48] We should pause and appreciate the enormity of the change in moral theology, as well as the methodological trend it may symbolize: it brings moral theology closer to traditional Christian mystical theology, in which sexual intercourse and romantic love have for centuries been used to symbolize the soul's relationship with God.

In addition, *Humanae vitae,* subsequent documents on sexuality, and all of John Paul II's writings on sexuality celebrate the depth and complexity of marital commitment. They recognize the profundity of a couple's vow not merely to be constant to each other but actually to embody Christ for each other, to open their love generously to the huge and unknowable task of child-rearing, and to enact these promises lovingly in the concrete yet mysterious act of sexual connection. Here the Church recognizes that intercourse confirms and strengthens a couple's mutual commitment of self-gift, reinforces their emotional bond, bestows joy and pleasure through generous sensitivity, and recalls or maybe even bestows sacramental grace. Clearly, this new vision is a gain: it better comprehends the experience of healthy marital sexuality and more faithfully reflects our understanding of the body's goodness and of the integrity of body and spirit. It sees a couple's continuing emotional and spiritual bond as part of the fabric of the marriage, not merely as fruits of it. And it installs profound reverence and respect for human dignity — both one's partner's and one's own — as a fundamental criterion of sexual relations.

This message is perhaps most prophetic not in the West, where at least romantic and spiritual visions of union are commonplace in the dominant culture, but in places like sub-Saharan Africa, in which young women in desperate economic situations gain some financial stability and social status by accepting support from men who have no intention of marrying them. In these and other exploitive situations, sex loses all of its unifying and symbolic value.

The growing edge of this new message is official teaching on individual agency and married sexuality. Many recent writings treat the couple as if they possessed a single will.[49] This is neither an orthodox belief nor a realistic foundation on which to build either sacramental marriage or an ethic of sexuality. It is not true to the Church's egalitarian vision of marriage, which in turn depends upon the traditional vision of moral agency, in which — although a couple can and must support each other in virtue and should strive to be partners in vocation — morally each spouse is and must remain an individual actor whose behavior and attitudes are independent of the other's. One's virtue cannot depend on what one's spouse does. Further, marriage is a social institution, in which obligations to God, self, children, and world must be met whether or not one's partner is willing to assist or to act virtuously. In a very real sense a person's spouse is part of the situation in which she must behave ethically rather than a co-actor indistinguishable from her. So, for instance, it may be perfectly true that regulating their fertility through planned abstinence can help couples "to drive out selfishness," making them better role models and partners.[50] But admonitions to *couples* to practice planned abstinence do not answer the question of what, for example, virtuous *women* are to do either when husbands ignore the admonition or when the situation implies that refusing sex will bring desertion, beating, exposure to disease contracted through men's subsequent use of prostitution, or other forms of violence.[51] The Catholic moral tradition has ample resources to develop this dimension of individual moral agency in marriage, and it must employ them if the new vision of married sexuality is to be faithful to that moral tradition.

In addition, the place of pleasure in sexual relations is ambiguous. Because John Paul II sees intercourse as the only sexual act in which a couple's mutual, total self-gift transcends them in possible conception and parenthood creating a unity and shared vocation larger than both of them, he rigorously condemns both noncoital sex and intercourse merely for the sake of pleasure (one's own or, apparently, one's spouse's). However, pleasure is still essential to the act, so much so that orgasm should as far as possible be simultaneous. He also instructs spouses to focus on each other (rather than on vocation or reproductive purpose) during sex; acknowledges that differences between male and female arousal patterns guarantee men's coital pleasure but render women's highly uncertain; and goes to great lengths to instruct men on their responsibility to ensure that their wives enjoy sex. His goal is to reemphasize the indispensability of loving intercourse to a healthy marriage; if wives do not feel loved and cared for in *the* act that is intended to create the couple as spouses, its purpose will fail and the marriage will disintegrate.[52] The additional effect is to install erotic playfulness, pleasure, and tenderness as staples of married life and love, elements without which the couple cannot realize their vocation. Yet in his 1994 letter *Gratissimam sane* John Paul II appears to step back from his earlier emphasis on pleasure-giving as essential to (though not constitutive of) marital self-gift, implying that subjective pleasure is not a measure of intimate union at all. This could in turn be read as a judgment that, although intercourse is necessarily pleasant for the male participant, a woman's lack of pleasure is irrelevant to the success of intercourse as a mutual moral embrace of marital vocation.[53] This leaves one wondering whether the meaning of marital intercourse entails mutual pleasure after all.

Yet overall the developing tradition's emphasis on marital union in sexuality, the Song of Songs, and the mystical tradition celebrate mutual desire and its generous, loving, playful fulfillment as a good in itself, and John Paul II has admitted in at least some writings that these goods are difficult for women to achieve in intercourse. It is appropriate to continue to ask whether non-procreative forms of sexual delight are not perfectly appropriate within committed unions, which — given our growing longevity — now often need to weather the changes and challenges of fifty or more years together rather than the average of ten to twenty that even very recent ancestors could expect. Longer unions may require larger, more sophisticated tool sets.[54]

The Community

Traditionally sexuality was primarily a matter of personal virtue, not social justice. Yet the tradition contains significant overtures to justice. Among its strengths, for example, is its condemnation of fornication on the basis of the injustice it does to the child conceived out of wedlock;[55] its irritating, tacit recognition that the person wielding greater power in a situation of possible sexual contact is the one to be addressed morally;[56] its more recent concern that couples strive for mutuality and equality; and above all, its current insistence that society supply political, economic, and social conditions that encourage healthy sexuality and family life to flourish. Recent commentators who identify consumerism, narcissism, poverty, low wages, illiteracy, unemployment, and poor health care as the real enemies of families and healthy sexuality can find ample support in Vatican documents.[57]

Yet to date Church teaching on sexual justice has been limited to prophetic denunciation of unhealthy social conditions. It also has not taken account of the theology of growth in virtue that it also espouses. Typically, official teaching expresses sympathy for the pressures married couples face but recommends that they persevere prayerfully in fulfilling the absolute norms of noncontraceptive marital sexuality.[58] For example, under China's one-child policy, which severely restricts the rights of children born in excess of a family's quota, a couple might prefer to avoid pressure for abortion by guaranteeing (not just discouraging) unwanted conception. This could mean practicing as much as 75 percent abstinence, in order to account for the vagaries of fertility cycles and for the false fertility signals created by stress. This might be possible for a chaste, mutually giving, prayerful married couple. But greater difficulties arise for a couple in which husband, wife, or both do not meet these conditions, when they have not yet achieved the virtue of chastity.

Further, the circumstances in which the sacramental meanings of sexuality are in fact most profoundly transgressed are defined primarily not by external pressures of family policy or by uncontrolled lust but by unjust use of power inside the sexual relationship. Traditionally, the common good language of social justice is the rubric for analyzing victims' rights and responsibilities in unjust situations. For example, if I am starving and must take food from another person in order to preserve my life, this is not stealing; this is in effect forcing society to fulfill obligations to me that it has neglected. It seems reasonable for victims of sexual coercion, whose lives and safety may also be at stake if they do not cooperate, also to behave self-protectively, to take for themselves the protection that their community has not granted them. In countries where child sex-workers are common, it may make less sense for an enslaved girl to risk her life by resisting violently and probably ineffectively, fleeing, or refusing to perform than to acquiesce regretfully, biding her time until she can plan an intelligent escape. The Church would obviously counsel men to stop visiting child prostitutes. But until the day when men utterly cease to do so, how can the young girls and boys who are their victims conduct themselves with integrity and self-love? The question for them is not self-control in the face of lust, but survival in circumstances of coercion. Similarly, as has already been mentioned, the culturally and legally enforced, relatively less powerful position of millions of women in comparison to their husbands creates a situation in which refusal to have sex risks loss of livelihood for themselves and their existing children. The Church would, of course, castigate the husbands for allowing social inequalities to permeate their intimate relations. But in the meantime, what are their wives to do?

The moral tradition has the tools to develop answers to these questions. When the issue is self- and other-defense in the face of abuse of power—circumstances we can expect to continue until the kingdom of God is realized fully—the rules that apply are normally not moral absolutes. For instance, just-war theory counsels us not to refrain from coercion and deadly violence (do not kill) but to use them in a measured way to preserve life and order (do not kill unjustly). Radical nonviolence is permitted, but—as it is potentially self-sacrificial—it is not required. Similarly, when sex becomes the field on which power is played out unjustly, the point may no longer be sexual purity but, as in war, legitimate self-preservation. It can be argued that we need a "just-sex" theory for cases of subtly or overtly coercive sex and that we will need it until the parousia.[59]

Reason

The Roman Catholic moral tradition affirms that creation is rationally organized; that through the intellect reason discovers ends and develops norms; and that through the will reason calms and directs the passions. Reason as interpreter of the structure, ends, and meaning of sexual reproduction has long shaped Catholic sexual ethics. But it also makes three important contributions of other kinds to the ethic of sexuality.

First, the lack of development noted under justice above points out not only an injustice but also a logical inconsistency: In every other area of life, circumstances of coercion matter. They do not simply lessen one's guilt; reasoning is developed that preserves one's virtue even when one is regretfully using coercive violence to defend oneself. This strategy is thought to be not dishonest, but realistic. In sexuality, however, coercive circumstances typically have not led to the general refinement of rules but to permission for priests to excuse individuals from rules on a case-by-case basis—usually on the basis of incompletely formed intentions, which implies that the actor is thoughtless and immature rather than carefully and faithfully reflective. This inconsistency is troubling. Integrity demands both the creation of justice in *societies* in which political, social, and economic conditions impede the development of a sacramental understanding of sexuality and systematic guidelines for *persons* who for the foreseeable future must live out their sexuality under these difficult conditions. Sin is no more easily uprooted from sexual relations than from international politics.

Second, one premise of the natural law moral tradition on which the Roman Catholic tradition depends is that grace completes nature rather than contradicting it. One consequence of this belief is that true virtue tends to integrate, support, and nurture our development on all levels from individual to global and from spiritual through emotional and intellectual to physical. A corollary is the belief that one sign of vice is the disintegration of these unities. Wisdom about holistic flourishing from medical, historical, philosophical, and other scientific sources is, and always has been, relevant to general judgments about ethical fittingness. It is our responsibility to continue this tradition by ensuring that our moral thinking reflects the best of the contemporary sources of this wisdom. On the basis of theological and methodological consistency, then, medieval assumptions about sexuality's purposes that are rooted in what was in the Middle Ages revolutionary wisdom from Aristotelian biology should be tested against contemporary insights from sociology and psychology and, if necessary, expanded or replaced.[60]

In that case, for instance, evidence about wholesomeness, balance, and longevity in committed homosexual relationships must be attended to. Much has been made recently of the destructiveness of homosexual unions to the stability of heterosexual marriage and family. The argument is that acceptance of sexual relationships that are not ordered to procreation is acceptance of a barren, disordered vision of sexuality and of matrimony, which will in turn infect and destroy not just homosexual couples but heterosexual marriage.[61] But honesty requires us to ask what it is about committed homosexual relationships and sterile marriages that permits them to be stable and fruitful, even without procreativity. *Humanae vitae* already affirms coitus's "natural adaptation to the expression and strengthening of the union of husband and wife" in infertile couples.[62] John Paul II himself has argued that "man masters 'nature' by exploiting more and more effectively the possibilities latent in it."[63] Is the traditional vision of the natural possibilities latent in sex too narrow?

Less radically, I have already noted new evidence of the necessity of touch for human health, and of the importance of sensuality for human bonding, that suggests procreation may not be the only end of physical affection. A parish pastor related the story of a nun who, having received the gift of a massage, wept during the therapy because it was the first time during her long celibate ministry that she had ever been touched with such love and care.[64] Clearly humans do and must experience love and care, like grace, through the body. If so, we need to develop a positive ethic of touch in addition to, and as a ground for, the developing negative ethic on abuse. It may be truer to our current best understanding of ourselves to view intercourse as a special, sacramental case of the ethics of touch rather than as the paradigm by which all touch is interpreted.

These three examples illustrate the inductive, expansive character of reasoning that is adequate to human dignity. In moral reasoning, analytical simplifications must always follow, rather than replace, thoughtful, broad reflection on persons, goods, and concrete circumstances.

Radical Discipleship Revisited

In what way might all of these considerations affect our discussions of sexual ethics? First, I would like to suggest that they already have. Most of them are operative among all parties to the Roman Catholic discussion of sexual ethics, although not all are realized to the same degree in all treatments. But, second, more consistently applied, they may alter the ways in which we describe and evaluate cases. For instance, the encyclical *Veritatis splendor* combines a call to radical discipleship and affirmation of moral absolutes, a tension that begs for concrete illustration. Reaching for biblical examples, John Paul II moves from the Gospel of Matthew's account of the failure of the rich young man to the story of Susanna in the book of Daniel (Dn 13). Ambushed in her own husband's garden by two powerful and lecherous judges, associates of her husband's, the chaste Susanna is given the choice between having sex with them or refusing and being reported to have committed adultery with yet another man. Susanna chooses the latter, is brought to trial, and is saved from condemnation to death only by Daniel's last-minute brilliant cross-examination of her accusers. John Paul II concludes:

> Susanna, preferring to fall innocent into the hands of the judges, bears witness not only to her faith and trust in God but also to

> her obedience to the truth and to the absoluteness of the moral order. By her readiness to die a martyr, she proclaims that it is not right to do what God's law qualifies as evil in order to draw some good from it. Susanna chose for herself the "better part": Hers was a perfectly clear witness, without any compromise, to the truth about the good and to the God of Israel. By her acts, she revealed the holiness of God.[65]

In his view, the judges were tempting Susanna to adultery, a violation of the vocational and affective unity that she shared with her husband, Joakim. She resisted that temptation in the face of apparently certain death, putting fidelity to her husband and to the laws of God above her own life.

Anyone who has experienced sexual coercion — or is close to someone who has — may feel rather odd about leaving the story here. What do our gleanings from the tradition contribute to further analysis of it? Certainly, as John Paul II agrees, sex-under-blackmail violates integrity and sacramentality for Susanna, Joakim, and the judges, although it is not obvious that moral responsibility for this violation should fall upon Susanna when it is the judges who both propose the act and threaten her life. Susanna is plainly temperate: she neither desires sexual contact with the judges, exhibits any wish to deceive Joakim, nor is tempted by any sort of favor offered by the judges (unless preservation of innocent life can be counted as "drawing some good" from adultery). Rather, she is the victim of two unscrupulous men's exploitation of a legal system unjustly weighted against women, and of a husband either so untrusting of her or so reluctant to risk his political reputation that he will not challenge her accusers.

Thus regardless of how the biblical author may have viewed sin, if we are faithful to our own moral tradition, we need not and perhaps cannot read this as a simple choice between chastity and adultery. We might, instead, read her as asserting her dignity at very high cost, perhaps in a last-minute attempt to call the judges' bluff. We must examine her words carefully. She is in checkmate. She is so powerless that simply by being cornered alone in her own husband's garden by the trespassing judges she receives a death sentence: " 'I am completely trapped,' Susanna groaned. 'If I yield, it will be my death [for committing adultery]; if I refuse, I cannot escape your power [that is, death again]. Yet it is better for me to fall into your power without guilt than to sin before the Lord' " (Dn 13:22–23). We might read her as saying, "if you are determined to kill me, let me at least die unviolated rather than violated." And then she seals her choice by screaming.

It is possible in fact to read this decision without a sexual reference at all, simply as an act of witness to human dignity in the face of inhumane oppression — also an act of radical discipleship, but with a slightly different justification.[66] From this point of view Susanna is a person of mature faith who goes beyond the simple norm of self-preservation to challenge two men who very much need to learn the lesson of respect for human dignity; in the process, she ensures that they will humiliate her only once, in an adultery trial, rather than two additional times, in coerced sex. One could not conclude from this that others in similar situations were required to behave similarly.

But even supposing that one views Susanna's choice as a simple one between sexual dissoluteness and chastity, when one reads her story against the backdrop of her exceedingly unjust situation it may teach more lessons than at first appear. If adultery is tantamount to apostasy, then Susanna would fall into the same category as Felicity and Perpetua, early Christian women who (despite their families' pleadings) refused to renounce their faith and were executed by the Romans. For centuries much was made of their willingness to renounce motherhood for the sake of their faith, implying that neither life nor any human attachment should stand in the way of fidelity to belief. One could argue then that if Felicity and Perpetua are required to sacrifice themselves for their faith, certainly Susanna (who apparently is not a mother) must do so. But a closer look reveals that Felicity and Perpetua do not abandon their responsibilities as mothers but seek out others to shoulder them: both find good, stable homes for their children before committing themselves irreversibly to death. All three women are in rare positions: they can witness radically in the most extreme way possible, by risking their lives for theological truth, without abandoning any important worldly responsibilities. It can be argued that Susanna was permitted to choose only the circumstances of her apparently inevitable death. Yet radical discipleship might not even have entailed death for Felicity and Perpetua had they not been able to find loving guardians for their children; one can argue that in their cases fidelity to divine calling might have included escape, recantation followed by quiet underground support of the Christian community, or some other solution that would have permitted them to care for their children.

Theological and methodological trends outlined in this paper force us to ask important further questions about radical discipleship. First, the courageous, radical, often ascetic witness of relatively unencumbered saints is inspiring. But the very definition of radical discipleship as a mature step that is the result of gradual developmental growth implies that the behavior of such saints cannot be imitated by immature Christians. Nor can their single-mindedness be imitated even by radical disciples with responsibilities for others. And so the behavior of "free agent" radical disciples cannot be installed either as a minimal standard or as a goal for the rest of us. If we begin with vocation — with holistic reverence for ourselves and others in the midst of concrete callings — we can begin to describe the character of true self-gift, an act that for virtuous people is not less holy for having to be divided among many responsibilities both to others and to self. Occasionally — especially in cases of coercion — self-gift may require making temperate sexual concessions like those we find in the ethic of self-defense.

Second, when we carefully examine traditional teachings on temperance, we discover that enjoyment of the simultaneously given and received pleasure of human touch is in fact integral to a life of balance and virtue. In addition, contemporary psychological writing suggests that whether married or not, we, and those we love, need each others' affectionate touch if we are to have the health and energy that a vigorous life requires. And spouses gain so much from loving sexual relations that John Paul II has characterized intercourse as practically indispensable to a healthy marriage. It is likely that love-making is essential to the health of any committed lifelong partnership. The pleasure of affectionate touch may then be not just acceptable within a life of radical discipleship but essential to it. This would be an unaccustomed place to begin an ethic of sexuality, but one with very solid traditional credentials.

Chapter 6

Celibacy

Decisive Moments in Its History

John O'Malley, S.J.

In the wake of the sexual-abuse scandal of the past few years, the requirement of celibacy for ordination to the priesthood in the Roman Catholic Church has become a topic of conversation among Catholics and non-Catholics alike. Despite the subject's currency in the media (or perhaps because of it), for most people, it seems, lots of questions remain. Why and how, for instance, did the celibate state become a prerequisite for ordination in the Western church? Those are the two questions I will address, but I do not pretend in these few pages to do anything more than provide a sketch of the history of the issue. I hope, however, that even such a brief treatment will be helpful in framing the other contributions in this volume and providing a long-range perspective. I divide what I have to say into two unequal parts. The first part consists simply in six points of clarification, so that we can be sure what we are talking about. In the second I will review the basic history.

First, three words that recur over and over again in the historical sources need to be defined: celibacy, continence, and chastity. Celibacy is today sometimes used as a synonym for sexual abstinence ("I've been celibate for a year"), but in our context it means, rather, not being married, being "single." That is the meaning it has even today in Romance languages. In Italian, *celibe* for a man means he is unmarried, a bachelor. Continence in the tradition we are concerned with means being married but not engaging in marital relations with one's spouse. In that tradition, continence is as important an issue as celibacy, as will become clear below. Chastity in the past and in the present is the virtue required of all Christians according to their state in life, whether single or married, and is opposed to the vice of lust. As such, chastity does not enter directly into the discussion below, but it is of course presumed as the motivation and the goal for all legislation on celibacy and continence.

Second, we are dealing here with the local or diocesan clergy, not members of religious orders. All members of religious orders, whether male or female, take a vow of chastity that at the same time commits them to the celibate state. The vow is the expression of a tradition different from that of the diocesan clergy. Third, for the diocesan clergy, celibacy is an ecclesiastical discipline, a ruling by the church for the church and therefore subject to change. It is not as such a doctrine or dogma. But a qualification is in order. There are a few scholars who, while admitting that the discipline of celibacy may be subject to change, argue that the tradition of continence for deacons, priests, and bishops is of apostolic origin and, hence, not subject to change, at least not for priests and bishops. That is very much a minority opinion, but it needs to be mentioned.[1]

Fourth, although the requirement of celibacy for ordination to the priesthood is a discipline or law, the official understanding of it, as indicated in the new *Code of Canon Law,* recognizes it as also a charism, a gift from God. The church ordains those who have received the gift, so that it does not so much impose celibacy as invite to ordination those who have the gift.

Fifth, I will be talking about the Western church, the Latin Rite, not about the Greek-speaking church before the Great Schism of 1054 nor about priests of other rites that are in communion with Rome. Priests from those rites (Ukranian, Melkite, and others) have different disciplines in this regard whose origins reach far back into their traditions. This means, finally, that even today there are priests from churches in full communion with Rome, hence fully Catholic, who are married. There are, therefore, legitimately married priests in the Catholic Church. The steady opposition of the American Latin-Rite hierarchy to the presence of married Eastern Catholic priests in North America has generally prevented married clergy from those churches serving here. This policy was formalized in 1929 with the Vatican decree *Cum Date Fuerit*. In recent years some bishops in the Ukranian and Ruthenian Catholic Churches in North America have not altogether followed this policy and seem to have suffered no penalty for their actions. Moreover, there are in the United States a small number of former Episcopalian priests, married, who have converted to Catholicism and are now legitimately functioning as Roman Catholic priests, that is, functioning within the so-called Latin Rite. They are not obliged to observe continence with their spouses.

With those clarifications in place, we can turn to the history of celibacy. I will begin with a few words about the Bible, and then describe three decisive moments — the fourth century, the eleventh, and the sixteenth. In the Old Testament, marriage was considered honorable and compulsory for all and to have many children was viewed as a sign of divine favor. Virginity as a state of life consecrated to God was unknown except possibly among the Essenes.

It is significant, therefore, that in the New Testament and related sources there is no indication that either John the Baptist or Jesus was married. Although the celibacy of John and Jesus is thus argued "from silence," which usually does not make for a strong case, it seems a solid argument here. Their celibacy can be construed as suggesting a shift in values. Indeed, celibacy undertaken "for the sake of the kingdom of heaven" (Mt 19:12) fits well with what we know to have been the focus of Jesus' life and preaching. Nonetheless, Peter was certainly married, since Mark tells us he had a mother-in-law (1:29–31). And Paul claims in 1 Corinthians 9:5 that Cephas (usually interpreted as another name for Peter) was accompanied by his wife on his apostolic journeys. We know nothing about the marital status of the other apostles.

Paul in that same epistle, chapter seven, holds up virginity, continence, and celibacy as Christian ideals. For him, writing in an eschatological context while awaiting the Second Coming, those ideals were helps toward a more fervent consecration to God. Paul even concludes that one "who refrains from marriage will do better" (1 Cor 7:38). He insisted, however, that these were gifts from God and were not granted to everyone.[2] When Paul wrote his letters, he was not married and affirms that he was celibate. But, on the basis of 1 Corinthians 7:8 ("To the unmarried and the widows I say that it is well for them to remain unmarried as I am"), some interpreters argue that Paul had been married and was now a widower. The first Epistle to Timothy (3:12) directs that "bishops" and "deacons" be "married only once." Exegetes are still arguing whether this stipulation forbade polygamy or remarriage. It is certain from this text, however, that being married was not only an option for these leaders of the Christian community but was taken for granted.

There is indisputable evidence from as early as the third century that even in the West many (perhaps very many) priests and bishops in good standing were married. Indeed, some popes were the direct descendants of married priests, bishops, or even other popes. The father of Pope Damasus (366–84), the important pope who was the friend of St. Jerome, was the son of a bishop whose see was probably in the suburbs of Rome.[3] Pope Felix (483–92), whose father was almost certainly a priest, was the great-great-grandfather of Pope Gregory the Great (590–604).[4] Pope Hormisdas (514–23) was the father of Pope Silverius (536–37).[5]

Being a married man with children was, obviously, no obstacle to the episcopacy or even the papacy. We know for certain that one of the fathers of the Western church, St. Hilary, bishop of Poitiers in the fourth century, who was declared a doctor of the church in 1851 by Pope Pius IX, was married and had a daughter named Apra. It is thus clear that during the patristic era and into the early Middle Ages celibacy, as such, was not in force. The Synod of Gangra, held in the first half of the fourth century, condemned in its fourth canon manifestations of a false asceticism, which included refusing to attend liturgies celebrated by married priests.[6]

Celibacy is one thing, continence another. Until the fourth century no law was promulgated for men being ordained to major orders prohibiting marriage before ordination and no law enforcing continence on men who were already married. We know, however, that by that time renunciation of marriage for those looking to ordination was not rare, nor was the practice of living apart from their wives by those who were married before ordination. There is no way of estimating how many conformed to these behaviors, but it is clear that at least in some places continence was considered normative and traditional by the time of Constantine's recognition of Christianity in the early fourth century.

We cannot underestimate the profound changes that that recognition brought with it. Among other things it helped fuel a sometimes fierce asceticism, leading some Christians to withdraw into the desert from a world that had become too friendly. This period marks the beginning of Christian monasticism. With the age of the martyrs over, Christians had to have other means of following Christ to the limits and laying down their lives for him. With St. Jerome, as well as other Christian writers in the late fourth and early fifth centuries, virginity for those espoused to Christ began to be extolled with new fervor and consistency.

The first legislation regarding our subject, however, slightly antedates Constantine's decisive actions. Around the year 305, nineteen bishops assembled from various parts of Spain for the Council of Elvira (near Granada). Also in attendance but not voting were twenty-four priests and a number of deacons and lay people. The Council promulgated eighty-one disciplinary decrees. Canon 33 is the one that concerns us, for it is chronologically the first of a long series of legislative measures extending down to the present dealing with the subject of marriage and the clergy. The text reads: "It has seemed good absolutely to forbid the bishops, the priests, and the deacons, that is, all clerics in the service of the ministry, to have relations with their wives and procreate children; should anyone do so, let him be excluded from the honor of the clergy."[7]

The decree takes for granted that some clerics will be married. What is prohibited is for them to have conjugal relations with their wives. The decree thus concerns continence, not celibacy. It seems likely, furthermore, that the decree was meant to deal with infractions of what was considered normative rather than to initiate some new practice. By the end of the fourth century, the Council of Carthage in 390 would justify its almost identical prohibition with the claim that it was legislating "what the Apostles taught and what antiquity itself observed."[8]

There is, however, one thing that is certainly new and extremely significant about canon 33 of the Council of Elvira: it made a practice or a tradition into a law, violations of which would be punished. From that time forward into the early Middle Ages councils, popes, and bishops issued a number of decrees enjoining continence on married men who had been ordained to the diaconate, priesthood, or episcopacy.[9] In 441, for instance, the Council of Orange in its twenty-second canon required married candidates to promise continence before they were ordained to the diaconate.[10] In reply to a question from Bishop Rusticus of Narbonne, Pope Leo I (the Great, 440–61), stated that wedded clerics should not give up their wives but live together in wedded love without the acts of love, so that a spiritual marriage might replace a carnal one.[11] Later, since such cohabitation looked suspicious, legislation began to appear discouraging it.

To summarize for this early period: first, continence has emerged as the ideal for the clergy. Second, the ideal sometimes claims to be based on the teaching of the apostles themselves. Third, aside from its claim to apostolicity, it is not clear just why and how this ideal emerged with such prominence. Arguments from ritual purity and allusions to Old Testament precedents appear in the sources.[12] We cannot rule out, moreover, the influence of various forms of Neo-Platonism and other philosophies of late antiquity. Fourth, as is clear from a decree of Emperor Justinian in 528, some Christians were concerned that bishops would squander on their wives and children resources given the church for worship and for the aid of the poor. Finally, and perhaps most significantly, what was originally an ideal or a tradition is in the process of becoming a law, with penalties attached for infractions.

The second decisive moment was the Gregorian Reform of the eleventh century, also known as the Investiture Controversy.[13] As the West began to recover from the many travails of the previous centuries, thoughtful people wanted to reestablish proper order in society and turned to old legal texts to help them do so. Two interlocking abuses among the clergy shocked reformers of the eleventh century — simony and incontinence. These abuses were related in that clerical offices were sometimes sold to the highest bidder, no matter what his morals, or were passed on, with their considerable revenues, from father to son. Secular rulers, moreover, used bishoprics and other prelacies to reward their followers. Surely the most shocking and blatant example of the abuses in the system (if it can be called a system) occurred in the tenth century with the papacy itself. Alberic II of Spoleto was lord of Rome and for three decades dictated who the pope would be, from Leo VII (elected 936) through John XII (died 964). The morally dissolute John XII was in fact Alberic's son, who died of apoplexy while allegedly committing an act of adultery.

By the eleventh century the renewed study of canonical texts from the patristic era revealed different norms for the ordering of church and society. Moreover, for thirty-five years beginning in 1049, a series of energetic popes emerged who were determined to set things right. Their principal weapon was the canonical collections that provided them with their blueprint. Two things were clear in that blueprint—secular rulers did not appoint bishops and continence was the rule for clergy. The popes launched a program of reform that, in the name of restoring the authentic past, created something new, especially a papacy with claims of authority far exceeding in theory and practice anything that had preceded it.

The movement began, however, with the more modest, but still formidable, goal of bringing the behavior of clergy and secular rulers into line with the reformers' interpretation of the ancient canons. To that extent it was a holiness movement. The fact that abuses, as the Gregorians saw them, resulted in church property passing into families was important to them because it meant a holy thing, a gift meant for God or the saints, was passing into secular use. Even so, it was a somewhat secondary issue to them. Primary was the restoration of right order, which because of the monastic ethos of the day had a sharply ascetical, even mystical, dimension to it. Widespread in that ethos was the persuasion that any sexual act, even for married persons, was gravely sinful.[14]

In any case, as a result of the efforts of the Gregorian reformers, the law of celibacy as we know it today emerged and definitively took hold. The very first of the reforming popes, Leo IX, for instance, presided with the German emperor at a synod in Mainz in 1049 that condemned "the evil of clerical marriage" — *nefanda sacerdotum coniugia.*[15] If this prohibition is to be understood as somehow qualified for those already married before ordination, it was not thus interpreted in its immediate aftermath.

Along with other sanctions for incontinent priests, the reformers forbade the laity to assist at the masses of priests they knew were not conforming to the requirement. They found an argument for their ideals in canon 3 of the Council of Nicea (325), which forbade clerics in major orders to have any women in their households except their mothers, sisters, or aunts. They interpreted the canon, incorrectly, as a prohibition of marriage. In 1059, St. Peter Damian, a cardinal and one of the most effective spokesmen for the Gregorian program, wrote his book "On the Celibacy of Priests" (*De celibatu sacerdotum*), which by its very title helped promote the trend and give prominence to the word itself.[16]

No aspect of the Gregorian movement went uncontested, including this one. Otto, bishop of Constance, absolutely refused to enforce with his clergy the directives regarding clerics and women. When Bishop Altmann of Passau tried to enforce them, his clergy drove him out of his diocese with armed force. A cleric, probably Ulrich, the bishop of Imola, took up the pen about 1060 in a defense of clerical marriage that assumed conjugal relations after the ordination. Ulrich's "Rescript" influenced other writings in the same vein that continued to appear into the twelfth century.[17]

Nonetheless, with the passage of time the absolute prohibition of married clergy gradually became accepted as the tradition of the church by a seeming majority of lay magnates and higher clergy. Although cohabitation with wives and concubines was expressly forbidden in canon 7 of the First Lateran Council (1123), the five hundred bishops assembled for the Second Lateran Council (1139), gave this development a fuller formulation, which would become classic. Canons 6 and 7 of that Council forbade all those in major orders (which now included subdeacons) from taking wives and, further, forbade the faithful from assisting at masses of priests they knew to have wives or concubines:[18]

> Canon 6. We also decree that those in the orders of subdeacon and above who have taken wives or concubines are to be deprived of their position and ecclesiastical benefice. For since they ought to be in fact and in name temples of God, vessels of the Lord and sanctuaries of the Holy Spirit, it is unbecoming that they give themselves up to marriage and to impurity.

> Canon 7. Adhering to the path trod by our predecessors, the Roman pontiffs Gregory VII, Urban and Pascal, we prescribe that nobody is to hear the masses of those whom they know to have wives or concubines. Indeed, that the law of continence and purity pleasing to God might be propagated among ecclesiastical persons and those in holy orders, we decree that where bishops, priests, deacons, subdeacons, canons regular, monks and professed lay brothers have presumed to take wives and so transgress this holy precept, they are to be separated from their partners. For we do not deem there to be a marriage which, it is agreed, has been contracted against ecclesiastical law. Furthermore, when they have separated from each other, let them do a penance commensurate with such outrageous behavior.

Although these canons are open to interpretation in the older sense of prohibiting marriage after ordination, they came to be understood as absolute prohibitions. From that time until the Reformation, the prohibition of marriage for all clerics in major orders was simply taken for granted.

The Reformation was the third decisive moment. Since Luther and the other reformers found no justification for clerical celibacy in the New Testament, they denounced it as just one more restriction on Christian liberty imposed by the tyrant in Rome. The reformers all married. Luther also argued that celibacy was responsible for the debauchery of the clergy. Although the demand for a married clergy was not at the center of the Reformation agenda, it in fact gave that agenda an institutional grounding that would serve it well. These ministers would be a powerful force resisting reconciliation with the traditional church until they could be assured that they could bring their wives and children with them as they continued to exercise their ministry.

The Reformation was certainly the most massive frontal attack that the traditions of clerical celibacy and continence had ever received. It had to be answered. The Council of Trent (1545–63) did not formally take up the matter until a month before it ended its eighteen-year history. The theologians deputed to deal with the matter were divided in their opinions, with a few of them maintaining that celibacy for the clergy was of divine law and could not be abrogated.[19] Most of them held more moderate opinions. The matter was further complicated by political pressure from the German emperor, Ferdinand I, and from the duke of Bavaria, Albrecht V, both devout Catholics who wanted celibacy abrogated. If abrogation were not possible, they at least wanted dispensations from it for their own territories. On June 17, 1562, Augustin Baumgartner, a layman and ambassador of Duke Albrecht to the Council, spoke at length before the bishops arguing for reform of the clergy, the granting of the cup to the laity, and the admission of married men to holy orders.[20]

Citing the information garnered from an extensive visitation of ecclesiastics in 1558, Baumgartner painted a dark picture. Out of a hundred parish clergy, only three or four were found not to have concubines or to be either secretly or openly married. Moreover, many of the best clerics were joining the "sects" so as to take a wife. Germany was therefore suffering a terrible priest-shortage. Unless remedies were applied, the drain especially of the better-educated clergy would only get worse. Almost all thoughtful persons acquainted with German affairs had come to the conclusion that "a chaste marriage is preferable to a contaminated celibacy" — *castum matrimonium contaminate coelibatu praeferendum.*

> [The situation will further deteriorate] unless, in accordance with the custom of the early church [*primitivae ecclesiae*], learned and well educated men who are married are admitted to holy orders so as to preach the word of God in an effective manner. It is, after all, not a divine law that requires priests to be celibate. As is clear from the historical documentation, married

men have been admitted to sacred orders — and not only to the dignity of the priesthood but even to the exalted heights of the episcopacy.[21]

The decrees and canons of the Council of Trent run to almost 300 pages in a standard English translation. Despite the urgency of the issue, you have to search hard in that collection of ordinances to find anything on our subject. In only two canons, which together amount to only a paragraph, did the council touch upon the matter. The canons are best interpreted as obliquely reaffirming the tradition of celibacy — but so obliquely as to amount to a decision not to decide. In canon 10 of session 24, November 11, 1563, the Council stated: "if anyone says the married state is to be preferred to that of virginity or celibacy, and that it is no better or more blessed to persevere in virginity or celibacy than to be joined in marriage, let him be anathema."[22]

In canon 9 the Council condemned the opinion that anyone obliged to celibacy by his state in life can enter into a valid marriage. The canon also condemned the opinion that the opposite view amounts to a condemnation of marriage, as well as the view that those vowed to celibacy but who judge they do not have the grace to observe it can contract marriage. "For God would not deny the gift to those who duly ask for it, nor allow us to be tempted beyond our strength."[23]

But the Council of Trent made no assertions about the origins of the tradition of celibacy/continence or about the importance or desirability of maintaining the tradition. It surely left open the possibility of exceptions, dispensations, and, seemingly, even of abrogation. German leaders postcouncil continued to press their case with Pope Pius IV. The pope, under pressure from King Philip II of Spain to stand firm, submitted the matter to a consistory of cardinals, wavered, and then finally denied the Germans' petition. His successor, Pope Pius V (1566–72), left no doubt that the matter had been definitively closed.

In the centuries that have intervened between the sixteenth century and the present the issue occasionally surfaced again, especially during the French Revolution, but by and large it has been quiescent in Catholicism until quite recently. Canon 12 of the 1918 *Code of*

Canon Law stated: "Clerics in major orders may not marry, and they are bound by the obligation of chastity to the extent that sinning against it constitutes a sacrilege."

At the Second Vatican Council (1962–65) the issue first arose in connection with the diaconate.[24] As is well known, the Council approved of allowing "permanent" deacons to be married, a significant departure from the tradition that required all in major orders to be celibate. A debate over obligatory celibacy for the priesthood was scheduled for the fourth period of the Council in 1965, but Pope Paul VI in a letter to Cardinal Tisserant forbade it from coming to the floor. "It is not opportune to handle this theme in open discussion because it requires great prudence and is of the greatest importance." In this regard Pope Paul reflected the opinion stated by John XXIII in a letter of June 25, 1962, "There are a number of reasons against putting before the fathers of the council such a difficult question, with all the consequences it could have for ecclesiastical discipline. It will fall to the competence of the Holy See to examine it and to adopt the measures that in its prudence it will deem opportune."[25]

The Council in number 16 of its decree on "The Life and Ministry of Priests" (*Presbyterorum ordinis*) reaffirmed the discipline and commended it "as in very many ways appropriate to the priesthood."[26] The decree admits that celibacy "is not of course required by the very nature of the priesthood, as is clear from the practice of the early church and the tradition of the eastern churches." However:

> Through virginity or celibacy preserved for the sake of the kingdom of heaven, priests are consecrated to Christ in a new and exalted manner, and more easily cleave to him with singleness of heart; in him and through him they devote themselves with greater freedom to the service of God and the people . . . and they are thus equipped to accept a wider fatherhood in Christ. . . .
>
> For these [and other] reasons, which are rooted in the mystery of Christ and his mission, celibacy was at first commended to priests, and was later imposed by law in the Latin church on all who were to be advanced to holy orders. As regards those destined for the priesthood, this synod once more approves and

> confirms that law, trusting to the Spirit that the gift of celibacy, so fitting as it is to the priesthood of the new covenant, will be generously given by the Father, as long as those who share in the priesthood of Christ by the sacrament of order, and indeed the whole church, humbly and earnestly ask for it.

In the current 1983 *Code of Canon Law,* created to incorporate the new measures enacted by Vatican II, the law of celibacy is found in canon 277. It reads thus: "Clerics are obliged to observe perfect and perpetual continence for the sake of the kingdom of heaven and therefore are obliged to observe celibacy, which is a special gift of God, by which sacred ministers can adhere more easily to Christ with undivided heart and can more freely dedicate themselves to the service of God and humankind."

Chapter 7

The Perils of Celibacy

Clerical Celibacy and Marriage in the Protestant Reformation

John Witte Jr.

THE CONTEMPORARY BATTLES over clerical celibacy and its abuses are nothing new. When mandatory celibacy was first universally imposed on the Catholic clergy in 1123, clergy and laity alike broke into riotous rebellion for more than two generations, and a good number of bishops and priests flouted these laws for several generations more. When the Protestant Reformation broke out in 1517, clerical celibacy and marriage produced some of the most bitter grievances over which the Western church ultimately splintered. Today, the exposures of child abuse by some enterprising Catholic clergy has rejoined these ancient battles within Catholicism and between Catholics and Protestants — and triggered all manner of media exposés, private law suits, and criminal prosecutions.

In this little essay, I would like to revisit the original Protestant case against clerical celibacy and for clerical marriage as it emerged in the sixteenth-century Lutheran Reformation. I shall then draw out a few implications of the significance of these historical battles for the theology and law of clerical celibacy and marriage today.

The Case of Johann Apel

We begin with a concrete case.[1] Our case comes from 1523. This is six years after Luther posted his 95 Theses in Wittenberg, three years after Luther's excommunication from the Roman Catholic Church, and two years after the Diet of Worms. At the time of the case, Luther was back in Wittenberg from the Wartburg Castle. The Lutheran Reformation was gaining real revolutionary momentum in Germany and beyond.

Our case involves a priest and canon lawyer named Johann Apel. Apel was born and raised in Nürnberg, an important German city, still faithful to Rome at the time of the case. In 1514, Apel enrolled for theological studies at the brand new University of Wittenberg, where he had passing acquaintance with a new professor of theology there, an Augustinian monk named Martin Luther. In 1516, Apel went to the University of Leipzig for legal studies. He was awarded the doctorate of canon law and civil law in 1519. After a brief apprenticeship, Apel took holy orders and swore the requisite oath of clerical celibacy. One of the strong prince-bishops of the day, Conrad, bishop of Würzburg and duke of Francken, appointed Apel as a cathedral canon in 1523. Conrad also licensed Apel as an advocate in all courts in his domain. Apel settled into his pastoral and legal duties.

Shortly after his clerical appointment, Apel began romancing a nun at the nearby St. Marr cloister. (Her name is not revealed in the records.) The couple saw each other secretly for several weeks. They carried on a brisk correspondence. They began a romance. She apparently became pregnant. Ultimately, the nun forsook the cloister and her vows and secretly moved in with Apel. A few weeks later, they were secretly married and cohabited openly as a married couple.

This was an outrage. Clerical concubinage was one thing. The records show that at least three other priests in Conrad's diocese kept concubines and paid Conrad the standard concubinage tax for that privilege. Earlier that very same year of 1523, another priest had fathered a child and paid the bishop the standard cradle tax and oblated the infant in the very same St. Marr's cloister that Mrs. Apel had just forsaken. Clerical concubinage and even fatherhood were known and were tolerated by some obliging bishops of the day. But clerical marriage was an outrage, particularly when it involved both a priest and a nun — a *prima facie* case of double spiritual incest.

Upon hearing of Apel's enterprising, Bishop Conrad annulled the marriage and admonished Apel to confess his sin, to return his putative wife to her cloister, and to resume his clerical duties. Apel refused, insisting that his marriage, though secretly contracted, was valid. Unconvinced, the bishop indicted Apel for a canon law crime and temporarily suspended him from office. Apel offered a spirited defense of his conduct in a frank letter to the bishop.

Bishop Conrad, in response, had Apel indicted in his own bishop's court — for breach of holy orders and the oath of celibacy and for defiance of his episcopal dispensation and injunction. In a written response, Apel adduced conscience and Scripture in his defense, much like Luther had done two years before at the Diet of Worms. "I have sought only to follow the dictates of conscience and the Gospel," Apel insisted, not to defy episcopal authority and canon law. Scripture and conscience condone marriage for fit adults as "a dispensation and remedy against lust and fornication." "My wife and I have availed ourselves of these godly gifts and entered and consummated our marriage in chasteness and love."

Contrary to Scripture, Apel continued, the church's canon law commands celibacy for clerics and monastics. This introduces all manner of impurity among them. "Don't you see the fornication and the concubinage" in your bishopric, Apel implored Conrad. "Don't you see the defilement and the adultery . . . with brothers spilling their seed upon the ground, upon each other, and upon many a maiden whether single or married." My alleged sin and crime of breaking "this little man-made rule of celibacy," Apel insisted, "is very slight when compared to these sins of fornication" which you, "excellent father," "cover and condone if the payment is high enough." "The Word of the Lord is what will judge between you and me," Apel declared to the bishop, "and such Word commands my acquittal."

Bishop Conrad took the case under advisement. Apel took his cause to the budding Lutheran community. He sought support for his claims from Luther, Philip Melanchthon, Martin Bucer, and other Evangelical leaders who had already spoken against celibacy and monasticism. He published his remarks at trial adorned with a robust preface by Martin Luther, and it became an instant best-seller.

Shortly after publication of the tract, Bishop Conrad had Apel arrested and put in the tower, pending further proceedings. Apel's family pleaded in vain with the bishop to release him. The local civil magistrate twice mandated that Apel be released. Jurists and councilmen wrote letters of support. Even Emperor Charles V sent a brief letter urging the bishop not to protract Apel's harsh imprisonment in violation of imperial law, but to try him and release him if found innocent. Apel was finally tried. He was found guilty of several violations of the canon law and of heretically participating in "Luther's damned teachings." He was defrocked and was excommunicated and evicted from the community. Thereafter Apel made his way to Wittenberg where, at the urging of Luther and others, he was appointed to the law faculty at the University. Two years later, Apel served as one of the four witnesses to the marriage of ex-monk Martin Luther to ex-nun Katherine von Bora.

This was a sensational, but not an atypical, case in Reformation Germany in the 1520s. Among the earliest Protestant leaders were ex-priests and ex-monastics who had forsaken their orders and vows, and often married shortly thereafter. Indeed, one of the acts of solidarity with the new Protestant cause was to marry or divorce in open violation of the Catholic Church's canon law and in open contempt of episcopal instruction. As the church courts began to prosecute these offenses of its canon law, Protestant theologians and jurists rose to the defense of their budding co-religionists.

Classic Arguments for Clerical Celibacy

Bishop Conrad's position in the Apel case was in full compliance with the prevailing Catholic theology and canon law of marriage and celibacy.[2] Prior to the sixteenth century, the church regarded marriage as "a duty for the sound and a remedy for the sick," in St. Augustine's famous phrase. Marriage was a creation of God allowing man and woman to "be fruitful and multiply." Since the fall into sin, marriage had also become a remedy for lust, a channel to direct one's natural passion to the service of the community and the church. When contracted between Christians, marriage was also a sacrament, a symbol of the indissoluble union between Christ and His Church. As a sacrament, marriage fell within the social hierarchy of the church and was subject to its jurisdiction.

The church did not regard marriage as its most exalted estate, however. Though a sacrament and a sound way of Christian living, marriage was not considered to be so spiritually edifying. Marriage was a remedy for sin, not a recipe for righteousness. Marriage was considered subordinate to celibacy, propagation less virtuous than contemplation, marital love less wholesome than spiritual love. Clerics, monastics, and other servants of the church were to forgo marriage as a condition for service. Those who could not were not worthy of the church's holy orders and offices.

This prohibition on marriage, first universally imposed on clerics and monastics by the First Lateran Council of 1123, was defended with a whole arsenal of complex arguments. The most common arguments were based on St. Paul's statements in 1 Corinthians 7. In this famous passage, Paul did allow that it was better to marry than to burn with lust. But Paul also said that it was better to remain single than to marry or remarry. "It is well for a man not to touch a woman," he wrote. For those who are married "will have worldly troubles." It is best for you to remain without marriage "to secure your undivided attention to the Lord" (1 Cor. 7:1, 28, 35, RSV). These biblical passages, heavily glossed by the early church fathers, provided endless medieval commentaries on and commendations of celibacy. They were buttressed by newly discovered classical Greek and Roman writings extolling celibacy for the contemplative, as well as by the growing medieval celebration of the virginity of Mary as a model for pious Christian living.

Various philosophical arguments underscored the superiority of the celibate clergy to the married laity. It was a commonplace of medieval philosophy to describe God's creation as hierarchical in structure — a vast chain of being emanating from God and descending through various levels and layers of reality down to the smallest particulars. In this great chain of being, each creature found its place and its purpose. Each institution found its natural order and hierarchy. It was thus simply the nature of things that some persons and institutions were higher on this chain of being, some lower. It was the nature of things that some were closer and had more ready access to God, and some were further away and in need of mediation in their relationship with God. Readers of Dante's *Divine Comedy* will recognize this chain of being theory at work in Dante's vast hierarchies of hell, purgatory, and paradise. Students of medieval political theory will recognize this same theory at work in the many arguments of the superiority of the spiritual sword to the temporal sword, of the pope to the emperor, and of the church to the state.

This chain of being theory was one basis for medieval arguments for the superiority of the clergy to the laity. Clergy were simply higher on this chain of being, laity lower. The clergy were called to higher spiritual activities in the realm of grace, the laity to lower temporal activities in the realm of nature. The clergy were thus distinct from the laity in their dress, in their language, and in their livings. They were exempt from earthly obligations, such as paying civil taxes or serving in the military. They were immune from the jurisdiction of civil courts. And they were foreclosed from the natural activities of the laity, such as those of sex, marriage, and family life. These natural, corporeal activities were literally beneath the clergy in ontological status and thus formally foreclosed. For a cleric or monastic to marry or to have sex was thus in a real sense to act against nature (*contra naturam*).

The Lutheran Position on Celibacy and Marriage

Johann Apel's arguments with Bishop Conrad anticipated a good deal of the Lutheran critique of this traditional teaching of marriage and celibacy.[3] Like their Catholic brethren, the Lutheran reformers taught that marriage was created by God for the procreation of children and for the protection of couples from sexual sin. But, unlike their Catholic brethren, the reformers rejected the subordination of marriage to celibacy. We are all sinful creatures, Luther and his followers argued. Lust has pervaded the conscience of everyone. Marriage is not just an option, it is a necessity for sinful humanity. For without it, a person's distorted sexuality becomes a force capable of overthrowing the most devout conscience. A person is enticed by nature to concubinage, prostitution, masturbation, voyeurism, and sundry other sinful acts. "You cannot be without a [spouse] and remain without sin," Luther thundered from his Wittenberg pulpit. You will test your neighbor's bed unless your own marital bed is happily occupied and well used.[4] "To spurn marriage is to act against God's calling . . . and against nature's urging," Luther continued. The calling of marriage should be declined only by those who have received God's special gift of continence. "Such persons are rare, not one in a thousand [later he said one hundred thousand] for they are a special miracle of God."[5] The Apostle Paul has identified this group as the permanently impotent and the eunuchs; very few others can claim such a unique gift.

This understanding of marriage as a protection against sin undergirded the reformers' bitter attack on traditional rules of mandatory celibacy. To require celibacy of clerics, monks, and nuns, the reformers believed, was beyond the authority of the church and ultimately a source of great sin. Celibacy was a gift for God to give, not a duty for the church to impose. It was for each individual, not for the church, to decide whether he or she had received this gift. By demanding monastic vows of chastity and clerical vows of celibacy, the church was seen to be intruding on Christian freedom and contradicting Scripture, nature, and common sense. By institutionalizing and encouraging celibacy the church was seen to prey on the immature and the uncertain. By holding out food, shelter, security, and economic opportunity, the monasteries enticed poor and needy parents to oblate their minor children to a life of celibacy, regardless of whether it suited their natures. Mandatory celibacy, Luther taught, was hardly a prerequisite to true clerical service of God. Instead it led to "great whoredom and all manner of fleshly impurity and . . . hearts filled with thoughts of women day and night."[6]

Furthermore, to impute higher spirituality and holier virtue to the celibate contemplative life was, for the reformers, contradicted by the Bible. The Bible teaches that each person must perform his or her calling with the gifts that God provides. The gifts of continence and contemplation are but two among many, and are by no means superior to the gifts of marriage and child-rearing. Each calling plays an equally important, holy, and virtuous role in the drama of redemption, and its fulfillment is a service to God. Luther concurred with the Apostle Paul that the celibate person "may better be able to preach and care for God's word." But, he immediately added: "It is God's word and the preaching which makes celibacy — such as that of Christ and of Paul — better than the estate of marriage. In itself, however, the celibate life is far inferior."[7]

Not only is celibacy no better than marriage, Luther insisted; clergy are no better than laity. To make this argument cogent, Luther had to counter the medieval chain of being theory that naturally placed celibate clergy above married laity. Luther's answer was his complex theory of the separation of the earthly kingdom and the heavenly kingdom. God has ordained two kingdoms or realms in which humanity is destined to live, the earthly kingdom and the heavenly kingdom. The earthly kingdom is the realm of creation, of natural and civic life, where a person operates primarily by reason and law. The heavenly kingdom is the realm of redemption, of spiritual and eternal life, where a person operates primarily by faith and love. These two kingdoms embrace parallel forms of righteousness and justice, government and order, truth and knowledge. They interact and depend upon each other in a variety of ways. But these two kingdoms ultimately remain distinct. The earthly kingdom is distorted by sin, and governed by the Law. The heavenly kingdom is renewed by grace and guided by the Gospel. A Christian is a citizen of both kingdoms at once and invariably comes under the distinctive government of each. As a heavenly citizen, the Christian remains free in his or her conscience, called to live fully by the light of the Word of God. But as an earthly citizen, the Christian is bound by law, and called to obey the natural orders and offices of household, state, and church that God has ordained and maintained for the governance of this earthly kingdom.

For Luther, the fall into sin destroyed the original continuity and communion between the Creator and the creation, the natural tie between the heavenly kingdom and the earthly kingdom. There was no series of emanations of being from God to humanity. There was no stairway of merit from humanity to God. There was no purgatory. There was no heavenly hierarchy. God is present in the heavenly kingdom, and is revealed in the earthly kingdom primarily through "masks." Persons are born into the earthly kingdom, and have access to the heavenly kingdom only through faith.

Luther did not deny the traditional view that the earthly kingdom retains its natural order, despite the fall into sin. There remained, in effect, a chain of being, an order of creation that gave each creature, especially each human creature and each social institution, its proper place and purpose in this life. But, for Luther, this chain of being was horizontal, not hierarchical. Before God, all persons and all institutions in the earthly kingdom were by nature equal. Luther's earthly kingdom was a flat regime, a horizontal realm of being, with no person and no institution obstructed or mediated by any other in access to and accountability before God.

Luther thus rejected traditional teachings that the clergy were higher beings with readier access to God and God's mysteries. He rejected the notion that clergy mediated the channel of grace between the laity and God — dispensing God's grace through the sacraments and preaching, and interceding for God's grace by hearing confessions, receiving charity, and offering prayers on behalf of the laity.

Clergy and laity were fundamentally equal before God and before all others, Luther argued, sounding his famous doctrine of "the priesthood of all believers." All persons were called to be priests for their peers. Luther at once "laicized" the clergy and "clericized" the laity. He treated the traditional "clerical" office of preaching and teaching as just one other vocation alongside many others that a conscientious Christian could properly and freely pursue. He treated all traditional "lay" offices as forms of divine calling and priestly vocation, each providing unique opportunities for service to one's peers. Preachers and teachers in the church must carry their share of civic duties and pay their share of civil taxes just like everyone else. And they should participate in earthly activities such as marriage and family life just like everyone else.[8]

This same two kingdoms theory also provided Luther with a new understanding of the place of marriage within this earthly life. For Luther, marriage was one of the three natural estates of the earthly kingdom, alongside the church and the state, and was essential to the governance of the earthly kingdom. The marital household was to teach all persons, particularly children, Christian values, morals, and mores. It was to exemplify for a sinful society a community of love and cooperation, meditation and discussion, song and prayer. It was to hold out for the church and the state an example of firm but benign parental discipline, rule, and authority. It was to take in and care for wayfarers, widows, and destitute persons — a responsibility previously assumed largely by monasteries and cloisters.

The marital estate was thus as indispensable an agent in God's redemption plan as the church. It no longer stood within the orders of the church but alongside it. Moreover, the marital estate was as indispensable an agent of social order and communal cohesion as the state. It was not simply a creation of the civil law, but a Godly creation designed to aid the state in discharging its divine mandate.

The best example of such an idealized marital household was the local parsonage, the home of the married Lutheran minister. The reformers had already argued that pastors, like everyone else, should be married — lest they be tempted by sexual sin, deprived of the joys of marital love, and precluded from the great act of divine and human creativity in having children. Here was an even stronger argument for clerical marriage. The clergy were to be exemplars of marriage. The minister's household was to be a source and model for the right order and government of the local church, state, and broader community. As Adolf von Harnack once put it: "The Evangelical parsonage, founded by Luther, became the model and blessing of the entire German nation, a nursery of piety and education, a place of social welfare and social equality. Without the German parsonage, the history of Germany since the sixteenth century is inconceivable."[9]

Contemporary Reflections

In one sense, these ancient battles over clerical and monastic celibacy and marriage are a world away from our common experience today. In another sense, they are the stuff of the very latest headlines. The recent media exposures of child abuse by selected Catholic clergy and of clumsy cover-ups by some of their episcopal superiors has rejoined many of these old issues, and redrawn many of the old battle lines between Protestants and Catholics.

It is, of course, easy for us Protestants today to sit back, content with the knowledge that we pointed out the perils of celibacy five hundred years ago, and replaced this odious institution with a happy system of marriage and family life for all. Just turn on CBN, tune in Sunday sermons, or read some Protestant periodicals, and you cannot help but sniff a thick new air of Protestant smugness, sometimes even triumphalism, about our great reforms of marriage and family life. If only those Catholics would follow us.

Before we Protestants become too content with ourselves, however, it is worth remembering that some of these early Protestant marital reforms, however meritorious, were not without their own enduring problems. Yes, the Protestant reformers did outlaw monasteries and cloisters. But these reforms also ended the vocations of many single women and men, placing a new premium on the vocation of marriage. Ever since, Protestant single women and men have chafed in a sort of pastoral and theological limbo, objects of curiosity and pity, sometimes even suspicion and contempt. These are stigmata which singles still feel today in more conservative Protestant churches, despite the avalanche of new ministries to help them. Yes, the Protestant reformers did remove clerics as mediators between God and the laity, in expression of St. Peter's teaching of the priesthood of all believers. But they ultimately interposed husbands between God and their wives, in expression of St. Paul's teaching of male headship within the home. Ever since, Protestant married women have been locked in a bitter struggle to gain fundamental equality both within the marital household and without — a struggle that has still not ended in more conservative Protestant communities today.[10] Add to this the ample evidence of wife and child abuse within traditional Protestant homes — Protestant minister's homes notably included — and the story is more sobering than might be imagined. We Protestants are not without our own institutional sins and shortcomings on matters of sex and marriage. We would do well to stop throwing stones at Catholics and start bringing bricks to help in the reconstruction of a better Christian understanding of sex, marriage, and family life.

That said, it must also be said that there seems to be something gravely amiss with the American Catholic Church's insistence on maintaining mandatory clerical celibacy—despite the mounting evidence of homosexual and heterosexual abuses among its clergy, and despite the rapid dwindling of eligible candidates within its seminaries. There is something strangely anomalous with a hierarchy that will ordain married Anglican and Orthodox priests to fill its vacant parishes, yet deny Catholic priests and seminarians any such marital option.

To be sure, the First Amendment free exercise clause mandates that the Catholic hierarchy be free to conduct its internal affairs without interference by the state. And to be sure, this constitutional protection frees the church to find its own internal resources to repeat, repair, or replace its rules of clerical celibacy as it sees fit. The First Amendment is one of our most cherished freedoms, which protects popular and unpopular religious practices alike.

But the First Amendment does not license violations of the life and limb of another, and does not protect corporate complicity and conspiracy. Child abuse is a very serious felony that the modern criminal law now punishes severely. And even mutually consensual sexual contact with a minor is a strict liability offense called statutory rape. Religious and secular clergy who engage in such sexual acts with minors must be aggressively prosecuted and must be severely punished if found guilty after receiving full due process. Bishops who harbor and hide such sex felons are accomplices after the fact and are just as guilty under modern criminal law as the sexual perpetrator himself. Church corporations who conspire in such subterfuge invite serious charges of corporate criminality and corruption.

The American church hierarchy today needs to stop hiding behind constitutional walls and sacramental veils and take firm public responsibility for its actions and omissions — ministering first and foremost to the abused victims and their families, exposing and evicting the clerical sex felons and accomplices within their midst, and getting on with their cardinal callings of preaching the word, administering the sacraments, catechizing the young, and caring for the needy. In medieval centuries past, the church and its clergy may have been above the law of the state, and thus privileged to deal with such clerical abuses by their own means, in their own courts, at their own pace. No longer. "Privilege of forum" and "benefit of clergy" have been dead letters in this country for more than a century. Clergy are not above the law. They should exemplify its letter and its spirit. The church is not above the state. It should set a model of justice and equity.

Few issues are as sublime and serious today as those involving sex and sexuality. Few crimes are as scarring as rape and child abuse. To rape a child is to destroy a child. To abuse a child is to forfeit one's office. No cleric found guilty of child abuse can continue in office. No Christian church found complicit in child abuse is worthy of its name. Bureaucratic wrangling and political lobbying are no way for the church to respond to recent events. Repentance, restitution, and reformation are the better course.

Chapter 8

Monastic Perspectives on Celibacy

COLUMBA STEWART, O.S.B.

FOR TWENTY-FIVE YEARS I have been a member of a large Benedictine monastic community. I have an academic interest in early monasticism, and have taught and written about monastic topics for some years. I also worked for several years in monastic formation in my monastery, including four years as formation director. My term coincided with the second wave of the national sexual-abuse crisis, which brought a good deal of media scrutiny to our monastery and the schools we sponsor. Several of our monks were accused of sexual abuse dating from the 1960s to the early 1980s, and we learned that one of our former abbots had abused younger members of the community. During the period of intense media coverage, I was very much involved in developing our public response to both allegations and the fact of sexual abuse by some of our monks. Meanwhile, I was also trying to explain to our new members why monasticism can actually be a path of ever-increasing openness to God and to one another.

My own perspective, then, is both professional and personal. As a vowed monk I continue to learn how to live my own celibate commitment with integrity as a member of a community that has done a good deal of painful sorting through issues of celibacy and sexual misconduct. I am very grateful to find wisdom and strength in the monastic tradition as it has been passed along in both the classic texts and the extraordinary monks and nuns I have known.

Celibacy has been a universal feature of Christian monastic life, and was a key marker of the pre-monastic Christian asceticism out of which the visible, formal monastic movement emerged in the fourth century. In the life of the church, monastic celibacy is the Ur-celibacy. It was normative for Christian monastic men and women before episcopal or priestly celibacy became common in churches of the East and West. The roots of monastic celibacy in pre-monastic Christian asceticism suggest that we need to consider the "ascetic" aspects of the practice of celibacy. The development of monasticism as a strongly identifiable movement in the church suggests that we need also look at some institutional or sociological aspects of monastic celibacy. In the brief window available today I can only point to some of the elements that have shaped monastic perspectives on celibacy in the past and then comment on what I would see as the monastic contribution to the discussion in the church today.

The scholarly work of researchers such as Peter Brown in his landmark study *The Body and Society*[1] has shown us the vastness of the early Christian sexual—and particularly ascetic sexual—landscape. As we focus on monastic sexuality in the early period, however, there is little evidence within specifically monastic writing of theological or even spiritual justification of celibacy. The significant literature comes from the broader world of Christian asceticism: the pre-monastic but certainly ascetic Origen, or the married but conflicted bishop Gregory of Nyssa. Early monks and nuns tended not to expatiate on the beauty of virginity or the mystical possibilities afforded by celibacy, with the rather embarrassing exception of Jerome. Augustine, in this as in so many things, is a case apart. His account of his own struggle with sexual urges is so personally contextualized, and his later theology of marriage and original sin is so polemically conditioned, that his perspectives on sexuality do not fit easily into the monastic literary tradition. His mentor Ambrose exalted virginity for young girls, but did so as a celibate bishop, not as a monk, and those young virgins in Milan were not properly speaking "monastic." As Brown has helped to remind us, monastic Christians inherited an ascetic worldview that saw sexuality as a powerful marker of human mortality, linked as it was to the reproductive cycle that made the survival of the species possible. Whether in Paul's heightened eschatology, the Syriac theology of deep identification with Christ the only-begotten One, Origen's Platonic imaging of the eternal, or Gregory of Nyssa's link between virginity and resurrection, celibacy meant opting out of the conventional understanding that human fulfillment could somehow be anchored in this world.

The excavation of specifically *monastic* attitudes about sexuality and the imperative of celibacy uncovers a strong emphasis on the danger of sexual attraction. In male monastic literature (almost the only kind we have), one readily finds examples of monastic anxiety about contact with women or cautions about same-sex urges toward younger monks, or among the young ones themselves. The literature about monastic women, predictably much scarcer and typically controlled by male editorial authority, is similar. The *Life of the Blessed Syncletica,* a fifth-century text that is the best example we have, is remarkably similar in approach to the male-oriented texts.[2] It urges nuns to imagine the face of their beloved disfigured by age and disease, and even to imagine tearing away its flesh as a reminder that the beauty by which they have been seduced is only skin deep.

What were they all so anxious about? An initial reading suggests an unwholesome preoccupation with the risk of "falling" into genital activity, either with another person or in masturbation. This line of thought was destined for long survival, even into the period immediately before the Second Vatican Council, when monks of my Congregation were brought up on the *Tyrocinium Religiosum,* an eighteenth-century text that forbade the novice to smell flowers, hold babies, pet animals, or, even worse, wear cologne: the next step would surely be the deadly peril of "particular friendship."[3]

A more nuanced reading points to a deeper concern about the power of obsession, and obsession's close links to memory and visual imagination. The main problem seems not to have been actually having sex, but *thinking* about doing so. Being absorbed in fantasy threatened the most fundamental mark of a monastic Christian, the freedom to follow Christ far and deep: into the farthest and deepest ranges of the heart, into the desert or some other distant place, into the spaciousness of inner silence. Any threat to that freedom was a serious problem. The monastic elders knew that our fiercest attachments are often not to things or even to people, but to our "thoughts" about them. The problem with obsessive thoughts is this: when our imaginations are preoccupied with thoughts of acquisitiveness or vindictiveness, we cannot pray. If we cannot pray, we cannot stand on the solid, real-time ground of our own truth and integrity. One of the litanies we regularly pray at Evening Prayer in our monastery asks God that we "remember our deeply rooted dependence on you." The practice of celibacy, the *intentional* practice of celibacy, like the other renunciations and obligations of the ascetic or monastic life, makes us remember that utter dependence.

This emphasis on the power of thoughts, traceable directly to Origen and earlier, was expressed most cogently by the monk Evagrius of Pontus, who as a young deacon in Constantinople had a disastrous affair with a married woman of high social status.[4] Escaping with his life but with his soul in tatters, Evagrius was set straight by another high-born woman in Jerusalem, the wise and formidable Melania, who packed him off to the Egyptian desert. Evagrius's writings, generated by his own experience and his encounters with savvy instructors such as Melania, her advisor Rufinus, the Egyptian monks Macarius the Elder, Macarius the Great, and others, created the first systematic treatment program for what today we might call addictive behaviors. Evagrius was also interested in the psychodynamics of dreams and the power of the visual imagination, another anticipation of modern approaches to sexuality.

One of Evagrius's students, John Cassian, has left us the most extended exploration of monastic sexuality in the entire monastic tradition. As I have noted elsewhere, when you add up all of the pages Cassian devotes to sex, the total exceeds that even of his discussion of prayer.[5] Cassian's writings on sexuality are both frank and disconcerting. His view of the body is problematic for us because of his Platonic anthropology and his antique understanding of biology. What is marvelous about his writing on sex, however, is his ease with the subject. He weaves together physiology, theology, and spirituality in a manner we can scarcely begin to emulate. Where else can you find someone who in the same paragraph can write about wet dreams, unceasing prayer, and purity of heart? Cassian shows us up as the prudes we are. What I want to emphasize here, however, is that Cassian moves beyond the typical emphasis on *restraint* of sexuality to a developmental understanding of what he describes as the move from "continence" (a.k.a., "celibacy") to "chastity." In this he points to that deep and lasting freedom meant to be the goal of every Christian life, when intention and behavior have become congruent. In a way that we might emulate, Cassian writes of the attainment of "integrity." Cassian had a keener sense than most of his — or our — contemporaries that preoccupation with control and restraint is enforced congruence, not a joyful harmony. But he also recognized that this harmony comes only with long practice and often painful experience, and most of all, with God's grace. In this he anticipates modern authors on celibacy who write of the development of celibate identity over a lifetime, and of its close link to a deep life of prayer.

The strategies the early monastic tradition developed to deal with obsessive thoughts and to foster the development of an integrated sexuality were both practical and attitudinal. The most striking was the practice of manifestation of thoughts, whereby one would go alone to an elder and simply report what was occupying mental and psychic space.[6] The idea was an uncensored and unashamed reporting, though it wasn't any easier then than now, and the literature abounds with stories of struggle and the need for pastoral sensitivity. Behind the *practice* of manifesting thoughts was the *attitude* of humility, which was their antidote to shame. Humility in their view was closely connected to compunction, a keen awareness of one's own frailty and sinfulness. This would become important in the sixth century for St. Benedict, who makes humility, understood in this manner, the centerpiece of his spirituality.[7] For him, humility meant utter transparency, the refusal to hide anything from a merciful God. As for compunction, Benedict never mentions prayer without mentioning tears. And how does one cultivate humility and compunction? Through the classic monastic tools of prayer, obedience, and fasting. Each one of those needs to be unpacked, but not alas here. But let me say simply one word that permeates all of these tools: Psalms.

So what does this mean for us? Clearly anyone in monastic or religious life today needs help in navigating the power of Eros. In a sexually saturated but very confused environment like modern Western society, a monastery or religious community should be a place of at least relative sexual sanity. One of the universal themes in monastic tradition is the offering of hospitality, to both strangers and friends. We should be able to provide a place, a space, where people can decompress from the relentless marketing of youth and beauty, romance and sexual desirability. This places a large burden on us to learn from the tradition we have received and to create a constructive dialogue between its theologically based worldview and the more subjective focus of modern psychology. And meanwhile we have to walk the talk.

I would also suggest that we learn to emulate the monastic men and women who were unafraid to speak about sexuality and spirituality in the same sentence. The modern monastic approach to celibacy should invite honest and unselfconscious conversation about sexual identity, about the challenges of celibate living, and about the social, ecclesiastical, or communal pathologies that inhibit celibate maturity. Such honesty is hard-won. Its exercise is difficult in a Catholic Church so anxious about celibate failure that it inhibits the transparency that would make celibate success more likely. The monastic tradition has much to offer if we can summon the courage to receive it.

Chapter 9

Celibacy under the Sign of the Cross

MARGARET A. FARLEY

WHILE WRITING AND SPEAKING FREQUENTLY on issues of sexual ethics, marriage and family, divorce and remarriage, same-sex relationships, and related topics, I have yet to address the question of celibacy. It seems both appropriate and timely to do so now, even though I believe the recent work of Sandra Schneiders, Peter Brown, Jo Ann McNamara,[1] and others has covered much of the ground I might have explored. Historians (such as Brown and McNamara)[2] have contributed immensely to our perspective on questions of religiously motivated celibacy, both for men and for women; and systematic analyses (in particular, those set forth by Schneiders)[3] have focused issues and argued for positions with which I am largely in sympathy. Nonetheless, my agenda and my perspective may be sufficiently different from those taken by other scholars that I will risk adding this essay to the conversation already in place.

I will attempt to do three things, each briefly. Drawing on the massive historical studies of others, I will look to history not for a complete narrative of the Christian practice of celibacy, but to give some content to the concept of celibacy as it has perdured through centuries. Then I will turn to contemporary problems that burden both the concept and practice of celibacy. Finally, but in response to these problems, I will propose an understanding of celibacy that may be fitting and useful for contemporary Christians. I will not explicitly address the question of whether celibacy should be required for the Roman Catholic priesthood (though I think it should not be), nor the question of the secular as well as religious importance of celibacy for persons in general, particularly contemporary women (though I think this is of great personal and political importance, especially for feminists). I will focus on celibacy in Western Christianity, because issues of sexuality vary from culture to culture and tradition to tradition, and I cannot here take on questions of so broad a scope. This in no way implies that I think traditional Christian understandings of celibacy cannot cross cultural divides.

It is an understatement to say that celibacy presents key questions for the future of traditionally celibate Christian communities. My goal is not to make recommendations in this regard but to contribute to work that needs to be done prior to such recommendations. My own ultimate interest is in celibacy as understood and practiced by women in Western Christian religious communities with so-called active ministries, though I hope what I say will have useful implications for the practice of celibacy in other contexts as well.

The View from the Past

What I am looking for here is the history of an idea, a creative concept, an imaginative understanding of the meaning of religiously motivated (in particular, Christianly motivated) celibacy. I do not, of course, think that concepts can be divorced from the concrete contexts and specific practices which shape them, but sometimes a concept crosses the divides of time and space, of gender and culture. It becomes part of a living tradition. "Celibacy" is such a concept.[4] It cannot be understood adequately apart from the specific historical contexts in which it was practiced, yet the meanings of one context tend to interact with meanings of another. Peter Brown's study of the practice of "permanent sexual renunciation" among men and women (mostly men) in Christian circles from 40 C.E. to 430 C.E. provides a good example of this. Brown pays attention both to context and to the development of a tradition as he weaves a narrative with multiple plots and characters, drawn from letters and sermons, philosophical and theological dialogues, lives of saints and fictional romance literature, polemical treatises and guides to prayer, works of art and inscriptions on tombstones.

Brown offers no incautious and sweeping generalizations, no superficial samplings of profoundly diverse experiences. Rather, what we are asked to examine in meticulous detail is an intriguing variety of places and times, persons and cultures. A repeated phrase of Brown's is "a different world"; this or that was a "different world" from the ones through which he led his readers in previous chapters. The Diaspora of Paul was a different world from the Palestine of Jesus. The meanings given to the human body and to human sexuality were therefore different as well. Cappadocia and Pontus were worlds away from the Egypt of the Desert Fathers, and Gregory of Nyssa's understanding of asceticism was a world away from Anthony's. The Latin traditions of sexual renunciation grew out of a world vastly different from either the drastic challenges of the East or the slow and humble patience of the monks at Sinai. Different times, different places, different particular histories, different temperaments: the forms and meanings of sexual renunciation have been myriad—complementary, paradoxical, contradictory, parallel, incompatible. They form a dazzling panorama, an intricately woven tapestry whose threads we can trace without blurring what they portray.

Think, for example, of the vast differences in the experiences of a commitment to celibacy by wandering young radicals, middle-aged post-maritally celibate bishops, desert solitaries, virgin women who remained within the households of their families of origin, wealthy women patrons of monasteries, celibate philosophers engaged in serene study circles, men and women participating in daring experiments of cohabitation, desert communities of women or men. Think of the differences in self-understanding in the experience of permanent continence undertaken in the belief that the soul can transform the body; or the belief that conversion of heart is helped by a celibate integration of affections in relation to God; or the conviction that sexual nonavailability of women to men can overturn gendered expectations; or beliefs that friendship can be greater if it transcends sexual intimacy; that human personal self-bondage can be undone only by rigorous asceticism that includes the repudiation of sex; that the death and resurrection of Jesus Christ can be entered into in a way that makes sex irrelevant. Brown finds all of these forms and rationales (and more) for permanent celibacy — emerging, developing, competing among themselves and competing with a view of married chastity. None of them were lived in a social vacuum; most of them were intensely debated; and thus did the option of sexual renunciation grow more real and more widespread in an unfolding Christian world.

Despite all of this variety — descriptive and normative — in understandings of celibacy, Brown insists that permanent sexual renunciation is a recognizably distinctive element of Christian morality in the four centuries he studies and later; and that it has had far-reaching cultural consequences, including the breaking of the "city's" control over the meaning and activities of the human body. But can these diverse practices of sexual renunciation inform a whole tradition, and if so, how shall it be characterized?

What began with Paul's opinion about celibate freedom in service of the gospel took quantum leaps when through the years it came to be seen variously as a substitute for martyrdom, a majestic ideal of virtue, a radical turn away from ordinary lives of marrying and raising children, a form of heroic asceticism that promised mystical experiences of God.[5] Specific contexts gave rise to idiosyncratic practices, but developing theologies both fueled these practices and held them, however loosely, together. Chief among these was a theology of sexuality that made sexual renunciation a logical choice for those who could make it.[6] Christianity, after all, emerged in the late Hellenistic Age when even Judaism was influenced by pessimistic attitudes toward sex. While early Christian writers and preachers affirmed sex as good, a part of creation, they also believed it to be paradigmatically injured by the destructive forces of the fall. The fathers of the church shared with Stoic philosophers, therefore, a suspicion of bodily passion and a respect for reason as a guide to the moral life. What prevailed in Christian moral teaching was a doctrine that viewed sex as good but seriously flawed — because its passion could not as such be controlled by reason. Like the Stoics, Christian leaders taught that sex can be brought back under the rule of reason by discovering and respecting its rational purpose—that is, the purpose of procreation. Its justification could only be found in its service to the species, as a necessary means to human reproduction (hence, there could be no morally good sex without a procreative intent, and in large part because of this, no sex outside of marriage).

Even within marriage, sex was considered a kind of duty, acceptable for its instrumental value; it could even as such still be tainted (a view held by St. Augustine, though not by many others).[7] At the very least, the experience of sexual passion was thought to prevent (for the time it lasted) an undistracted contemplation of God. Hence, marriage was extolled as a graced institution and as a remedy for lust, but it was better to forego marriage (and sex) in order to free the spirit for union with the divine, as well as to free an individual's time and energies for service of the gospel.

A theology of sexuality combined, then, with a theology of marriage that heightened the value of celibacy. While mainstream Christianity was never a world-denying or body-denying religion, the early church fashioned theological perspectives that relativized the importance of marriage and family for centuries to come. As Rowan Greer has shown, the church in late antiquity manifested at least three attitudes toward marriage and family, the combination of which yielded a deep ambivalence.[8] First, there was a seeming rejection of family ties, sometimes even open hostility toward the family. The Christian message was a sword of division, setting family members against one another (Mt 10:34–39; Lk 12:51–53). All Christians were asked in some sense to leave all things, including father, mother, spouse, and children (Mt 12:25, 22:30; Lk 20:35). Believers lived in anticipation of a new age, which would exclude marrying and giving in marriage. Closely related to this, the early Christians saw the church itself as their family. For those who had to leave their former families, the church itself was their new home (Mt 10:29–30). On the other hand, Christians also believed that marriage and family in the ordinary sense could be affirmed, not abolished, within the new life of faith. Against Gnostics of all kinds, Christian preachers (Augustine the foremost among them) affirmed the goodness of marriage and its importance in God's plan. But the message remained ambiguous, with attitudes of rejection, substitution, and affirmation continually in tension. In such a context, a rationale for celibacy was not difficult to understand.

Threads in theologies of sexuality and of marriage were pulled forward into a theology of the human person that raised the choice of celibacy into a magnetic ideal. A celibate lifestyle offered a way to heroic virtue, to perfection in the love of God and neighbor. Holiness was connected with bodily discipline and with the heights of contemplation. Relieved of ordinary responsibilities (and in the case of women, freed from coerced marriages, limited lives of drudgery, and the often painful burdens of endless childbearing), individuals could control their own bodies and map out whole new horizons of human freedom. By the second century, Christianity had become a religion for the young; for many, celibacy had become the lifestyle of choice.[9] By the Middle Ages, there was a whole world of celibate priests, monks, and nuns, a whole culture sustained on the assumption that celibates can embrace a holy way in the church and in the reign of God.

Along with theologies of sexuality, marriage and family, and human perfectionism, there grew through the centuries a theological and practical connection between celibacy, community, and the "care of souls." Added to this, and gradually transforming it, was the expansion of care of souls to the care of whole persons, especially persons in desperate need. From Basil the Great's "hospitals" in the fourth century to the monastic centers in the early Middle Ages, and from the mendicant friars of the high Middle Ages to the eighteenth- and nineteenth-century orders of nuns dedicated to the care of the poor, celibacy was a way both to union with God and to love and service of one's neighbor. The relentless logic of a way of life that was not only an end in itself but a contributor to this world yielded a descriptive concept of celibacy and its normative rationale.

At the heart of the concept, in summary, was the belief that celibacy offered a unique and privileged access to union with God, primarily because it was conducive to prayer — to contemplation, meditation, even mystical experience of the presence of God. But access to God was also a matter of wholeness in the individual self, achieved through sexual renunciation as a primary form of asceticism, both negative (the control of disruptive and conflicting desires) and positive (the liberty of spirit that was thereby achieved). Celibacy was, therefore, a way to holiness, to perfection of the highest human capabilities, shaping a readiness for the reception of God's grace in this world, and all the while witnessing to hope for a new world to come. As a way of life, it aimed to refine capacities for love of both God and neighbor. Most of the time it was understood as a higher and better way (than marriage) of imitating the life of Jesus Christ (though it was never considered automatically or absolutely so).[10] Hence, despite its multiple and varied manifestations through the centuries, celibacy in a Christian context came to incorporate the general conceptual elements of a lifelong commitment to sexual abstinence, non-marriage, *imitatio Christi,* freedom from ordinary familial responsibilities — all for the sake of union with God, perfection of the self, and service to one's neighbor in the context of the reign of God. These conceptual and purposive lines were set and remained with astonishing consistency through most of the subsequent history of the church.

Both the concept and its rationale have been subject to critique, however, from individual Christian (as well as secular) thinkers, political leaders, and in the twentieth century, proponents of psychological theories that judge celibate lifestyles to be unhealthy. In the history of Christianity, there is no doubt that the paradigmatic critique of celibacy was rendered in the sixteenth century by leaders of the Protestant Reformation. Not only the concept and the rationale of celibacy made it vulnerable, but the concrete historical failures in its practice readied it for the broadsides delivered by the major reformers.

Theologies of sexuality, marriage and family, perfectionism, and even forms of neighbor-love came under particular attack by Martin Luther.[11] In fact, questions of sexual behavior played an important role in the whole of the Reformation. Celibacy was challenged not just in its scandalous nonobservance but as a Christian ideal. Marriage and family replaced it among the reformers as the center of sexual gravity in the Christian life. Luther (as well as John Calvin, for that matter) was deeply influenced by the Augustinian tradition regarding original sin and its consequences for human sexuality. Yet Luther developed a position on marriage and sex that was not dependent upon the traditional procreative ethic. Like most of the Christian tradition, he affirmed marriage and sexuality as part of the divine plan for creation. But he shared Augustine's pessimistic view of fallen human nature and its disordered sex drive. Like Augustine, Luther thought of sex as an indomitable drive, difficult to control and tainted by sin. Luther was convinced, however, that the best remedy for disordered desire is not celibacy but marriage, wherein sex can be domesticated, tamed, by the multiple responsibilities of wedded life and children. Luther was not the first to advocate marriage as the cure for unruly sexual desire, but he took on the whole of the tradition in a way that no one else had.

In Luther's view, sexual pleasure itself in one sense needs no justification. The desire for it is simply a fact of life. It remains good so long as it is channeled through marriage into the meaningful whole of life. What there is in sex that detracts (or distracts) from the knowledge of God is indeed sinful, but even a procreative aim cannot provide it with a special "justification." If it cannot be justified, it has simply and finally to be forgiven, as do the sinful elements that are inevitable (according to Luther) in all human activity. The "place" of its forgiveness is only within marriage and a family.

The Protestant Reformation, then, did little to change fundamental Christian assessments of sex. Yet it drastically altered the assessment of celibacy. The paradigm for Christian daily life was now marriage and family. A lifelong commitment to celibacy became thoroughly suspect as a realistic possibility for individuals (the indomitability of sexual desire precludes sexual abstinence for all but a very few). And since (by the higher Middle Ages) it was frequently associated with a life of supposed poverty, but one that depended on alms from the genuinely poor, celibacy was judged to be not only unrealistic but marked by laziness and moral turpitude.

Even more importantly, Luther rejected perfectionism on theological grounds.[12] All persons are justified by the grace of God in Jesus Christ, yet all remain sufficiently sinful that progress in internal transformation is not to be expected: *simul justus, simul peccator.* Seeking perfection is, rather, sinful in itself, since it is essentially self-centered. It contaminates faith in God (for it seeks salvation in "works-righteousness") and prevents a full-blown love of neighbor.

The primary *ethical* demand made on Christians is indeed, according to Luther, love of neighbor. But it is in the secular, nonsacramental institutions of marriage and family that individuals learn obedience to God, patience, and the required forms of neighbor-love. After 1523, therefore, Luther shifted his emphasis on marriage as a "hospital for the incurables" to marriage as a "school for character." This did not mean that Luther simply turned desires for holiness in a new direction. Rather, he continued to reject perfection altogether as an authentic Christian concern.

The Catholic Reformation (or so-called Counter-Reformation) absorbed scarcely any of the critiques of the ideal of celibacy or its goals. It did take seriously the quite accurate charges of widespread nonobservance among celibates. Catholic church leaders moved, therefore, to strengthen the discipline (primarily through "enclosure") that might better protect and promote celibacy as a valid choice among Christians.[13] By and large, however, the Protestant critique remains still to be addressed at practical and theoretical levels alike. Combined with other problems that haunt the concept, rationale, and practice of committed lifelong celibacy this critique must finally be taken into account in the development of theologies of celibacy. Only by doing so will constructive proposals make sense in the "different world" of contemporary cultures and the church. I turn, then, to problems of the present that are in important ways still problems from the past.

Problems in the Present

Problems with historical theologies of sexuality, of marriage and family, and of the human person are not the only problems to be faced in validating Christian choices of committed lifelong celibacy. Developments in contemporary theology that correct historical inadequacies sometimes serve only to sharpen the questions for a celibacy rationale. A "view from the present" is therefore needed to complement a "view from the past" if we are to clarify the full set of challenges that constructive proposals regarding celibacy must take into account.

First, past theologies of human sexuality no longer serve well the authentication and promotion of lifelong committed celibacy. Pessimistic views of sex have yielded to theologies of embodiment and sexuality that at least aim to integrate reason and emotion, body and spirit, desire and love. Far from being seen as a drain on individuals' strength and power, sex is believed to enhance the capabilities of the person as a whole. Today, sex is not even thought to be a distraction from prayer. On the contrary, it has become a truism that it is not sex that gets in the way of contemplation, but work (or whatever form of pressured and all-encompassing activity characterizes responsible lives in contemporary society).

No one any longer argues that sex is the paradigmatic location of the damage from original sin. Sexual desire can still have negative consequences (as in exploitation, repression, oppression, betrayal), but celibacy is not the remedy for all such evils.[14] Moreover, freedom for service may still be secured at the price of celibacy, but there are those whose experience shows that too much "availability" can be as counterproductive as too little. The challenge to celibacy, then, is that there are very fine ways, holy ways—other than lifelong celibacy—to live out the sexual dimension of human life. There are ways, to put it sharply, that appear to be just as conducive to union with God, service of the neighbor, and fulfillment of the human person. Given the personal cost of celibacy, why should anyone choose it?

Similarly, historical problems with theologies of marriage and family are superseded by contemporary insights and valuations. But in this development, also, traditional rationales for celibacy may be weakened if not destroyed. The twentieth century has in some sense seen a giant step taken in the church's positive affirmation of the family. Again and again in papal encyclicals, statements of episcopal synods, documents of Vatican II, and so forth, the family has been hailed as not only the foundation of society but even "the first cell of the church," the "domestic sanctuary" of the Christian community.[15]

Today arguments are made (primarily in defense of rights of the family) for marriage, family life, and parenthood as intimate to the identity of the individual, rooted in the core of what it means to be a person.[16]

The very concerns that led Christians of the past to relegate the family to secondary importance in the Christian life have been revisited in the light of new understandings of human relationships, connections between public and private spheres, the secular and the sacred, and salvation history.[17] Previous assumptions that marriage and family are "things of this world" that must be transcended for the sake of the reign of God, or that they are less conducive (than celibacy) to growth in a whole and absolute love for God and a universal love for all humankind, are now modified and even discarded. Today Christian theology is less likely to think of marriage as involving a "divided heart" and more likely to ponder the ways in which God can be found in creation, especially in created persons. Theologians are less likely to conceptualize marriage as an "indirect" way to union with God and more likely to see special relationships as participations in and helps toward Christian *agape*. Once again, then, what rationale can be given for lifelong celibacy that fosters it as a choice among Christians?

When it comes to contemporary theologies of the human person, there has been no abandonment of the view that moral development and growth in holiness are possible and even required. Luther's view has not found resonance in the Roman Catholic psyche. The attack on "works-righteousness" has indeed chastened Catholic theology, but the net result has been stronger, more persuasive, theologies of grace and theologies of human freedom.[18] Moreover, in both Protestant and Catholic theologies, character development and theories of virtue are once again central to a comprehensive Christian theological ethics. Similarly, postmodern dismissals of the continuity of the "self" are not finally persuasive for human persons whose experience of life includes the promise of an unlimited future in relationship with God.

What does provide yet another challenge to rationales for celibacy, however, is the gradual move in Catholic theology to develop the notion of a universal call to holiness. Always implicit in Catholic belief, it nonetheless was obscured by the emphasis on celibacy as a response to this call. Thomas Aquinas had argued in the thirteenth century that it is a matter of "precept," of moral obligation, that all are called to love God with a whole heart[19] with the implication that this is possible in all walks of life. But it took Vatican II to identify once and for all the radicality of the vocation of all Christians, and in one fell swoop the tensions between "precepts" and "counsels" were almost swept away.[20] But if all morally good ways of life can be the "means through which and the basis upon which" an individual grows toward the fullness of her perfection, then it is less clear why anyone would choose lifelong celibacy, given the genuine renunciation that it involves.[21] If "grace is everywhere,"[22] and the way that grace works is through ordinary lives, private or public, in church or family or chosen community, then is there a particular rationale left to be articulated for lifelong celibacy?

Celibacy and Its Future

No doubt the most important Christian response to contemporary questions of whether or not religiously motivated lifelong celibacy makes sense is that Jesus himself has shown the way. Yet no one thinks she or he can exactly replicate Jesus' life. There are requirements for discipleship, but celibacy is not one of them. Having no general command to imitate Jesus particularly as celibates, Christians must probe the legitimacy of this option in their own time and place and in their own personal circumstances. Hence, it is not superfluous to respond to the problems of celibacy in the face of changing understandings of human sexuality, marriage and family, and the call to holiness.

Celibacy must be an authentic way not only of living, but, in particular, of living one's sexuality. What was a difficult life choice for past generations becomes more difficult still in a pan-sexualized culture like our own. Whatever the rationale for such a choice, it must be able to stand when past groundings seem no longer reasonable, or when understandings and practical possibilities of sexual choices are legitimately transformed. Deep in the Christian tradition is a sexual theology and ethic that values marriage and procreation on the one hand and singleness and celibacy on the other. Why is this so? We have come well beyond the view that sex as such is as likely to be evil as to be good, and we can also move beyond the view that a life without genital sexual activity is against nature. Even if all theory should be for this latter view, the experience of those who lead celibate lives is too often against it. Whether celibacy is chosen or graciously accepted, many of those who live it manifest in their lives not only happiness and well-being but the heightened dignity that comes with human fulfillment.

Committed lifelong celibacy has always been only an alternative way—an alternative to marriage and to life in a family, and also an alternative to singleness without a focused permanent commitment to celibacy. As such, it has offered a way of relating to God and to neighbor that is of value in itself, but also revelatory of the meaning of sexuality for the Christian community and the wider society beyond. Whatever the aberrations in some past historical settings, celibacy has always held the potential of challenging existing power relations, liberating individuals for the unexpected, breaking the bonds of gender stereotypes, and resisting the social construction of sexual meanings in any era. There is no reason to prevent the option of religiously motivated lifelong celibacy from fulfilling these functions today.

The twenty-first century brings its own sexual problematic, and it is one for which celibacy is not irrelevant. The work of the French philosopher Michel Foucault was preoccupied with a question that his massive history of human sexuality was not finally able to answer: how did contemporary Western culture come to believe that sexuality is the key to individual identity? How did sex become more important than love, and almost more important than life?[23] Celibates have no more of an answer to that question than anyone else. But the option of celibacy keeps such a question in perspective and perhaps even alive. Celibacy represents the possibility that genital sex need not be at the heart of every profound human relationship, and that sexual intensity, lived celibately, can empower the human person as a whole.

Perhaps particularly for women in the twenty-first century, committed lifelong celibacy holds the possibility of resisting and transcending gender stereotypes that continually threaten to limit the spheres within which women (and men, for that matter) may live and work. In an era when the importance of gender is more and more questioned — whether in marriage, partnerships of all kinds or roles in the family, church, and society — celibate individuals and groups provide perspectives and insights of critical importance to all. Genital sexual renunciation need not (ought not, and probably cannot) render individuals sexless or gender-free, but it can expand the horizons against which gender and sex gain meaning. Moreover, in a time when population growth is less of a problem than ever before (when, in terms used by Peter Brown, there is no need to "replace the dead")[24] celibates can help to make visible the multiple forms of fruitfulness that characterize human relationships and endeavors.

Moreover, despite my earlier positive theological review, traditional concepts and rationales regarding marriage and family are themselves under challenge. For whatever reasons (including the greater acceptability of same-sex unions, the volatility of contemporary societies, the development of reproductive technologies), it is difficult to know what counts as "traditional" family. And whatever form a family takes, issues of structural justice have become central to its viability and its worth. Every form of human power — religious, legal, political, economic — is being brought to bear on the family. "Family values" are frequently not pious or innocuous slogans but coercive agendas for controlling the family, as often to its detriment as to its gain. Celibates along with everyone else have a stake in the outcome of this social confusion.

This means that, for example, it will not do for celibate women and men on the one hand, and spouses and parents (or single persons, partners, single parents, etc.) on the other, to compete with one another for some kind of pride of place in the church or society. Contemporary discourse about sexuality, about the nature and roles of men and women, serves all persons ill if it closes off their options, determines the limits of their activities, and yields yet again gendered hierarchies in every sphere. Hence, if the alternatives open to individuals are pitted against each other, both women and men must refuse the temptation to vie for what any others judge to be a "better" way. Oddly enough, if celibates have a stake in a stable outcome of social confusion regarding marriage and family, so sexually partnered persons and their offspring have a stake in whatever new understandings emerge for celibacy. After all, most human relationships — all but a limited number in any person's life — are celibate.

Every authentic way of life incorporates relationships that are intrinsically good and hence constitutive of the fullness of life toward which they are also a means. In so far as love of God requires love of neighbor — not just as a test or a sign, but as the way in which God is to be loved — marriage and family offer particular ways of loving. It is, as Karl Rahner insists, false to say that "two loves, the love for God and Christ on the one hand, and the human love which finds its fulfillment in marriage on the other, are opposed to one another as rivals."[25] God is not one particular among many, not in competition with human objects of love. To love anyone truly is to encounter, in Martin Buber's terms, the "Eternal Thou."[26] Past distinctions, then, between celibate love for God as "direct" and a love for God in and through marriage as "indirect" are no longer adequate. The possibilities we have of union with God are not determined by the ways in which we live our sexuality (except in so far as everything in our lives has something to do with our way of loving God).

Committed lifelong celibacy, as I have already said, has always been only an alternate way of living, but it has been an *alternate* way. Despite newer insights into the shared goals and rationales of every authentic way of Christian living, the different ways are not conflatable. If we are more adequately to *distinguish* yet value diverse ways of life — in particular, celibate and married walks of life — a focus on some particular aspects of both ways of life may be useful. These aspects include different forms of intimacy, different witnesses to hope, different patterns of living.

Briefly, then, we can observe that differences in possibilities for human interpersonal intimacy are more telling than anything else. There are forms of intimacy that belong to sexual partnerships but not to celibate relationships. At the heart of the renunciation that is intrinsic to lifelong celibacy is a letting go of some of the richest, most passionate yet tender, most all-encompassing forms of intimacy given to human persons. This is an intimacy that is not limited to genital intimacy, but overflows into the daily sharing of all of life with another person in so far as that is possible. Of course, such intimacy frequently encounters the many forms of struggles that are also part of blending lives together. Even and perhaps only through these struggles are the depths of this intimacy discovered and forged.

Not all human interpersonal intimacy is foregone by a commitment to celibacy, since the intensity of friendships — precisely without genital content — can sometimes surpass the intimacy of those who are sexually partnered. Yet at the heart of the renunciation that is intrinsic to lifelong celibacy is a letting go of sexual and marital intimacy. Something is lost for celibates when it comes not only to the intensities of sexual relationship but to a particular kind of sharing of the fabric of everyday life. When a commitment to celibacy is religiously motivated, when it is undertaken in response to a perceived call, then the reasons for renunciation and loss are lodged in a relationship to God and to the people of God, both of which offer new possibilities for intimacy in shared lives and labors. And such a call can include casting one's lot with others, in community, ministry, and friendship. Hence, the processes toward and the realities of intimacy are not the same in different walks of life. Intimacy may not be measured, but it takes diverse forms.

Lifelong celibacy, chosen for the sake of the reign of God, has from early Christian centuries been valued in part as a witness to an unlimited future — an embodiment of eschatological hope in a world to come. In the twentieth century, eschatology turned more to this world than a world beyond, so that marriage and family have become a sign of hope in a new way. That is, the very decision to bear children requires hope in the future of this world, whatever its tragedies and terrors. Both perspectives are important, one must say. The danger that hope will be wishful thinking, a "pie in the sky" kind of hope that never attends to the needs of this world, is countered by eschatological demands that we (whether celibate or married) work for justice and the mending of the world. But on the other hand, if hope in another world without care for this one is a mistake, so too is hope in this world without belief in the continuity between this world and its transformation by God into another. Those in either walk of

life, married or celibate, are called to hope in both ways. Neither detracts from the other if their primary embodied witnesses coalesce into the kind of theological hope without which we cannot live.

When one focuses particularly on one or the other vocation, there are things to be said that cannot be said only by comparison. In each vocation there is need for a home — if not a dwelling place, at least a home in the heart of God and the hearts of some others. In each vocation a life is laid down, again and again. In each vocation there is fulfillment and nonfulfillment, rejoicing and waiting, in the mystery of the already and not-yet. In each vocation, there is waxing and waning of courage and energy and devotion and love. Each vocation is in itself a life and a ministry.

In the story of each person's life is the story of God-relatedness and neighbor-love. Neither of these loves is reducible to the other, and both are required as the foundation, the integrated way, and the goal of authentic vocation. There is more than one kind of neighbor-love and more than one kind of love of God. Just as there is more than one kind of love in diverse experiences of marriage and family, so there is more than one kind of love in diverse experiences of lifelong celibacy. The fullness of love that God gives to God's people encompasses them all.

But were I to speak primarily (and in general) of lifelong committed celibacy, I would have to emphasize somewhere that such a life is a little like living on a park bench — without a home or a place to lay one's head. Though a Christian celibate life is certainly not "world-denying," nonetheless to embrace it is fundamentally a decision to "leave all things" for the sake of the reign of God. Unlike marriage and family, a celibate vocation is not really first a part of the "order of creation." It may be that there are goods that are attractive to some who choose lifelong celibacy, goods that they respect and love and need not leave behind. Yet the experience of many who make the choice of lifelong celibacy in a Christian context is frequently charged with radicality in a way that most other commitments are not.

This form of choice of Christian celibacy makes sense only for the sake of love — or better, for the sake of at least a desire to love God with one's whole heart and soul and mind and strength, and to love one's neighbor as one's self. That is, it makes sense only if it is a way to refine human capacities for love, to find in faith the union that is love, and to express love in action. The goal of this life is given first in the yearning that prompts it and then in the ongoing desire that sustains it. The central rationale for this life may be found, finally, in the desire to pick up one's very being and place it down again in utter affirmation of God; and in so doing, in profound love of and solidarity with the near neighbor and far. This is true of all vocations in one way or another, for all great loves are in some profound sense  crucified loves. In each vocation a life is laid down somewhere along the way, and perhaps again and again. In each there is fulfillment and nonfulfillment, rejoicing and waiting, in the mystery of the already-not-yet. Each vocation is both life and ministry, and perhaps also mystery. But a celibate vocation makes sense only under the sign of the cross — which is a sign, after all, not of death but of life; not of betrayal but of relationships that hold.

Chapter 10

Homosexuality and the Church

CHRISTOPHER WOLFE

MOST OF THE DISCUSSION about homosexuality and the teaching of the Catholic Church in America today is beside the point. That is, most of it simply challenges the Church's unalterable teaching on the intrinsic immorality of homosexual acts, a teaching which cannot be changed because it is solidly rooted in Scripture and has been the constant teaching of the Church from the beginning. The discussion is an unfortunate manifestation of how many American Catholics have been formed much more by their culture than by the Church. Why and how that has happened is a large discussion in itself, embracing *la trahison des clercs*, the decline of confident leadership and authority in many of the local churches, and the enervation of faith in an affluent and hedonistic society.

It is distressing to see so much effort diverted to an unhelpful discussion of *whether* the Church should teach that homosexual acts are immoral, because it prevents discussion of other important matters that is urgently needed. These include, most importantly: how to help Catholics understand, live, and explain the Church's moral teachings; how Catholics can effectively offer the substance of the Church's teachings as the best answer to so many individual and social problems in our pluralistic society — though typically offering it, not as "the Church's teachings," but as simply "the truth about the human person"; and how to dramatically improve the Church's pastoral response to Catholics afflicted with same-sex attractions.

In this paper, I will focus my discussion on the question of how to deal pastorally with young Catholics experiencing same-sex attractions and temptations. I think I can do this best in the form of a letter to an imaginary son of a friend, who reaches adolescence and experiences same-sex attractions and is wondering how to respond to them. (For the more academic purposes of this book, however, I will add subheadings and endnotes that would normally not be part of such a letter.)

◆ ◆ ◆

Dear Jim,

Your dad just told me about your recent conversation, in which you told him about your sexual attractions to other guys (and lack of attraction to girls) and that you are wondering how you can deal with this, especially in light of your faith. Since our families have been friends for a long time, and most importantly because I am your godfather, I thought that maybe I could take the liberty of sending you this letter, hoping to help you understand some of the aspects of this topic a little better, and to suggest how you might respond to these feelings.

I'm sure that the feelings or questions didn't just arise overnight. In fact, I can't say that it comes as a shock to me. You haven't seemed to have many close friendships among your peers at school, your parents have mentioned, and you haven't really gotten involved in sports and the more typical male activities (though, of course, there's lots of variation among those with same-sex attraction on those points).[1]

It's probably been years now since you began to wonder whether you are just made different from others (i.e., from those with heterosexual attractions). And I wouldn't be surprised to hear that some of the guys your age have picked up on it and treated you less than charitably. And, perhaps most of all, in your wondering and questioning and uncertainty, you must have felt very alone — afraid to ask other people about it, often feeling like a freak yourself, fearing (all too justifiably) the reaction of many others, especially (less justifiably) your parents.

So, at this point, you're asking yourself. Who and what am I? Is this my identity? Am I a "homosexual"? What should I do?

Maybe you've already come in contact with some people who tell you that this IS your identity, and it's a good thing, and you have nothing to be ashamed of.[2] I know there's a GLBT group at your school, and that the school has established a program to prevent harassment of homosexuals and lesbians — a good end in itself, but unfortunately the program goes well beyond that purpose, since its counselors establish contact with any students who raise questions about their gender identity and encourage those who wonder about their same-sex attractions to embrace their homosexuality and view it positively.[3] Perhaps they have referred you to some of the literature — an incredible growth industry these days — that proclaims the naturalness, the legitimacy, the equality, and the goodness of an actively homosexual life.

Probably you don't hear much on the other side of the issue. And, unfortunately, when you do, it may be people who just react with a kind of instinctive loathing — the idiots who go around calling people like you "faggots." Even the ones who are kinder, like your parish priest (whom I've known for a long time), really don't know much about homosexuality and can't offer a persuasive account of what the Church teaches, and why. (They know it says that homosexual acts are wrong, but couldn't really give good reasons. In fact, they haven't given a homily on the Church's teaching on sexual ethics for years, and nothing they say even suggests that they have studied John Paul II's extraordinary reflections on "the theology of the body."[4])

So, my guess is, these last few years have probably been pretty hard ones for you. I'm really glad you finally talked to your dad. Keeping this inside, trying to grapple with it alone, is not the way to go — though I understand your confusion about where you might actually get help in coming to terms with it. I want to suggest that you can get help, and that this crisis that you face may be an opportunity, though a difficult one, to really grow as a human being and as a Catholic.

The first thing I want to say to you is this. What you are — your deepest and truest identity — is not defined by your sexual feelings or inclinations. What you are, most fundamentally, is a child of God. Like every other human being, you are called — you have the vocation — to holiness. And that holiness includes — as one important, though subordinate, element — a call to chastity. There are no second-class citizens in the kingdom of heaven: all (irrespective of feelings or tendencies they do not choose or will, including same-sex attraction) are called and can respond to God's love and commandments.

Since I know you take your faith seriously, you should start by looking at what the Church says about the question of homosexuality. By "the Church," I mean those who have been entrusted by Christ with the authority to maintain and pass on the deposit of the faith, namely, the hierarchy. It's tougher these days, of course, for many people to give any credence to the hierarchy, since some priests and bishops have behaved terribly over the years, unconscionably taking advantage of their position to engage in sex with young men, or protecting those that did. (And dissenters in the Church have readily used these lamentable acts as a potent weapon to further detach ordinary Catholics in the pews from any spirit of humble submission to the Church's leaders.) If the authority of priests and bishops rested on their personal qualities, it would be easier to understand why people's faith has been shaken (even though the percentage of priests engaging in such acts is low, and many of the bishops were misled by advice from mental health professionals who assured them that this "problem" could be overcome by a relatively brief sojourn at some facility). But bishops have authority, not because they are smarter or better than other people (though we are gratified when they have those gifts), but because they have received the power to teach, govern, and sanctify through the sacrament of Holy Orders that extends back to Our Lord Himself. Whatever their personal qualities, and whatever their personal sins, when they teach with and for the Church, they are God's chosen instruments. I suppose God could have done without them, writing his message to men in the sky for each new generation. But he wanted to establish a Church and to give all-too-fragile men — which is what all of us are, after all — a cooperative role in the redemption.

The Church on Homosexuality

So, what does the Church teach on homosexuality? The best starting point is the *Catechism of the Catholic Church,* since that book is intended to provide people with a basic statement of the Catholic faith, especially as it has been developed in Vatican II and the subsequent Church documents interpreting and applying its teaching.

What the *Catechism* says is basically the following: (paragraph 2357) (1) Homosexuality has taken many forms in different centuries and cultures, and its genesis remains largely unexplained; (2) Scripture presents homosexual acts as acts of grave depravity; (3) tradition has always declared that homosexual acts are intrinsically disordered; (4) they are contrary to the natural law, because they close the sexual act to the gift of life and they do not proceed from a genuine affective and sexual complementarity; (5) they can never be approved (paragraph 2358); (6) The number of men and women who have deep-seated homosexual tendencies is not negligible; (7) (in the revised text of the *Catechism*) the homosexual inclination is objectively disordered and constitutes for most who experience it a trial; (8) homosexuals must be accepted with respect, compassion, and sensitivity, and every sign of unjust discrimination should be avoided; (9) those with homosexual tendencies are called to fulfill God's will in their lives, and homosexuals who are Christians are called to unite the difficulties they encounter from their condition to the sacrifice of Our Lord's Cross (paragraph 2359); (10) Homosexual persons are called to chastity; (11) they should gradually and resolutely approach Christian perfection (a) by the virtues of self-mastery that teach them inner freedom, (b) at times by the support of disinterested friendship, and (c) by prayer and sacramental grace.

This is the section on homosexuality itself. It cannot be understood, however, without looking at the broader context of the Church's positive teaching on the beautiful meaning of sexuality in which it is, literally, located.[5] That teaching is much too rich and extensive to summarize here. (You should re-read it and bring it to prayer, however, trying to understand its depths.) For our purposes, I would single out these aspects: First, sexuality is by its nature oriented to the union of spouses who commit themselves to each other and whose physical union — the sign of their complete self-giving — is always open to love and life; second, everyone is called to live the virtue of chastity, according to his or her state in life (consecrated virginity, marriage, the single life); and third, chastity requires the freedom of self-mastery — it cannot be reduced to a biological or psychological need or imperative.

Some people claim that the Church's teaching should be discounted or ignored because the Church has not "taken into consideration" the "experience" of homosexual people, including Catholics who experience same-sex attractions. The Church must listen to their experience, it is said, and this will lead to an appreciation of the contribution gays can make to the Church.

It's certainly true that the Church should listen to people of all sorts. How can we bring the gospel to them, if we don't genuinely love them and listen to them with our hearts, even when we know they are wrong about some things? And, yes, we can and should learn many things from others, even people who don't live in accord with important moral principles. (From homosexuals many of us have learned of the lack of affection and moral support they so often face in their lives, and in the Church, too.) And, yes, people who experience same-sex attractions, and those who succumb to them at times — after which they can and need to seek the forgiveness that all of us sinners must ask for — can make tremendous contributions to the Church.

But, having recognized all that, the Church cannot rest its moral teaching on the subjective experiences of various individuals. To take a simple example: Catholics should listen to, and learn from, and appreciate the contribution to the Church of people who are racists (there were well-intentioned American Catholics, historically, who defended the South's chattel slavery, for example, as well as Catholics who strongly opposed desegregation, and were excommunicated for it) — but without conceding that their experience, or their subjective interpretations of it, should affect the content of the Church's moral teaching on racism. It is God's law — expressed both in revelation and in the natural law — that must be the basis for the Church's teachings. And that law clearly prohibits homosexual acts, as the

Catechism says. So the relevant experiences of homosexuals in the Church *that are compatible with Church teaching* — for example, their testimony to the unkindness with which they have been treated, or the loneliness they have felt in the Church — are very important for us to take into account. But "experiences" that are rooted in a rejection of Church teaching, such as their sense of completeness or fulfillment in homosexual activity, cannot be "accepted" as a good on the basis of their subjective feelings.

Well, let's get back to your situation and your very natural questions and concerns. First, you know that you did not "choose" to have same-sex attractions. So how can you understand them? Did God make you that way? And, if so, does he thereby "validate" those attractions and make them legitimate to pursue?

Causes of Same-Sex Attraction

Let's start with the question of the cause of homosexual feelings and attractions. Some moral conservatives treat same-sex attraction as if it were simply a choice. That's a mistake, for the most part. (There are some instances where that is true, but those are very exceptional.)[6] The *Catechism* is right to point out that there are significant limits to our knowledge about the causes of homosexuality, but I do think that some things can be said, which are worth knowing.

For example, some people argue that homosexuality is genetically or biologically determined: some people are simply "wired" to be homosexual. This is important to some people because they believe that, if some people are "made" homosexual, they should have a right to act on those inclinations. (More on that later.)

I think that, despite the limits of our knowledge, there is enough evidence to show that the idea of genetic *determination* of heterosexuality is simply wrong. You see articles on the front pages of newspapers pretty regularly trumpeting new studies that makes such claims; the studies that test and do not confirm the initial studies tend to be reported much farther in the back of the newspapers, but they are there.

The best discussion of this issue can be found in an article by Dr. Jeffrey Satinover, a former Fellow in Psychiatry at Yale University. The chapter, which reviews our knowledge of genetic causes of various conditions and then surveys some of the published research on genetics and homosexuality, is worth a careful read. It sensibly insists on the limits of our present knowledge, but it also points out the extent to which what we *do* know undermines the claim that homosexuality is genetically determined.[7]

For example, identical twins have identical genes. If homosexuality were genetically determined, then where one twin is homosexual, the other would be, too. But that is the case, according to one well-known study, only 50 percent of the time. Moreover, since identical twins typically are raised in the same environment, a good part of that 50 percent may be due to environment rather than genes.

Moreover, fraternal twins in the same study had about a 22 percent concordance rate for homosexuality, while biological brothers (who have the same share of genes fraternal twins do) have about a 9 percent concordance rate — which suggests that there is some "twin factor" unrelated to genes. And, to add another complicating factor, nonbiological (adoptive) brothers — who have no significant genetic similarity — had a concordance rate of 11 percent (about the same as biological brothers), a finding that seems to support the importance of environmental factors.

It is plausible, of course, that genetic influences play some limited role, but this role is likely to be indirect rather than direct — i.e., not determinative. The analogy Satinover gives is this: no one is genetically determined to be a basketball player, but genes for height and athleticism certainly would affect the likelihood of becoming a good basketball player.

Another analogy: alcoholism has long been suspected to have a genetic component, e.g., Northern Europeans seem to be more susceptible to it. A recent line of analysis explaining this fact is the following: there isn't any gene directly related to alcoholism per se, but the harsher climate and light conditions of northern areas affect the development of the nervous system and its response to stressors, or anxiety — and this renders people in this group more susceptible to alcohol, because alcohol is a classic anti-anxiety agent. So the genes don't "cause" alcoholism, but they may put some people more "at risk" for it.

The idea that even the limited genetic influence may be indirect is also supported by the simple observation that homosexuality doesn't simply die out—which, given the sterility of homosexual acts, would be the ordinary tendency if the condition was genetically caused. If the genetic influences (even in their limited form) are indirect, however—that is, if they do not code for homosexuality per se—that would explain why those genes do not adversely affect heterosexual reproduction.

(Note that this discussion has this side implication: if the evidence indicates that homosexuality is not genetically determined, but we see a cascade of studies purporting to show that it is, might this not indicate that what we are seeing is a politically motivated scholarship rather than true scholarship? Anyone familiar with scholars will not find it hard to believe that political predilections can influence supposedly scientific studies, and especially the interpretations thereof.)[8]

Finally, what about the implications of the claim that homosexuality is genetically caused? If same-sex attractions *are* genetically determined, what would follow from that fact? We still couldn't accept the proposition that all genetically determined conditions are morally equal. Why not? Well, think about the implication of the fact that various mental illnesses are pretty clearly influenced by genes. If schizophrenia or paranoia are sometimes influenced by genes, for example, would we say that makes schizophrenic or paranoiac behavior legitimate or unobjectionable? If some people are more disposed by their genetically based temperaments to violence or anger or cowardice or lust, would that make displays of violence or anger or cowardice or lust by them unobjectionable?

The fact is that material nature is sometimes defective. Sometimes bad genes cause very unfortunate conditions, including physical deformations and diseases, and also disordered moral tendencies. Genes don't legitimate what they cause, since some of their effects are acknowledged by all to be afflictions and others dispose people to act in ways we all would consider wrong. So even if homosexual feelings were genetically caused, that wouldn't prove they should be treated as "natural" and legitimate, or that people should act on them.

If genes don't "cause" same-sex attractions, but are, at most, a predisposition, then what does cause it? It seems clear that there is no single "cause" of homosexual attractions, but a variety of factors, none of which is determinative. (That is, for every person who has a given factor and is homosexual, it is easy to find others who have that same factor and are not.) The cause in any given case is, frankly, a complex mix of factors about which we have pretty limited knowledge.

The clinical experience of many psychiatrists and therapists does, however, point in the direction of various environmental factors, perhaps most importantly, developmental disorders stemming from problematic relationships with parents.[9] The basic idea is that each individual in some sense has to "achieve" his gender identity by going through a developmental process, and in some cases — especially where the ordinary relationships with parents are disrupted (sometimes in ways that are not overt) — this process is short-circuited.

That heterosexuality is the "normal" end of this process is almost self-evident. Human beings are animals, after all, even if they are rational animals, and the purpose of sexual differentiation in animal species is clear: it's for reproduction.[10] A development of even a rational animal that utterly frustrates that intrinsic capacity of sexual activity is *prima facie* a distortion of normal development. (This doesn't mean that looking at human beings as animals is a completely adequate way of looking at them. The teaching of the Church on sexuality emphasizes that this capacity that human beings share with animals must be elevated and transformed into a truly human capacity. Nonetheless, the elevation of the capacity of a rational animal should ordinarily respect the inherent purpose of that capacity.)[11]

Now, if developmental problems — in ways not entirely clear to us — are the cause of same-sex attractions that is not to say that every homosexual has a "bad" father or mother. The relationship between parent and child can be affected by many adventitious and subjective factors. Still, clinicians find that it is a very common occurrence that homosexuals have fathers who are, in various ways, experienced as "distant" fathers, and/or mothers who are experienced as very controlling. (Your dad is a friend of mine, but no one would say that he is a particularly warm person, and his excessive commitment to his professional life has drawn him away from the family — and you — quite a bit, hasn't it?) Lesbians often have had the experience of a father who deserted the family, or was personally very distant, or was an alcoholic or abusive, or some combination of these, and/or a mother who was extremely weak. In cases such as these, and in other cases, such as the trauma of sexual abuse, it is not surprising to discover that ordinary gender identity development is thwarted.[12] (Again, we have to remember that many people affected by these various factors are not homosexual. It's just that when they are present the chances of developing same-sex attractions are clearly greater.)

You will undoubtedly have pointed out to you that contemporary psychiatry and psychology no longer regard homosexuality as a mental disorder; that the American Psychiatric Association removed homosexuality from its Diagnostic and Statistical Manual in 1973. While that is true, it doesn't follow that the removal was based on genuine scientific grounds, or that it was justified. It simply means that gay rights activists were able to muster enough political power within the APA to accomplish this objective. (Again, any scholar who is a member of a professional organization will be aware that some issues can become intensely politicized and be dealt with more on ideological than scientific grounds.)[13]

Moreover, the situation is complicated by the fact that psychiatry and psychology are deeply shaped by normative assumptions about human nature and the human good, which are really borrowed from moral philosophy — and a training in psychiatry is no guarantee of expertise in moral philosophy.[14] The changing attitudes of many contemporary practitioners in those fields simply reflect the increasing spread in our culture — perhaps especially in its intellectual elites — of various forms of moral relativism (at least with respect to "self-regarding" action, or "victimless crimes").[15]

The Possibility of Change

I want to make another important point, Jim, about the implications of understanding homosexuality as a developmental disorder, despite the fact that it is controversial. That is the possibility that in some cases same-sex attractions can be overcome, and replaced by a normal heterosexual life. It is necessary to be careful here, because the reversal of something as deeply rooted, psychologically, as same-sex attractions cannot be treated as simple or routine. Even those who recognize the possibility of overcoming same-sex attractions by working through developmental disorders with a competent therapist ("reparative therapy"), and especially with the support of religious means (e.g., programs similar to the 12–Step program employed by Alcoholics Anonymous) admit that such change is not easy.[16] Nor is it morally necessary, as Fr. John Harvey, the founder of Courage, a wonderful Catholic program for people with homosexual temptations, is careful to point out.[17] It is an entirely legitimate choice to live with, and resist, one's homosexual attractions, living chastely in spite of them. But it does need to be said that it is also legitimate, and generally desirable, to make the effort to transform one's sexual attractions, when it seems possible. Interestingly, one of the main actors in the removal of homosexuality from the DSM-II in 1973, Dr. Robert Spitzer, has come around to the view that change is possible. Intrigued by claims made by some "ex-gay" protestors at a psychological association meeting, he embarked on a study to determine whether such change was really possible. Spitzer — who is still a supporter of homosexual rights — concluded in his study that the evidence showed that some people, with strong motivation and the appropriate support, were indeed able to change their sexual orientation.[18]

I don't know whether that is an effort you will consider making. You are young, not habituated to a life of homosexual activity, and you want to be serious about your faith, and those are some indications that it is worthwhile for you to take a serious look at the possibility. Moreover, even if you decide not to pursue it, some discussion with a good Catholic psychiatrist or therapist is likely to be valuable for you in trying to understand and come to grips with these feelings you experience.[19] So I would encourage you to look into it. But it's also worth remembering that the key question is not what our feelings are, but what our free choices and acts are.

Personal Identity and Same-Sex Attraction

At this point, I should make clear an important fact that is an obvious implication of this analysis. The fact that a person has same-sex attractions is not necessarily — indeed, not typically — due to any failure on his own part. People with homosexual attractions generally do not choose them but find themselves afflicted by them. In that sense, it is entirely right to say that persons with same-sex attractions ought not to view themselves as somehow personally and intrinsically evil or bad — any more than should a person who is born with a physical deformity or who has had some handicap inflicted on him by some event. At the same time, a homosexual orientation, since it is objectively disordered, is never in itself something to be "celebrated," as some gay advocates (even in the Church) do. We always come back to this fundamental point: you are not essentially defined by feelings beyond your own control. You are defined, ontologically, by the fact that God created you, and, on the supernatural plane, by the fact that God the Son has redeemed you, and morally, by the choices you make, with the grace of God, either to follow His Will for you or to reject it.

Now there are many people who want to tell you that you are, in fact, defined by your sexual attractions, and that there is therefore nothing wrong in acting on them, since that is your supposed "nature." In particular, I think a very influential assumption that many people have is that sex is an imperious need, and that therefore there is a natural right to sexual gratification, and that any view denying such a right is rigid, inhuman, and uncompassionate. Such a view, I think, denigrates sex, by denying its full humanity — by considering it, not as a matter of free choice, but as a biological imperative.

There is a strong, inarticulate sense among many ordinary people that this view entails a fundamental injustice. Given the undeniably great power of the sexual urge, and the role that it ordinarily plays in human maturing and fulfillment, they think, how can we deny its realization to anyone? Isn't this to condemn a person to a life of frustration and alienation?

It would be wrong of me to deny that the mastery of the sexual impulse is often difficult, and that — especially in the disordered state of our souls due to original sin and our own personal sins — it can entail genuine affliction or suffering. For example, we can see how very often a heterosexual man or woman, despite a deep desire for conjugal love and family, never meets the person who can be his or her spouse, and suffers greatly (from loneliness and/or from sexual tension). Such people, on the Church's understanding, are not authorized to engage in sexual activity outside of marriage, simply to fulfill emotional needs or relieve sexual tension. Rather, they are called by the Church to respond to these particular circumstances that constitute the mysterious design of Providence in their lives.

And this is as good a place as any to decry the "double standard" that some conservatives apply to sexual activity by heterosexuals and homosexuals. The teaching of the Church with which you are familiar — that conjugal love must by its nature be open to love and to life — implies important limits on heterosexual activity: the search for pleasure or intimacy does not justify premarital or extramarital heterosexual activity or sexual activity within marriage that denies the essential connection of the unitive and procreative meanings of the conjugal act, any more than it justifies homosexual activity. Those who would authorize heterosexual activity that pursues pleasure or intimacy while deliberately choosing to make that activity sterile violate the meaning of our sexuality, just as those who would authorize homosexual activity do. In both cases, an essential element of the inherent meaning of sexual activity — openness to life — is denied.

This leads us to another objection to the Church's teaching. Some people contend that sex that denies openness to children must be validated because certain forms of married sex that are accepted by all (e.g., postmenopausal sex and sex between married persons where one of them is infertile or sterile) are not essentially different.[20] That contention, I think, overlooks a key distinction, based on the nature of truly conjugal union. What makes fully marital sex distinctive is that a husband and wife, each of whom would be incapable of bringing into existence another human being, unite to form "one flesh," becoming a single unit that has that extraordinary capacity (not always actualized) to "embody" their union in the form of a child. Understanding this makes it possible to see the fundamental difference between (a) human sexual acts in which the nature of the act is deliberately changed, making it something less than a full one-flesh communion (the partners being rendered incapable of forming a single reproductive unit, e.g., by contraception or truncated sexual activities such as oral or anal sex), and (b) marital sexual acts where the act engaged in is fully a one-flesh communion, but where an obstacle in the human "matter" (due either to ordinary deterioration of bodily capacities, or to some special defect) prevents the act from being able to achieve actual reproduction (such as marital sex where at least one spouse is infertile or sterile). In the former case, the procreative significance of the act is attacked and denied, while in the latter it is fully preserved and respected even though the physical capacities of the spouses lack the actual present capacity for procreation. Homosexual sex, like contraceptive sex, involves deliberate engagement in a *kind* of sexual activity that is inherently sterile, whereas the latter cases do not.[21]

Compassion

Many people will tell you that the teaching of the Church is defective because it lacks compassion. In your darker and more difficult moments, your flesh may cry out in the same way. What about the sexual frustration you may experience, the personal anguish that continence may entail, you may ask?

It will be a difficult struggle sometimes, of course (as it is sometimes for chaste unmarried heterosexuals, and even for married heterosexuals), but this does not mean that the Church's exhortation to live such a life is uncompassionate or insensitive to suffering.

It is only a small part of the answer, but it is at least worthwhile noting, that in a very basic sense, the Church's teaching is compassionate in ways that should be obvious to any rational person. First, with respect to male homosexuals, the injunction to abstain from homosexual activity has a very important, indeed an immense, practical benefit: they are likely to live a lot longer. The central defining (though not the only) male homosexual activity is anal intercourse. But anal intercourse is extremely unhealthy. It is not just a question of HIV/AIDS, though, of course, that is enormously significant. There is a wide range of other medical pathologies associated with homosexual activity, e.g., hepatitis, liver cancer, pneumonia, internal bleeding, multiple bowel, and other infectious diseases.[22] Male homosexual sex, in particular, is simply unsafe sex. At the very least, those who wish to legitimize homosexual activity should be brought up short by the fact that the life expectancy of male homosexuals is drastically shorter than that of other men, not by years, but by *decades*.[23] (This is only one reason, but it is one reason why I am so glad you have not begun to experiment with homosexual activity in response to your same-sex feelings — I want you to live a long and happy life!)

Another potential harm for homosexuals is the greater likelihood (the fact that one is more "at risk") of a more promiscuous sexual life. Studies sympathetic to homosexuality confirm that the number of sexual partners for male homosexuals greatly exceeds the number for heterosexuals. (One study found that the average number of sexual partners for white male homosexuals was about 550.)[24] The problem with such promiscuity is not just physical (e.g., increased risk of STDs). Nor is it merely the abstract violation of a moral norm. Moral norms have a purpose: they prevent us from doing things that undermine genuine human fulfillment and happiness. Promiscuity creates emotional vulnerability and/or insensitivity, which undermine the conditions for genuine friendship and love. One of the defining features of the lives of many promiscuous homosexuals is loneliness and the desperate (unsuccessful) attempts to overcome it.

There is another harm suffered by homosexuals — in this case by lesbians as well as male homosexuals — that should make us wonder on which side compassion lies. Homosexuals will never know the incredible experience, the joy of seeing their love *embodied* in a new human being. They can raise other people's children, or one of them can cooperate in the artificial production of a child (via artificial insemination, for example), but they cannot bring into existence, through the act in which they most fully express their love for each other, another person. That is a terrible loss. It suggests that, where change of sexual orientation is possible, homosexuals should be encouraged to pursue it, rather than giving in to their same-sex temptations.

Still, none of this is to deny the fact of the very real difficulties that can arise from not being able to actualize our sexual capacity in conjugal acts. The right insistence on chastity, especially in the form of the complete continence required of single heterosexuals, divorced Catholics, widows and widowers, and homosexuals, does not deny the difficulty and even suffering necessary to achieve the kind of self-mastery necessary to achieve it. It says, rather, that suffering can often be an occasion for personal growth and happiness, even in the face of difficult circumstances. It is not an altogether pleasant or comforting truth that a life which involves some suffering can be good and meaningful, and it is understandably difficult, for those who suffer, to accept such exhortations cheerfully when they come from those who do not seem to share their suffering. But it is, nonetheless, an important truth about life — one that our modern affluent, secularized society has great difficulty acknowledging.

For a Christian, moreover, there is that dimension of suffering not available to unbelievers: it is a share in the Cross of Christ. Difficulties and suffering, while never transparently "intelligible" to us on this side of heaven, are an opportunity to identify with the life of the Son of God become man, who chose to suffer to show his love for mankind and thereby showed us that suffering can be redemptive, both for ourselves and for others.[25]

Having said that — for it needs to be said, especially in these days when the Cross is no longer seen as an essential element of Christian life by so many Christians — I don't want to present a life in accord with Christ's teaching as a painful duty that must, unfortunately, be undergone, merely as a prelude to happiness in some other life. I want to tell you once more that you are called by God to be a saint, to be happy with the joy of a Christian in this life, transforming all the ordinary events of your life — many of them wonderful opportunities for various forms of genuine self-fulfillment, in work, in leisure, and in friendship with men, with women, and with God Himself in contemplative prayer — into occasions of loving God and your brothers and sisters.

The means to live this life are the same that are available to every other Catholic confronting his or her own personal struggles: the sacraments (especially the Eucharistic sacrifice, including frequent reception of Holy Communion, and recourse to God's merciful sacrament of reconciliation), spiritual direction, daily personal conversation with Our Lord in prayer, awareness of the presence of God throughout the day, devotion to Our Lady, good friendships, and the ordinary requirements of the ascetical struggle (avoiding idleness and near occasions of sin, rejecting temptations quickly and emphatically but peacefully, humility, and "beginning again" after falls).

In one sense, you are fortunate. In the past, many people in the Church — probably most people in the Church for many centuries — would have regarded you without any understanding, and indeed often with fear, contempt, or loathing. Those days, despite the lingering attitudes and actions of some misguided people, are gone, thank God. There is a better, if still limited, understanding of the nature of homosexuality, as something generally beyond the control of those who experience it, and quite distinct from the deliberate choice to engage in homosexual activity. Most importantly, as the teaching of the *Catechism* indicates, all of us are called to treat those who experience same-sex attractions with respect, compassion, and sensitivity, and without unjust discrimination.

Some defenders of homosexual activity have attempted to impute homosexuality to saints of the past, and to use this as a way of defending their dissent from the Church's teaching. I don't doubt that some saints may have had same-sex attractions, though I deny that saints acted on them. But the limited attitudes of the past probably made it impossible for a person to admit that he had such attractions and still be considered a saint. In our own day, I think that people with same-sex attractions will often choose to keep that fact private because there is usually no reason to parade publicly our moral struggles with internal tendencies to disordered acts. But it is likely enough that others who have struggled with same-sex attraction will come forward — often enough, in order to help others experiencing them — and live lives of holiness, and that some of them will be canonized. That holiness is what I wish for you, Jim. I want to see you become a canonizable saint, with or without the attractions that you did not choose to have, but which you can choose to recognize as a disorder to be resisted — just as all of us have to resist, and all the saints in the history of the Church have had to resist, disorders within us. Instead of regarding those inclinations as imperatives that you must obey, you can master them, with the grace of God, and turn your attention to the other wonderful things God is asking you to do, whatever they may be.

Let's keep talking about this, and many other things. The last thing in the world you want to do is to feel that you have to bottle this up and work it out on your own. You need to know that your family and friends love you a lot, and that we'll always be there to help you in whatever way we can.

Your affectionate godfather,
Chris

Chapter 11

Following the Still Small Voice

Experience, Truth, and Argument as Lived by Catholics around the Gay Issue

JAMES ALISON

IN THE MIDST OF the recent crises which engulfed the Boston Archdiocese, Fr. Bryan Hehir made a call for adult discussion in our church. This is my attempt to provide a resource to enable that conversation to develop. One of the things about adult discussion is that it presupposes people who are both capable of being wrong, and yet who take responsibility for what they say. One of the things about Catholic adult discussion is that, in addition to those two dimensions, it should be charitable and generous-spirited towards differing opinions within the discussion. Please forgive me in advance if I fail to live up to these demanding criteria, but I will certainly try to attend to them, and will expect to be held to them.

My first intention is to try to create a sense of "we." I am not by my words seeking to create party spirit, but rather to work out who the "we" is when we say that we are Catholic. For this reason I am deliberately not setting out to talk uniquely about experience, truth, and argument as lived by gay and lesbian Catholics. That rather assumes that there is a certain sort of "we," a gay and lesbian Catholic "we," which has a special sort of experience and that I am some sort of privileged exponent of the experience of this "we." To start in this way would be to start by setting up sides for some sort of confrontation. I would be delivering to you a set of arguments which you could use to wield against other Catholics, and this would be, from my perspective, a failure of charity and of Catholicity.

Instead of this I want to take a step back from experience, truth, and arguments as lived by gay and lesbian Catholics, and raise the more ecumenical question of these matters as lived by Catholics, period. In other words, as something lived by all of those of us who are Catholics independently of our sexual orientation.

Now it is of course impossible to be comprehensive about the experience of Catholics as regards the gay issue, but there are some suggestions which I can make which point to what I would hope we can all consider to be elements of shared life which are ours by virtue of being Catholics who have been alive in the last twenty to fifty years, give or take a few. The first of these is the emergence among us of the phenomenon which we might now call "the gay thing." Fifty years ago, the word "gay" was only occasionally used with its current meaning, and the idea that there might be public discussion of loving relationships between people of the same sex except in the most shocked or whispered terms would have been incomprehensible. Yet, now, fifty years later, this is increasingly normal at every level of society, and indeed is being legislated for in more and more countries with fewer and fewer objections.

Fifty years ago there were hardly any figures who were publicly known to be gay, and such gay characters as existed in the media tended to be either heavily coded, as in the plays of Tennessee Williams, or depicted as depressive, self-hating, and prone to suicide. Now we have a major musician and his same-sex partner walking up the aisle of Westminster Abbey to play for the funeral of Princess Diana, with the BBC commentator's recognition of the partner being beamed throughout the world, while over the last ten years, programs broadcast all over the planet like *The Real World, Will and Grace, Queer as Folk,* and most recently *Queer Eye for the Straight Guy,* have introduced a different set of images: good, bad, risible, provocative, gentle and so forth, but definitely different, into the public consciousness.

And of course this has affected Catholics just as much as anyone else. In fact, as far as we can tell from surveys, practicing Catholic lay people are significantly more likely to be completely relaxed about gay people than their practicing Protestant counterparts, for reasons which may be interesting, and which I may have a go at suggesting something about later.

Fifty years ago, if someone had suggested that as many as half the men serving in the priesthood were homosexuals, that person would be assumed to be a bigoted anti-Catholic agitator who might be expected to go on in their next breath to claim that nuns regularly ate droves of the small babies who had been illegitimately born in their convents. Yet now someone who claimed that 50 percent of men currently in the priesthood are gay would not be considered mad, or anti-Catholic. Many, myself among them, would hazard that 50 percent seems a conservative estimate, at least in major metropolitan dioceses.

Whatever the figures were fifty years ago, and whatever they are now, one thing is certain: an angry denial that half the priesthood was gay fifty years ago and an angry denial of it now would be greeted by Catholics with entirely different reactions. Fifty years ago, an angry denial would have been expected, now an angry denial would be regarded as a sign that the denier was either ideologically driven or was suffering from some sort of extraplanetary mind warp.

I point this out not because I want to claim that it is a particularly Catholic thing, but rather because there is no evidence at all that being Catholic makes any of us less likely to have been affected by this huge change in social perception which has worked its way through English-speaking society, and, at different speeds and in different ways, through at least those other societies with whose languages and cultures I am familiar.

So here is the first point. In the first place what I call "the gay thing" is something which has just happened, and is just happening, to all of us, whatever our own sexual orientation is. You can be as straight as you like, but being straight is no longer the same as it was when there was no such thing as "gay." Our picture of what it is to be male or female has undergone, and is undergoing, huge changes which affect us not only from without, but from within. We find ourselves relating, whether we want to or not, with each other, and with ourselves, in new ways as a result of something which is far bigger than any of us and which is just happening.

Now please note that none of this makes any claim about whether this change is good or not, nor does it make any claim about what, if anything we should do about it. It merely notes that it has happened and is happening to all of us, Catholics and non-Catholics alike.

Now our experience as Catholics is not only that we have experienced this change, but we have also experienced our religious authority reacting to this change in particular ways. And this is not a matter of merely noting that religious authority has, from time to time, spoken out on these matters in the years since 1975, and that their pronouncements have reached us. We have all, religious authorities, lay people and clergy, undergone the changes together, and we have lived with each others' reactions to those changes. One of the things worth pointing out, given the passions that this subject raises, is how few and far between have been the public pronouncements of Catholic religious authorities in this area, until very recently, especially if we compare them to the abundance of such pronouncements emerging from Protestant churches. There has been much more reticence to speak about the gay issue than might have been expected. And this for two obvious reasons: it has not been a particularly important matter for the Catholic laity until recently; and the clerical world has been, in this area, a glass house in which it was not wise to throw stones, and discretion seemed the least scandalous option.

This too is part of the Catholic experience: our undergoing the change which has permeated society has been mediated to us not only through television and so on, but also through a discretely, but nevertheless, thoroughly, gay-tinted clerical system. In other words, unlike many Protestant groups, as Catholics we have never really had the option available to us of seriously pretending that we didn't know any gay people, or that there weren't any gay people in our Church. The result is that for us, part of the experience of "the gay thing" as Catholics has been a set of reactions provoked not so much by the official pronouncements of the Church as by the way the clergy live in relation to those official pronouncements: whether they have reacted by being honest, dishonest, frightened for their jobs, open about their partners, leaving, staying, being blackmailed or whatever. This "living with the change" by living with the way in which the clergy are coping with the change is very definitely part of the Catholic experience of this issue. It too is entirely independent of the ideological slant or the moral position taken by Catholics who are reacting to all this: some such Catholics may excoriate the dishonesty, some may lambaste a modernist plot to infiltrate seminaries and go on to demand that the gays be weeded out, some may be puzzled that there should be so many, or that so many should stay despite everything. Nevertheless, the comparative discretion with which this matter has been treated by Catholic religious authority over the last thirty or so years, and the clear presence of a clerical caste in which dealing with "the gay thing" having come upon us, usually rather quietly, is going on all around us, has been an ineluctable part of the Catholic experience in this area, whether we have been aware of it or not.

Now, here I want to say the obvious thing: that our access to the question of truth in this area has not been independent of this experience. Indeed it has only been through this experience that the issue has gradually begun to crystallize into questions of truth. And this is because one of the ways in which "the gay thing" has come upon us has not been merely that outsiders, non-Catholics, start to agitate about this issue; it is not something which is merely felt from outside pressure. Rather, "the gay thing," of its nature, happens within us. And I don't mean merely within the Church considered as a numerical body in which a similar percentage is gay to that found in the rest of society. I mean within the lives of people within the Church. It has become an ineluctable part of how we find ourselves coming to be adult humans at this period, whether or not we are ourselves gay or lesbian, that some of our number find it increasingly important, and at a younger and younger age, to identify themselves as gay or lesbian, aware that this is something they find themselves to be, that the label makes sense to them and is going to be an important dimension of their lives: it is going to be one of the ways they find themselves articulating their relationship with each other, family, friends, employers, and of course, Church. And of course, they are aware, as are their contemporaries, that it is a word which is associated with a certain moral courage.

I guess that everyone knows that the kid who "comes out" at high school, or the student at university is being to some extent brave. I think that this point has much more importance than is usually attached to it. For most gay people, as for an increasing number of their straight contemporaries, "the gay thing" is not in the first instance anything to do with sex. It comes upon us as something to do with how we relate to other people in our peer group — whether we stand up for the effeminate kid who is being bullied by the jocks in the class, or whatever. And this kind of group dynamic through which "the gay thing" comes upon us is extremely important for our moral and spiritual development. It is here that we learn to stand up for the weak, or, in my case, to my shame, how to hide myself, join in the crowd of haters and "pass" for straight until a later time. And the interesting thing is that in this sense "the gay thing" comes upon straight kids as well — they too make moral choices, know what is right and wrong here. More and more adults and kids are reporting that straight kids are increasingly reluctant to go along with gay bullying, whether they see it being done by fellow students or by adults. This is not because they have become hedonistic, oversexualized decadents. It is, on the contrary, because they seem to sense that such behavior is unworthy of them: they are less than straight if they need to beat up on the gay kids.

But part of the Catholic experience has been that alongside the way in which this process of moral and spiritual growth is happening as young people start to react to the way "the gay thing" is irrupting into our midst, has also been the way in which Church authority appears to regard "the gay thing" as exclusively an issue to do with sex — and simultaneously to ignore the experienced moral dimensions that "the gay thing" has in the lives of those who are undergoing it. This leads to a disjunction being lived by us as, on the one hand, we learn all about good Catholic values like solidarity, refusal to beat up on the weak, respect for the other, and on the other hand, we perceive that in order to handle "the gay thing" themselves, Church authorities (which often enough include such lay authorities as run Catholic educational enterprises), reduce the whole matter to sex. They are often enough notoriously bad at dealing with any of the lived moral issues which those not dependent on the clerical system for their employment have perceived to be psychologically and spiritually central to dealing with the whole "gay thing" — being brave, coming out, putting friendship at risk, being socialized transparently, and so on.

And this of course leads to one of the further disjunctions that is part of the Catholic experience of "the gay thing": the different sorts of truth-telling which "the gay thing" has brought upon us. On the one hand we have people who can be "out" as gay people, who can say "I am," and who are in all our parishes, neighborhoods, and so forth, and for whom truth-telling involves a certain form of sincerity, and desire to be transparent in their dealings with others, often quite pacifically so, sometimes infuriatingly and provocatively so. And on the other hand we have people who cannot say "I am." At least in public. And for whom truth-telling in this area involves talking about a "they." It involves an attempt to give an objective description of who "they" are who are being talked about, even when a considerable number of people suspect that the person saying "they" would be more honest to say "we." Yet, and this is important, the official characterization of the "homosexual person" in the recent documents of the Vatican congregations is something which can only be applied to a "they," because even when the person talking is referring to himself, he is accepting the need to treat part of his "I" as a "they," as something that can never be brought into a personal relationship, can never become part of an "I" or a "we," never be addressed as "thou." That's what is implied by saying that an inclination "must be considered to be objectively disordered."

This too is part of the experience of living as a Catholic as we undergo the "gay thing" — that there is a disjunction between two different sorts of truthfulness, neither of which seems quite adequate: the one because it suggests that sincerity is really all it takes to be honest, and that one can grasp an identity as gay and then "be" that thing, be wholly implicated in it, and the other because it suggests that truthfulness — holding fast to an official definition of what is true — requires dishonesty, makes self-knowledge the enemy of truth, and removes someone from the ordinary demands of charity and solidarity.

I've tried to deal elsewhere with the subject of honesty in the Church, but here I would just like briefly to indicate that it seems to me that the challenge for us as Church now, and as Church widely perceived to have an honesty deficit, is to understand that honesty is not the same as either sincerity or "holding to objective truth" because both of those involve a certain grasping onto something. Honesty is something undergone as a gift of being brought into truthfulness by being given a self-critical faculty, and it can never be grasped. It is precisely appreciated by others when they see someone undergoing an experience of dealing with something which is making them more truthful. I don't want to major on this now, merely to point out that my choice of approach to this talk, which may or may not have been successful, is because it seems to me that we are more likely to reach truthfulness if rather than battling each other with incommensurable forms of truth, we start to learn to tell the story of what we have been undergoing together.

What I would like to do now is point out that we have, as Catholics, a number of resources to help us work our way through some of these disjunctions, resources which I think we are in fact using already. I'd like to try to highlight how just one of these comes into play. Curiously, I'm going to look at an unlikely resource, which I consider to be absolutely central to our finding our way through this particular upheaval: the Catholic Doctrine of Original Sin.

One of the principal points of conflict at the time of the Reformation in the sixteenth century was the view of human nature held by each side of the discussion. The Reformed side tended to hold a view of human nature which claimed that after the fall, having been created good we became radically corrupted.[1] We are saved by God imputing to us a counter-factual goodness which is not really ours at all, but which is made available for us to put on, by Jesus' sacrifice on the Cross. The important thing about this for us here is what it means about our moral and spiritual life. It means that all our "goodness" is so much fakery, not real goodness, and God's goodness must be given to us through our being ordered to behave in ways which have nothing to do with our natural inclinations. God may order us to go totally against our natural inclinations, because our natural inclinations have been totally corrupted, and there is no proper analogy between what we think of as good, what we desire, and what really is good, what we should desire.

The sort of life story which this underlying theology asks us to tell about ourselves is one involving a radical conversion: how once I was a sinner (and so behaved in certain ways) but now, very suddenly, I am saved, and I have a completely new life story, one with no real organic continuity with my old life story. One where there is a real rupture. Whoever I was is now dead, and now there is a new "I," someone totally new.

Now perhaps you can see how this understanding of Original Sin and salvation would affect the discussion concerning "the gay thing" which I have just described as having come upon us, if we were strict heirs of the Reformed tradition. It would, in a sense, make life much easier for us by making it much clearer. Because we could say "Well, this business of 'the gay thing' coming upon us is what you would expect in a corrupt and depraved humanity. It is merely another wave of decadence and corruption. Anyone who is given the gift of being saved by Jesus must just obey the biblical commands, however little sense they may make. Given that the Bible, which is God's Word, and not affected by corruption, clearly teaches that homosexuals are a bad thing, and that God created man and woman for each other, it is quite clear that one of the signs of someone being saved is that they are learning to obey God's command which includes not being gay, and they should in fact be undergoing therapy to become straight. The new nature which they are receiving from God is certainly straight, so we can expect them to cease to be gay as part of being converted. Homosexual desire is intrinsically evil. Only divinely given straight desire is intrinsically good."

The reason I say that this would make life easier for us as Catholics is as follows: it would enable us to make a deduction from the teaching of the Church about who we really are, and dismiss any social changes taking place as so much evil. Being Catholic would then be a matter of being on the obedient side of things, not the disobedient, and of course, anyone who agreed that being gay is part of who they really are, rather than the ghastly corrupt former person that they should be leaving behind, isn't really a Catholic, just a hell-bound sinner. Following this model, we couldn't and shouldn't learn anything about ourselves from what is going on around us, from what is just happening to us, because we can't start from there; it is totally untrustworthy. We can only start from something which comes from God covering us over and giving us an entirely different story. A moral command is good because it is a moral command come from God, not because it causes any sort of flourishing of any sort of inclination of our own.

Now, strange though this may be to some of your ears, this is not the Catholic faith. The Catholic faith concerning Original Sin and salvation is slightly and subtly different from that of the Reformed tradition, and because of that, we have the possibility of quite a different way of dealing with "the gay thing." The Catholic understanding, as set out by the Council of Trent, whose ardent fan I am, is that the word "desire" (*epiqumia*), which the Apostle Paul sometimes uses in such a way as to give the impression that he considered it a purely negative thing, has never been considered by the Church to be a purely negative thing, to be sin in the strict sense of the word. Desire is in fact an entirely good thing which is, in the case of all of us, very seriously disordered, so that the way we find it in us is as something which comes from sin and inclines us towards sin, but which is nevertheless capable of being gradually transformed and ordered by grace so that we are brought to a flourishing starting from where we are. This means that in the Catholic understanding grace perfects nature, takes something which, while good, is severely damaged, and transforms it starting from where it is, whereas in the "radical corruption" account of the Reformed tradition that I gave you, grace cannot transform nature, because nature has become instrinsically corrupt. Grace has to abolish the old nature and start again.[2]

Now, as you can tell, this means that any story of salvation told by Catholics is of rather a different sort from the one I outlined to you earlier. It means that because our nature is not radically corrupt, just accidentally corrupt, and because grace perfects our nature and meets us starting from where we are, salvation then looks like our undergoing a process of divinely initiated transformation, together, in and as Church. It also means that the whole wave of changes in society which "just happen" and which are bigger and more powerful than any of us, are not simply entirely evil and corrupt, but are part of what enables us to be brought into being, which is in itself something good. Furthermore, these waves of change in society may be, amongst other things, ripples out from the way the leaven of the Gospel and the Kingdom is working in the midst of humanity, destroying our belief in the culpability of our victims and so enabling us to come to learn who we really are and how we can learn responsibility for what is. So, such waves of change need to be worked through, understood, discerned, analyzed slowly and carefully, not just written off. It also means that where we are is not an entirely untrustworthy place from which to start, and something of what is true and good can be discerned and learned in the midst of all this mess. And this is something vital: it also means that we can, over time, learn things about who we are as human beings such that what had seemed to be moral commandments turn out to be commandments which are not moral, because they go against our flourishing.[3]

You remember that in the picture of the Reformation understanding I gave you it didn't matter at all whether something leads to our flourishing or not. What matters is that it is right because it is commanded by God. In the Catholic understanding it is not the case that something is right because it is commanded by God, rather something is commanded by God because it is good for us: this is what you would expect from a good Creator who wants to make something even better out of his good creation, messy though it may look. But this means that in the Catholic understanding it must be possible for us as humans to learn that something which appeared to have been commanded by God can't in fact have been commanded by God, because it goes against what any of us can see leads to human flourishing. And this means that we can learn that we are not rebelling against God, but doing his deepest will when we learn that something which seemed to be holy and sacred is neither holy nor sacred, but a way of diminishing people. This of course lays upon us a huge burden of intelligence and responsibility in working out what really is God's will for us.

The funny thing about this Catholic understanding is that it is one of the parts of Catholic teaching that Catholics generally do really "get" at a pretty instinctual level. That we are all in a mess together, none really better than the other, but that we are all rescuable, and must be merciful to each other, is a kind of basic default understanding of Catholic interrelationship with each other. The notion that the Church is a refuge of sinners, that Our Lady has a soft spot for us in our weakness, and that no one should really be thrown out is kind of written into our souls. And I think that because of this, it is not surprising that one of the typical Catholic ways of dealing with "the gay thing" just having happened among us is to say "Well, of course, it does seem to go against the Church and all that, but, well, if she just is that way, well then, what do you expect, she must just get on and be the very best sort of lesbian, and I hope she finds happiness." I suspect that the ease with which Catholic lay people have got their heads around the idea of at least some sort of marriage for gay couples is related to this.

In contrast to this, the official teaching in this area has come to seem more and more out of line with the default self-understanding which I have been describing, because it seems to be creating an exception to the general rule of Original Sin, which applies to everybody, equally. It seems to be suggesting that there are some people to whom the Catholic understanding of Original Sin should not be applied, and instead, a Protestant understanding should be applied, but only in their case. This disjunction, I should say, is becoming increasingly evident as "the gay thing" has come upon us, and is seen by more and more Catholics to have something to do with "who people are" rather than with "what they do."

In the old days, the discussion was entirely about "acts" — there is an undisputedly ancient Christian tradition of objecting to sexual acts between persons of the same sex. And of course, you can condemn acts without saying anything at all about the being of the person. But over the last fifty years or so, this distinction has become ever less tenable, as people we would now call "gay" have begun to say "I am gay, it's not just that I do certain sexual things which are same-sex acts, but I just find myself being in a way which is best defined as gay, and which has to do with far more of me than sexual acts, furthermore there are other people like me, and we have recognizable traits in common, we can be studied, and we don't appear to be less healthy, more vicious than straight people" and so on.

Well, here is where Church authority had a problem: while the discussion was about acts, the acts could be prohibited, and yet the person could be urged to flourish and find appropriate happiness. But as it became clearer that the acts and a certain sort of person belonged together, were more or less well bound-up as part of a package, Church authority was stuck with a dilemma: "Can we maintain the traditional prohibition of certain sorts of acts if they are merely natural functions of the being of the person, capable of being exercised well or badly as that sort of person grows and develops? No, we can't. So we have to make up our minds: either we just concede that the traditional prohibition doesn't apply to those for whom growing and developing in this way is natural, and only applies to those for whom to engage in such things would be to leave their typical usage; or we have to insist that the traditional prohibition does apply, in which case it must be true that gay people aren't really what they say they are, but just have intrinsically disordered desire and must obey the commands of the Church even though these don't seem to help them flourish. But if we do that, we come perilously close to the Reformation position of seeing some part of people as incapable of flourishing, as something which must simply be abolished and covered over by grace, so that they become something different."

This is a difficult dilemma: how could Church authorities both maintain the traditional prohibition, one which was at least tenable before it had become clear that "some people just are that way," and yet not simply declare a person to be intrinsically corrupt? You must remember that shortly before they were dealing with this, Paul VI had maintained the traditional prohibition of any sexual act which separated the procreative from the unitive function of sex. So Church authorities could scarcely say, "Well, such acts as separate the procreative from the unitive are wrong for straight people, but fine for gay people." The phrase they came up with is a pretty good compendium of the difficulty they had in dealing with the dilemma.

As you probably know, the phrase says that "the homosexual inclination, though not itself a sin, constitutes a tendency towards behavior that is intrinsically evil, and therefore must be considered objectively disordered."[4]

Let's unpack that a little bit. In the first place, those who wrote it show they are good Catholics by indicating that the homosexual inclination is not itself a sin, for no Catholic can understand someone's basic pattern of desire to be intrinsically corrupt. That would be a Reformed position. However, they move on rather fast from this recognition that the homosexual inclination is not itself a sin, and I'd like to slow down a bit. For there is more than one way of recognizing that an inclination is not in itself a sin. There is the way, for instance, that would be true of all heterosexuals. All heterosexual humans find that the package of their growing up and their sexual desire is extremely difficult to humanize and to socialize in an appropriate way. Many heterosexual people find that it takes a long time before they are able to find themselves capable of a monogamous relationship in which each is capable of treating their spouse as an equal sharing the responsibility for procreation, if, indeed, they are ever able to get there. But in principle, the notion that their inclination is a good thing, but is always encountered by them in a distorted way, referred to in official teaching as "concupiscence," and that their salvation is, in part, worked out in their creative struggle with their concupiscence, is quite comprehensible.

So, the question arises: is the homosexual inclination, which is not in itself a sin, a subsection of heterosexual concupiscence? Or is it its own sort of concupiscent desire? This is an important distinction. If the homosexual inclination were a subsection of heterosexual concupiscence, then it would be something that couldn't lead to anything good in itself. It would simply be a symptom of the sort of thing that goes wrong in a basically heterosexual human being, like lusting after someone to whom you are not married, or wanting sexual relationships with as many partners (of the opposite sex) as possible. And of course, the life of grace would gradually lead the person whose heterosexual concupiscence takes the form of a homosexual inclination toward recovering an ordered pattern of heterosexual desire, and this would be public and visible in the relationships of the person concerned.

If on the other hand, the homosexual inclination were its own sort of concupiscent desire, then it would be something which does lead to something good in itself. It would have all the capacity for things to go wrong that exist in the case of heterosexual desire, but, just like heterosexual desire, it would also have the capacity for something to go right. That is, the life of grace would lead the person with the homosexual inclination to become less possessive, more merciful, more generous, more honest, more faithful, but without changing the gender of this person's potential or actual partner(s), and this would be public and visible in the relationships of the person concerned.

Now I would like to point out that both of these are perfectly possible interpretations given the Catholic doctrine of Original Sin. What the doctrine does not allow us to do is simply to refuse on *a priori* grounds the possibility that a long-term, persistent pattern of desire, may, after all, be a sign of how the Creator's love for us wills us to flourish. And therefore we cannot simply refuse the possibility that we can come to learn that what seemed like a subsection of heterosexual concupiscence may just be a different thing. In other words, the Catholic doctrine of Original Sin does allow the possibility that we come to discover, over time and with difficulty, that, in a regular minority of the population, long-term stable same-sex desire just is, and is the basis from which they flourish, rather than that which has to be "dealt with" in some way before they can begin to flourish.

Given the possibility of this distinction, you can see why I think that the Congregation for the Doctrine of the Faith rushed rather fast into their next claim: that the homosexual inclination "constitutes a tendency towards behavior that is intrinsically evil, and therefore must be considered objectively disordered."

The only circumstance in which it would be true that behavior tending to be a homosexual inclination was intrinsically evil is if it were simply true that there is no other intrinsic human pattern of desire than the heterosexual one, tending towards marriage and procreation, and therefore that the homosexual inclination is a subsection of heterosexual concupiscence. And this is what the Congregation for the Doctrine of the Faith implies is in fact the case, as a deduction from its own teaching on marriage and procreation.

In other words, from the Church's teaching on marriage and procreation an attempt is being made to reach a deduction about empirical truth concerning what really is. To flesh this out further: an aspect of revelation, here from the moral sphere, is being asked to bear the weight of defining truth in an anthropological sphere, where whatever is true in this sphere might instead be reached by empirical means. This same intellectual pattern did not work well in the Galileo case, and it did not work well with Genesis's account of Creation in six days. We would be wise to be extremely suspicious of it here.

Now it is, of course, perfectly conceivable that we will eventually discover (rather than presume) that all human beings are intrinsically heterosexual. But this is not a conclusion to which we are obligated either by the Church's teaching on Original Sin, or by the Church's teaching on marriage. Yet here a deduction from the Church's teaching on marriage is being used to try to foreclose the sort of process of discovery which is allowed for by the Church's doctrine of Original Sin.

And logically enough, if the homosexual inclination were indeed a subsection of heterosexual concupiscence, leading to nothing in itself, then of course it would be true that it must be considered objectively disordered. Here I would like to point out that I have nothing against the notion of an inclination being objectively disordered per se. We would all consider kleptomania to be objectively disordered. But we have come to this conclusion after studying people who are affected by it (rather than those who are just thieves) and seeing what it is that it is a distorted form of, and how those affected can be helped back into a more pacific possession of their own goods and respect for other people's. And this is the point: we can learn what is objectively disordered or not from studying people, their relationships, their habits, their happiness and so on. Our objectivity is gleaned from within the process of discerning experience, of learning. It is not reached by appealing to an *a priori* deduction from revelation which is supposed to cut short any process of discovery.

And of course, by yoking together, on the one hand, the concession to the Church's teaching concerning Original Sin and, on the other, an *a priori* deduction about intrinsically evil acts, the Congregation for the Doctrine of the Faith does leave us with a *de facto* Reformed teaching regarding the relationship between the homosexual inclination and Original Sin. What it concedes verbally it removes existentially. Anyone who lives with a homosexual inclination is taught that it is in itself not a sin, but that on the other hand, it can lead to nothing starting from itself, and that if they don't find that the process of grace in their life tends to make them heterosexual, then they must just be paralyzed as sexual beings. Existentially, this is no different from the Reformed position that homosexual desire is intrinsically corrupt and must be just covered over. It is, if you like, a piece of Catholic icing perched precariously atop a Protestant cake.

Well, here is our lived disjunction all right, and it is a disjunction between two forces of Catholic doctrine which hadn't been on a collision course before, but have entered into collision as part of the way that "the gay thing" has come upon us all. For the moment, it looks as though the only way to maintain the traditional Catholic prohibition of same-sex acts is to act as though the homosexual inclination were in fact an intrinsically corrupt desire, even though this is something alien to a Catholic anthropology, because the moment you consider that "being gay" is not an individually defective form of heterosexuality, but is just something that is, then the Catholic understanding of Original Sin would oblige you to regard grace as transforming that way of being, which is as much in need of transformation as its heterosexual equivalent, and as much in need as its heterosexual equivalent of all the help it can get, starting from where it is. A phrase like marriage as a "remedy for concupiscence" comes to mind. And of course, the Catholic understanding of Original Sin is such that we can in fact learn, with difficulty and over time that certain ways of being just are, are given, are part of being human, and as such are capable of leading to flourishing and sharing the divine life.

This, too, is part of Catholic experience: at the moment, it does appear from official discourse that everything to do with being gay is somehow an exception to the ordinary teaching of the Church about grace. The moment you apply the Church's ordinary teaching about grace to any aspect of life as a gay or lesbian person, then it is going to lead to all the things which it is in fact leading to, and most ordinary lay Catholics are aware that it is leading to: growth in healthy self-esteem, creative ways of living together, new forms of religious life, enriched sacramental participation, recognition and respect for different forms of flourishing, including appropriate legal guarantees against mistreatment, discrimination and so forth, some sort of marriage laws and eventually publicly recognized religious blessings of such partnerships.

Well, this point of disjunction is where we are at! Now, I think it very unlikely that any Church authority will suddenly wake up and say, "Good Lord, we've been missing the whole point of our own doctrine of Original Sin!" My ambition here is more minimalist than that. I merely want to point out, for the day when Church authority finally gets tired of heading up the dead end of trying to make spiritual and political sense out of its own current teaching, that there is a perfectly good Catholic way out of their cul-de-sac which is available for them whenever they want it. They are not condemned, like characters in a Greek tragedy, to carry on being paralyzed by the fatality of their own teaching, just as we are not.

My suggestion for us as Catholics at this point is this: if the Vatican congregations really want us to believe that there is something so wrong with being gay that it in fact constitutes an exception to the ordinary teaching of the Church about grace and Original Sin, then they must try a great deal harder to make their case. Or alternatively, they must demonstrate, not just to those whose livelihood depends on their publicly agreeing to it, but especially, as an urgent pastoral priority, to ordinary gay and lesbian Catholics that there is no such thing as being gay; that what we call "being gay" is a mistake, and is simply a severely defective form of heterosexuality. If the Vatican congregations can do that, then they stand a chance of being able to show that the intrinsic heterosexuality of the falsely gay person can flourish, and thus that their own teaching is compatible with the ordinary teaching of the Church about grace. However, if they can't do that — if they can't produce regular and sustained witnesses to heterosexual flourishing emerging without violence from the life stories of people who had assumed they were gay on something like the same scale as there are regular and sustained witnesses to gay and lesbian flourishing emerging without violence from the life stories of people who had been taught that they were heterosexual, then they should reconsider their definition.

However until they come up with their demonstration, and the burden of teaching effectively is surely on the teachers who have insisted so loudly on their unique role as teachers, then, faced with the disjunction, any ordinary Catholic should stick with the ordinary teaching of the Church, held uninterruptedly and reaffirmed by a major Church Council, about grace and Original Sin, and learn to apply it to their lives and the lives of those around them. And this means starting where we are, and not where someone else tells us we must be considered to be. One of the geniuses of the Catholic doctrine of Original Sin is that rather than it being a form of general accusation of how wicked we are, it is in fact a recognition of how we are all in the same boat as regards wickedness, and that it is a really terrible thing to do to judge others, because in doing so we become blind to the way we are judging ourselves.[5] Any way of characterizing people which makes them an exception to the general rule, by suggesting that they have a different kind and degree of original sin than others is of course a defection from the Catholic faith, because it is giving permission to judge them, when the whole purpose of the doctrine is to make such permission impossible.

You may have noticed that my title was "Following the still small voice." And you may also have noticed that I have got to what must surely, please God, be the end of the talk without making any reference to the title. So I would just like to make explicit that the title is a reference to what I hope to have been hinting at all along. I take it that one of the joys of being Catholic is that we are not a group united by an ideology, nor a group who adhere to a text, nor a group under the command of a leader or set of leaders, but a group being brought into being along with an ordered way of life as we undergo a certain form of listening, listening to a crucified and risen victim as he shows his forgiveness of us and undoes our ways of being together, which tend to be judgmental, violent and so on, so that we can share God's life forever. What keeps us as Catholics, and what is the central element of experience and truth as lived by Catholics in the gay issue, is that we can count absolutely on the crucified and risen Lord, present in our midst especially in the Eucharist, who is gradually teaching us how to reinterpret our world in such a way that we build each other up, and do not fear the truth which will set us free. The presence of the crucified and risen Lord teaching us, together, as Catholics to inhabit Words like "Go and learn what this means, I want mercy and not sacrifice" or "the Sabbath is made for humans, not humans for the sabbath," His Presence *is* the still small voice that is at work through and in all our debates and disjunctions, and will always be opening us up to being made anew starting from where we are.

Heaven and earth will pass away, but my words will not pass away.[6]

Those words are the living interpretative presence of One who loves us starting exactly where we are, One who reaches us in the midst of all the collapses of what seemed sacred, and the coming upon us of new dimensions of ourselves which seem terrifying until we learn to look at them through the eyes of One who loves us so much that he longs to be us, and longs for us to be free and happy with him, forever.

That we are learning to relax, together, through hearing His words, into being loved, is, surely, the central Catholic experience.

Chapter 12

Descriptions and Prescriptions

Proposed Remedies for a Church in Crisis

STEPHEN J. POPE

MULTIPLE DESCRIPTIONS AND EXPLANATIONS have been put forth regarding the church's crisis and many prescriptive proposals have been advanced to address them.[1] I would like to examine three attempts to understand and respond to the crisis, beginning with the efforts of conservative columnist George Weigel, and then returning to the work of legal scholar John Witte and psychologist Naomi Meara. Each of these authors offers a distinctive description of the crisis and advances a solution, or set of solutions, intended to address it. This presentation highlights ways in which normative or prescriptive presuppositions influence the descriptions of states of affairs that need to be remedied as well as prescriptions proposed to address them.

George Weigel: Crisis of Infidelity

One distinctive and clear position has been put forth by columnist George Weigel.[2] Weigel properly describes the problem as multifaceted: sexual, political, social, ecclesiastical, etc. His essay "Fidelity Crisis" begins with a series of questions about the nature of the crisis. The crisis involves sexual malfeasance and negligent bishops, but also others: seminary professors, self-deceived priests who doubt, silently or otherwise, the church's teachings, and moral theologians whose refusal to assent to these teachings encourages others in the "culture of dissent."

This scenario seems to presume that a golden age existed before the 1960s, a time period during which there was less sexual exploitation, deeper piety, greater obedience, more consistent development of moral virtue, greater holiness, and more moral integrity in the church. He argues that widespread dissent from *Humanae vitae* led to a pervasive "ecological crisis" of authority in the church in which individual Catholics started to feel free to disregard moral doctrine. Erosion of obedience in one area led, like falling dominos, to a downward spiral of moral deterioration that eventually culminated in the actions of Paul Shanley and John Geoghan.

Weigel's diagnosis sets the stage for his prescription: return to the gospel (which he regards as nearly identical to obeying the Catholic Church), enforce discipline, correct and, if necessary, root out wimpy and semi-orthodox priests from parishes, theologians from seminaries, and bishops from their dioceses. Weigel really has a vision of Catholicism on steroids: he insists that leaders of the church should be chosen on the basis of their fidelity to Christ and their "vision, determination, and grit." Part of the problem has been substituting social science for doctrine. He heaps scorn on the excessive role given by church authorities to the social sciences, and especially psychology, within seminary formation programs, spiritual training, and episcopal decision making. Weigel pronounces, on the basis of what information it is not clear, that: "In recent decades, education for chastity has been dominated by seminary psychologists and psychiatrists. This must end." Though he does not mention it, he might be thinking of the fact that psychiatric testimony led some bishops to make disastrous decisions to return abusers to active ministry.

Weigel's *The Courage to Be Catholic* gives special attention to gays in the priesthood. He distinguishes between the "gay" man who "makes his homoerotic desires the center of his personality and identity" and the homosexual man who recognizes the disordered nature of his sexual desires.[3] Other conservative Catholics have held that since most of the crimes were committed against pubescent boys, they ought to be characterized as "homosexual sins." Weigel does not advise gays to seek marriage to heterosexual women as a remedy for their lust. John Witte doesn't either, of course, but this silence would lead Weigel, I think, to argue that Witte misses an important dimension of the crisis — not just generic lust, but homosexual lust. And Weigel certainly does not propose, with Andrew Sullivan, that gays ought to take up a commitment to gay marriage. Since the main problem of the crisis is not chaste celibacy but its absence, homosexuals must have the courage and self-discipline to embrace chaste celibacy.

In response to Weigel it can be pointed out, first, that his distinction between "gays" and chaste celibate men who happen to be homosexual proposes an overly simplistic dichotomy. Catholic moral theology admonishes every person — gay or straight — not to make sex "the center of his [or her] identity and personality." The issue here is promiscuity and concupiscence, not sexual orientation.

Second, Weigel's prescription rides on the general assumption that all gay men have the psycho-emotional capacity to live as chaste celibates for their entire lives. Yet the 1983 *Code of Canon Law* teaches that chaste celibacy is a *special gift* not given to every Christian (or to every gay). It is a gift of grace, a special charism, and not a natural endowment.[4] Weigel thus boxes himself into defending a norm that obliges millions of people to adhere to a strenuously difficult rule of life for which they are suited neither by nature nor by grace.

Third, Weigel's religious framework obscures some highly significant facets of the crisis. He views the failures of the bishops largely in terms of lack of enforcement. Nowhere does he acknowledge, as have many observers before him, that the exclusively male culture of the clerical world may have led to a style of decision making that contributed to the problem. Nor does he consider the problem of unaccountable power, or power accountable only up the chain of command — indeed, Naomi Meara might worry that the highly centralized model of the church he adopts from John Paul II may well contribute significantly to the problem. Exclusively vertical accountability can undermine collegiality. This problem was highlighted by the uneven voluntary compliance with the norms of the 1992 National Council of Catholic Bishops — norms which if implemented would have prevented some later cases of clerical sexual abuse. Unlike Meara, Weigel ignores qualities of the bishops that encouraged negligence: a preoccupation with avoiding public scandal, myopic clericalism, a lack of compassion and pastoral care shown to the victims of sexual abuse and their families, and the cover-up of crimes.

Fourth, Weigel scapegoats those whom he deems "dissenters." Commentators admit that the negligent behavior of offending bishops was more disturbing than the sexual abuse which it facilitated. Weigel holds dissenting theology significantly responsible for the crisis, but he offers no evidence for even a vague *correlation* between episcopal negligence and anything having to do with the academic discipline of moral theology. In fact, many of the most negligent bishops received their theological education in "safe" seminary courses based on approved textbooks. It is hard to imagine Cardinal Egan, Bishop McCormick, or Bishop Daily even reading and considering, let alone being influenced by, the arguments of those moral theologians like the Rev. Charles Curran or the Rev. Philip Keene, S.S.[5] (both of whom were actually punished by the Vatican for their writings on sexual ethics).

One of the striking ironies of this situation is that the most notoriously permissive figure in the entire affair was Boston's Cardinal Law, an archbishop who certainly had what Weigel calls the "courage to be counter-cultural." It is hard to imagine how Weigel could explain the fact that this prelate — a cardinal held in the highest honor by John Paul II, known for his unwavering loyalty to the Vatican, most likely to be regarded as "unimpeachably orthodox," and prone not only to condemn those whom he considered morally lax and misguided theologians but even to initiate curial investigations of them — would also be responsible for some of the worst moral outrages in the history of the Catholic Church in the United States.

Fifth, Weigel advances an excessively sweeping dismissal of social science in general and psychology in particular. Rather than the intellectual engagement encouraged by Meara and exhibited in Witte's historical work, *From Sacrament to Contract*, Weigel seems to propose intellectual flight. It is true that a respected study by Philip Jenkins argues that the adoption of therapeutic modes of reflection by bishops may have contributed to the problem, but Jenkins's starting point is demographic rather than theological: the shortage of priests discouraged bishops from diminishing their numbers even more by relying on a punitive approach to transgressors.[6] This trend, however, warrants the wholesale dismissal of neither therapeutic advice nor psychological expertise, a fact recognized recently by the Vatican,[7] nor the valuable role played by psychological screening and monitoring in seminaries over the course of the last decade.[8] From what we know at this point, there seem to be relatively few cases of sexual abuse from priests trained in the 1990s as contrasted with those who went through the seminaries in the 1960s through the 1980s. The difference appears to be due in part to much greater psychological savvy on the part of those involved in seminary admissions and formation. This is obviously not to suggest that the gospel should be replaced by psychology — no Catholic would ever propose that it should — only that the latter can be in *service* of the former. Weigel's normative framework makes him more prone to see competition between these sources rather than the more typically Catholic relationship of complementarity. Though he wants to display the "courage to be Catholic," his own position winds up rather Manichean when it comes to the findings of social science.

John Witte: Crisis of Lust

Witte's "The Perils of Celibacy" offers a second way of understanding the relation between descriptive and prescriptive modes of discourse dependent on the theology of Martin Luther. The man-made rule of celibacy is a breeding ground of immorality, argued Luther, and marriage at least provides some "remedy against lust"[9] if not a sacramental avenue for sanctity. Luther attacked clerical celibacy first and foremost because it reflected an idolatrous commitment to works-righteousness: the assumption that celibacy pleases God more than matrimony and "earns" the celibate's way into heaven. Luther's proposal was not merely a matter of slightly modifying the sacramental system. It raised profound and far-reaching theological questions about the relations between creation and redemption, and nature and grace, which cannot be examined in a brief presentation. It involved a new notion of the minister not as mediator between God and humanity but as holding only one vocation among other, equally significant vocations in the world that serve the neighbor. Luther considered clerical celibacy, and the aura of the supernatural with which it was imbued, to be particularly demented because it conferred special privileges and powers that could be exploited in the venting of sexual desires upon weaker individuals. Better to allow some controlled expression of sexual desires in wedlock than to let them run rampant under cover of clerical darkness — a lower goal but one best suited to restrain sin, always Luther's preoccupation when it came to ethics.

Luther neither disparaged marriage nor reduced it to a condition like prostitution — a lesser evil that the state ought to tolerate, Augustine thought, because it allowed less virtuous men to blow off sexual steam.[10] He recognized marriage as "God's work and commandment," a holy condition blessed by God. But he argued that ministers are men and men are incapable of meeting the high standards expected of celibate priests by the Catholic Church.

Witte concurs with Luther that the Catholic Church would be better off removing such a stringent standard for priests. He readily admits that Protestant ministers have not always been models of sanctity and sexual virtue, but argues that, "there seems to be something gravely amiss with the American Catholic Church's insistence on maintaining mandatory clerical celibacy — despite the mounting evidence of homosexual and heterosexual abuses among its clergy. . . . "[11] The church ought to "stop hiding behind constitutional walls and sacramental veils and take firm public responsibility for its actions and omissions," to face the fact that "clergy are not above the law," and to set an example of "justice and equity."[12]

In response to Witte's position it can be said, first, that the proposal to eliminate mandatory celibacy is of course not an exclusively Protestant argument. Questions have been raised by Timothy Radcliffe, O.P., the former master general of the Dominicans and even by Cardinal Roger Mahoney of Los Angeles. Marquette theologian Michael Fahey, S.J., argues that "married priests would emancipate the church because they would be better connected to normal life. Unmarried priests are simply less sensitized to the needs of children."[13] He also speculates that allowing marriage would help to alleviate the spread of priestless parishes — of which there are now about twenty-five hundred in the United States.

Even Weigel could agree completely with Witte's concluding general exhortation for accountability and reform without accepting his rejection of chaste celibacy. Enforcing the Charter for the Protection of Children and the Norms enacted by the bishops in 2002 will do a lot to prevent the sexual abuse of minors by the clergy in the future. Indeed, some argue that, had they been enforced by the bishops, the provisions of the 1983 *Code of Canon Law* were sufficient to address the problem.[14]

Second, turning to the specific question of sexual abuse, Witte's argument rests on the unverified assumption that married priests are relatively less likely than celibate priests to commit sexual abuse of minors (note: the issue is not only celibate/single men vs. married men, but celibate priests vs. married priests). Unfortunately we do not, at least to my limited knowledge, have studies substantiating this position. On even the crudest measure, Witte's argument will be undermined if it turns out, as Cardinal Ratzinger (now Pope Benedict XVI) among others has asserted, that the percentage of sexually abusive married men is higher than that of celibate clergymen. In any case, most celibate priests have not been accused of sexual abuse, and, conversely, many married men have been found guilty of this kind of crime.[15]

Third, it is probably not particularly helpful to categorize all acts involving the sexual abuse of minors — from pedophilia and forced rape to seduction — as species of the "vice of lust." This issue raises important questions about how to relate psychological and moral accounts of action — a question perhaps better examined by Naomi Meara than me. It seems particularly inappropriate to regard marriage as a "remedy" for the sexual abuse of minors, at least if it suggests that the desires that motivate the abuse are more or less like the healthy sexual drives of adults with the exception that they are directed to inappropriate objects. Common sense suggests that the psychological problems that lead to the sexual abuse of minors would find little "remedy" in marriage. Timothy Radcliffe holds that a problem lying beneath these kinds of crimes is often a profound emotional immaturity — an inability to form true friendships based on equality, emotional intimacy, and mutual respect, a tendency to regard all relations in terms of submission or dominance, and a compensatory desire to engage in sexual relations based upon unequal power. Entering into marriage, in and of itself, cannot "remedy" men who are emotionally malformed in this way.

Fourth, vice is corrected by conversion and moral growth, not by having an "outlet." The "remedy for lust" argument, at least on the surface, seems to construe the problem of lust in hydraulic terms — pressure builds and must be released. In contrast, the Thomistic tradition more helpfully thinks of passions in terms of habituation and transformation. Rather than a "remedy," moreover, marriage can actually aggravate dormant vices and emotional flaws that might remain less pronounced in single life. Augustine, for one, was alert to the danger of lust within as well as outside of marriage.[16]

Fifth, Catholics, including Weigel and Meara, part ways with Witte and Luther over the *sacramental* significance of marriage.[17] This comment is not meant to be anti-ecumenical, only to indicate that the differences here run fairly deep. Today the church has a healthier, more balanced, and more interpersonal understanding of marriage than one finds in Luther, the neo-scholastic moralists of the last century, or Augustine, for that matter. According to *Gaudium et spes,* marriage involves not only procreation but "the good of the whole person." It taught that marital love "can enrich the expressions of body and mind with a unique dignity, ennobling these expressions as special ingredients and signs of friendship distinctive of marriage.... Such love pervades the whole of [the spouses'] lives."[18] The intimate partnership of authentic Christian marriage is "caught up into divine love and is directed and enriched by the redemptive power of Christ and the salvific action of the Church, with the result that the spouses are effectively led to God and are helped and strengthened in their lofty role as fathers and mothers."[19]

The theology of the Council does not necessarily lead to a complete dismissal of Witte's noble attempt to resuscitate the "remedy for lust" argument, but it does require a personalist interpretation of it, a move assisted by substituting the classical theological term "concupiscence" for "lust." "Concupiscence" refers to the fractured, impersonal, and potentially destructive nature of disordered human desire in all its dimensions. Concupiscence finally lies in the will rather than in the senses. It has traditionally been expressed through the symbolism of disordered sexual appetite, but its inner reality constitutes disintegration at the hands of any desires that do not serve the good of the person. Meara is right to suggest that psychology can be enlisted to assist the process of integration, but its success also depends on conversion and commitment that is proportionate to the self-knowledge gained in therapy.

Christian marriage thus has negative and positive dimensions. Negatively, it offers a remedy to concupiscence by correcting a lack of integrity, disharmony, and improper self-direction — this is the implied emphasis of Witte's "remedy for lust." Its positive function is expressed in the language of sanctification — this is Weigel's focus. As Walter Kasper puts it, "sanctification includes two elements: being taken into the service of God and his work in creation and redemption (*consecratio*) and being made inwardly capable of carrying out that service by sanctifying grace (*santificatio*)."[20] The language of "sacrament" and "covenant,"[21] the terms of choice for marriage in the Second Vatican Council, better communicates this positive interpersonal and ecclesial meaning of Christian marriage than do the terms "institution" or "contract."[22] The alternative to the vice of lust is neither celibacy nor marriage, but the virtue of chastity.[23] Every Christian, married or celibate, ought to live chastely. Those committed to chaste celibacy must live the virtue of continence,[24] abstention from sexual pleasure, while the married live conjugal chastity.

Naomi Meara: Crisis of Mistrust

Naomi Meara offers a third construal of the crisis. Whereas Weigel is determined to restore obedience and Witte wants to control lust, Meara focuses on rebuilding trust.[25] Speaking as a social scientist, she points out that the church is subject to the same social pressures and psychological dynamics of social influence as is any other social body. Her approach is consistent with a theology that acknowledges the church as a divinely instituted but thoroughly *human* institution.

According to Meara, the dynamics of trust include compliance with the requirements issued by various forms of power, identification with what is regarded as attractive, and internalization of what is taken to be credible. As the crisis of the church unfolded and the bishops' credibility and attractiveness waned, they increasingly attempted to exert control — and with diminishing success. Appearing to abide by the model of authority endorsed by commentators like Weigel, they failed to understand that genuine authority rests on the ability to elicit trust rather than on the authoritarian power of command. From Meara's perspective, Weigel's highly disciplinary view of church polity runs the risk of aggravating this situation of alienation rather than moving beyond it.

To be fair, the American bishops vary among themselves and so shouldn't all be tarred with the same brush, but there are recurring patterns among some of the most offensive bishops. Meara agrees with Weigel when she notes that "the primary mission of the hierarchy is to inspire holiness and to foster care,"[26] but she departs from Weigel in relying on social scientific insight to understand this process. She suggests that if the bishops wish to regain their authority (as opposed to retaining their institutional power) they need to reverse this process and begin to exercise an array of virtues found in the moral practices of other professionals, including transparency, integrity, humility, thoughtfulness, and truthfulness. Episcopal leadership depends on developing some badly needed virtues that have hitherto not been a strong part of their professional repertoire as bishops.

Whether these particular men can cultivate these virtues at this point in their lives and careers, after decades of socialization in the clerical world, is hard to determine. Meara notes that accountability as well as trust can be built into the structures and processes in both the church and the civil legal system — hence the need for lay-constituted review boards, mandatory reporting laws, reliance on civil authorities to investigate allegations of sexual crimes, etc.

Some critics would call into question the practicality of Meara's moral and psychological advice. They argue that virtues are exercised within the context of institutional structures and the offending bishops do not seem eager to change significantly the way in which the church functions. Some leaders of survivors groups would doubt her assumption that the offending bishops have good intentions. In their view they simply want to make minor adjustments, ride out the wave of bad publicity, allow the emotional turmoil to dissipate, and return to business as usual while avoiding any hint that a sexually abusive priest would remain in active ministry.

Conclusion

Where does this leave us? All three authors call for moral reform, but would seem prone to judge the other proposals further to aggravate an already severely strained situation. This analysis briefly traced three quite different views and assessments of the current crisis in the Catholic Church. A completely uninformed reader beamed in from Alpha Centuri might be forgiven for thinking that each of these authors is addressing a different crisis. The same crisis is regarded, respectively, as a crisis of infidelity, a crisis of mistrust, and a crisis of lust. In some sense of course it is all three—and then some. How observers understand the priorities among the various facets of the crisis is not a purely empirical or factual matter, even less so are the solutions they offer. Meara and Weigel, for example, offer two different sets of virtues aimed at two different sets of problems. Whereas Meara proposes openness, prudence, respectfulness, compassion, and humility, Weigel insists on the virtues of courage, clarity, vigilance, obedience, zeal, and unwavering loyalty. Both sets of character traits are laudable and valuable *in general* but they address quite *different particular* sets of problems.

Weigel, Witte, and Meara work from fields outside of theology but they all rely on a variety of normative sources, including normative theological and especially ecclesiological presuppositions that remain more or less unexamined in their essays, and for understandable reasons. What counts as a crisis depends on what one takes as normative human relationships, including those within the church. Their normative views of the church and Christian identity thus influence in a decisive way how they select and interpret evidence, what counts as problematic and how the problem is understood and diagnosed, and the prescriptions that they craft to address them. It is clear that the entire subject matter of the crisis, both its conditions and potential solutions, needs to be related comprehensively to extensive systematic theological examination of the church, Christian identity, and Catholicism.

Witte's proposal to drop the requirement of celibacy, if not to make marriage mandatory for clergy, flows from an egalitarian view of the church shaped by a Protestant emphasis on the "priesthood of all believers." Witte would be appreciative of the Second Vatican Council's increased appreciation for the common priesthood of the whole people of God, the universal call to holiness and marriage as a special vocation. Witte's implicit ecclesiology would also accept Meara's advice regarding the need to build trust, especially beginning on the local level. He would also concede that married clergy can be as guilty of clericalism and the abuse of power as celibates. Optional celibacy for the secular clergy might reinvigorate and galvanize the priesthood, at least in some communities, not only because it provides a "remedy for lust" but also for the positive reason that it provides an avenue for growth in moral integrity and in Christian discipleship, both prerequisites to competent ministry.

Meara's proposal to increase intellectual engagement with the sciences reflects the Catholic instinct to seek harmony between human intelligence and faith. Her position would judge Weigel's single-minded emphasis on holiness, piety, and conformity to the Catholic moral code to be psychologically naïve, sanctimonious, unrealistic, and even morally irresponsible. She could retain the general virtues Weigel endorses — who, after all, could be opposed to authentic obedience to genuine authority — but in a wider ecclesiological context that acknowledges the importance of the human dynamics of trust among equals within Christian community.

Weigel's hierarchically structured church regards the problem as one of disorder rooted in disobedience. His normative perspective, as we have seen, leads him to suspect that Meara's reliance on psychology detracts from the distinctively Christian and Catholic identity of the church. Meara is informed by faith as well, but I suspect that her interpretation of that faith, and particularly her inclusive, feminist ideal of the church, leads her to view the problems and their solutions in ways quite different from Weigel.

All this is to say that the "facts" do not speak for themselves. This is not to recommend a lazy tolerance of all construals of this crisis whatsoever. Some interpretations, and therefore some prescriptions, will be more adequate to the situation and its history than others. The desire to find out the truth, to come to a more genuine and accurate understanding, leads us to acknowledge the importance of dialogue with those who do not share identical interpretations of the religious and moral convictions proper to Catholicism. The search for wisdom on these matters must include an openness not only to different but even contrary points of view. How we understand the "norms" — especially regarding the life and structures of the church — and the "facts" — data, experiences, statistics, empirical tendencies — are both relevant to how we struggle to interpret the current crisis, how it developed, and how we might construct policies and adopt attitudes that make it less likely to be repeated in the future.

Notes

Chapter 1. Rebuilding Community, Naomi M. Meara

1. Richard A. McCormick, S.J., *The Critical Calling: Reflections on Moral Dilemmas since Vatican II* (Washington, D.C.: Georgetown University Press, 1989), 57.

2. Bruce Jennings, Daniel Callahan, and Susan M. Wolf, "The Professions: Public Interest and Common Good," *Hastings Center Report* 17, no. 1 (February 1987 Supplement): 5.

3. American Psychological Association, "Ethical Principles of Psychologists and Code of Conduct," *American Psychologist* 57, no. 12 (December 2002): 1060–73; Project of the ABIM Foundation, ACP-ASIM Foundation, and European Federation of Internal Medicine, "Perspectives: Medical Professionalism in the New Millennium: A Physician Charter," *Annals of Internal Medicine* 136, no. 3, 5 (February 2002): 243–46.

4. James F. Drane, "Character and the Moral Life: A Virtue Approach to Biomedical Ethics," in *A Matter of Principles? Ferment in U.S. Bioethics*, ed. Edwin R. DuBose, Ronald P. Hamel, and Laurence J. O'Connell (Valley Forge, PA: Trinity Press International, 1994), 301–3; John B. Bennett, *Collegial Professionalism: The Academy, Individualism, and the Common Good* (Phoenix, AZ: Oryx Press, 1998), 36; Naomi M. Meara and Jeanne D. Day, "Possibilities and Challenges for Academic Psychology: Uncertain Science, Interpretative Conversation and Virtuous Community," in *Virtue Obscured and Retrieved: Character, Community and Psychological Practices*, ed. Alan C. Tjeltveit and Blaine J. Fowers, *American Behavioral Scientist* 47, no. 4 (December 2003): 459–78, see especially 464–65.

5. Naomi M. Meara, "Virtues and Credibility: Foundations for Trust" (paper presented at Restoring Trust: Perspectives after Dallas, A Workshop for Bishops and Other Church Leaders, Notre Dame, Ind., November 2002), 5–6.

6. Chester Gillis, "Cultures, Codes and Publics," *America* 187, no. 3 (July 29, 2002): 8–11.

7. Eugene C. Kennedy and Sara C. Charles, *Authority: The Most Misunderstood Idea in America* (New York: Free Press, 1997), 2–5.

8. Kenneth S. Pope and Jacqueline Bouhoutsos, *Sexual Intimacy between Therapists and Patients* (New York: Praeger, 1986), 57–68; Melba J. T. Vasquez, "Sexual Intimacies with Clients after Termination: Should Probation Be Explicit?" *Ethics and Behavior* 1, no. 1 (1991): 45–61.

9. Albert Bandura, *Social Learning Theory* (Englewood Cliffs, NJ: Prentice Hall, 1997), 86–101.

10. Craig Haney, Curtis Banks, and Phillip Zimbardo, "Interpersonal Dynamics in a Simulated Prison," *Journal of Criminology and Penology* 1, no. 1 (February 1973): 69–97.

11. Craig Haney and Phillip Zimbardo, "The Past and Future of U.S. Prison Policy: Twenty-Five Years after the Stanford Prison Experiment," *American Psychologist* 53, no. 7 (July 1998): 709–27.

12. Kim Harper and Jennifer Steadman, "Therapeutic Boundary Issues in Working with Childhood Sexual-Abuse Victims," *American Journal of Psychotherapy* 57, no. 1 (January 2003): 138–39.

13. John Tracy Ellis, *American Catholics and the Intellectual Life* (Chicago: Heritage Foundation, 1956), 13–59.

14. A. G. Sertillanges, O.P., *The Intellectual Life: Its Spirit, Conditions, Methods,* trans. Mary Ryan (Westminster, Md.: Newman Press, 1920, 1956), 3–41.

15. John Paul II, *Ordinatio Sacerdotalis: Apostolic Letter of His Holiness John Paul II on Reserving Priestly Ordination to Men Alone* (Washington, D.C.: United States Catholic Conference, 1994), 2.

16. Congregation for the Doctrine of the Faith, "Reply to the Dubium Concerning the Teaching Contained in the Apostolic Letter Ordinatio Sacerdotalis," *Osservatore Romano* 22, no. 47 (November 1995): 2.

17. "Concerning the Reply of the Congregation for the Doctrine of the Faith on the Teaching Contained in the Apostolic Letter Ordinatio Sacredotalis," *Osservatore Romano* 22, no. 47 (November 1995): S2–3.

18. Bennett, *Collegial Professionalism,* 41.

19. Meara and Day, "Possibilities and Challenges," 460–70.

20. American Psychological Association, "Ethical Principles of Psychologists," 1060–73.

21. Bennett, *Collegial Professionalism,* 36.

22. Olvar Lovaas and Tristram Smith, "Early and Intensive Behavioral Interventions in Autism," in *Evidence-Based Psychotherapies for Children and Adolescents,* ed. Alan E. Kazdin (New York: Guilford Press, 2003), 325–40; Thomas L. Whitman, "Self-Instruction, Individual Differences, and Mental Retardation," *American Journal of Mental Deficiency* 92, no. 2 (September 1987): 213–23; Lisa Blackmore-Brown, *Reweaving the Autistic Tapestry* (London and Philadelphia: Jessica Kingsley Publisher, 2002), 254–73.

23. John G. Borkowski and Nithi Muthukrishna, "How Learning Contexts Facilitate Strategy Transfer," *Applied Cognitive Psychology* 9, no. 5 (October 1995): 425–46; Jeanne D. Day and Luis A. Cordon, "Static and Dynamic Measures of Ability: An Experimental Comparison," *Journal of Educational Psychology* 85, no. 1 (March 1993): 75–82; Luis A. Cordon and Jeanne D. Day, "Strategy Use on Standardized Reading Comprehension Tests," *Journal of Educational Psychology* 88, no. 2 (June 1996): 288–95; Erika E. Bolig and Jeanne D. Day, "Dynamic Assessment and Giftedness: The Promise of Assessing Training Responsiveness," *Roeper Review* 16, no. 2 (December 1993): 110–13.

24. Heinz Kohut, *The Analysis of Self* (New York: International Universities Press, 1971), 1–34; Heinz Kohut, *The Restoration of Self* (Madison, Conn.: Inter-

national Universities Press, 1977), 249–66; Michael J. Patton and Naomi M. Meara, *Psychoanalytic Counseling* (Chichester, U.K.: John Wiley & Sons, 1992), 3–96.

25. Linda Brooks and Linda Forrest, "Feminism and Career Counseling," in *Career Counseling for Women,* ed. W. Bruce Walsh and Samuel H. Osipow (Hillsdale, N.J.: Erlbaum, 1994), 87–134; Mary M. Brabeck and Laura S. Brown, "Feminist Theory and Psychological Practice," in *Shaping the Future of Feminist Psychology: Education Research and Practice,* ed. Judith Worrell and Norene Johnson (Washington, D.C.: American Psychological Association, 1997), 15–35; Judith Worrell and Norene Johnson, eds., *Shaping the Future of Feminist Psychology: Education Research and Practice* (Washington, D.C.: American Psychological Association, 1997), 1–14, 245–48; Mary M. Brabeck and Kathleen Ting, "Feminist Ethics: Lenses for Examining Ethical Psychological Practice," in *Practicing Feminist Ethics in Psychology,* ed. Mary Brabeck (Washington, D.C.: American Psychological Association, 2000), 17–35.

26. Norma Radin, "The Role of the Father in Cognitive, Academic, and Intellectual Development," in *The Role of the Father in Child Development,* ed. Michael E. Lamb (New York: John Wiley & Sons, 1981), 379–428; Joseph H. Pleck, "Paternal Involvement: Levels, Sources, and Consequences," in *The Role of the Father in Child Development,* 3rd ed., ed. Michael E. Lamb (New York: John Wiley & Sons, 1997), 66–103.

27. Henry Abramovitch, "Images of the 'Father' in Psychology and Religion," in *The Role of the Father in Child Development,* 3rd ed., ed. Michael E. Lamb (New York: John Wiley & Sons, 1997), 19–32.

28. E. Mark Cummings and Patrick T. Davies, "Emotional Security as a Regulatory Process in Normal Development and the Development of Psychopathology," *Development and Psychopathology* 8, no. 1 (Winter 1996): 123–39; E. Mark Cummings and Patrick T. Davies, "Effects of Marital Conflict on Children: Recent Advances and Emerging Themes in Process-Oriented Research," *Journal of Child Psychology and Psychiatry* 43, no. 1 (January 2002): 31–63.

29. E. Mavis Hetherington and M. M. Stanley-Hagan, "The Effects of Divorce on Fathers and Their Children," in *The Role of the Father in Child Development,* 3rd ed., ed. Michael E. Lamb (New York: John Wiley & Sons, 1997), 191–211.

30. Michael E. Lamb, "Predictive Implications of Individual Differences in Attachment," *Journal of Consulting and Clinical Psychology* 55, no. 6 (December 1987): 817–24; Norma Radin, "Primary-Caregiving Fathers in Intact Families," in *Redefining Families: Implications for Children's Development,* ed. Allen W. Gottfried and Adele E. Gottfried (New York: Plenum, 1994), 11–54.

31. Elliott Aronson, *The Social Animal,* 8th ed. (New York: Worth Publishers, 1999), 34–40.

32. Suzanne C. Thompson and Shirlynn Spacapan, "Perceptions of Control in Vulnerable Populations," *Journal of Social Issues* 47, no. 4 (Winter 1991): 1–21.

33. Aronson, *The Social Animal,* 35–36.

34. Abramovitch, "Images of the 'Father,' " 32.

35. "Call to Be Catholic: Church in a Time of Peril," 1996, New York: National Pastoral Life Center. *www.commonground@nplc.org* (April 11, 2003).

36. McCormick, *The Critical Calling*, 57.

37. Eugene C. Kennedy, *My Brother Joseph: The Spirit of a Cardinal and the Story of a Friendship* (New York: St. Martin's Press, 1997), 159.

38. Stephen J. Pope, "Human Evolution and Moral Responsibility: Beyond the 'Free Will Determinism' Conundrum," *Theoforum* 33, no. 3 (October 2002): 365–85.

39. Catherine Mowry LaCugna, *God for Us: The Trinity and Christian Life* (San Francisco: HarperSanFrancisco, 1973), 335–48.

40. Eugene C. Kennedy and Victor J. Heckler, *The Catholic Priest in the United States: Psychological Investigations* (Washington, D.C.: United States Catholic Conference, 1972), 3–16.

41. Mary Catherine Hilkert, *Speaking with Authority: Catherine of Siena and the Voices of Women Today* (Mahwah, N.J.: Paulist Press, 2001), 9–141.

Chapter 2 / Heaven Is a Place on Earth? David Cloutier

This paper was originally presented at the 2005 annual convention of the Catholic Theological Society of America. I want to thank William Mattison and Lisa Cahill for their follow-up comments and discussion during our session.

1. Mireya Navarro, "Spreading the Pope's Message of Sexuality and a Willing Spirit," *New York Times*, June 7, 2004, 1(B).

2. The interviewees had participated in either or both of the following programs: a viewing and discussion of an eight-part video series of Christopher West's lectures, sponsored by the Students for Life organization at CSB/SJU, and a discussion series led by Fr. Tom Knoblauch, sponsored by the Diocese of Saint Cloud.

3. One might wittily suggest it depends on whether your authority on young Catholics is Tom Beaudoin or Colleen Carroll. For references to these and other authors discussing the question at hand, see David Cloutier and William C. Mattison III, introduction to *New Wine, New Wineskins: A Next Generation Reflects on Key Issues in Catholic Moral Theology*, ed. William C. Mattison III (Lanham, Md.: Rowman & Littlefield, 2005), 1–23.

4. When mentioning "the rules," interviewees did not usually specify which ones. Rather, their concerns were directed toward an alternative catechesis in sexuality to simply stating a set of prohibitions.

5. David Cloutier, "Moral Theology for Real People: Agency, Practical Reason, and the Task of the Moral Theologian," in *New Wine, New Wineskins: A Next Generation Reflects on Key Issues in Catholic Moral Theology*, ed. William C. Mattison (Lanham, Md.: Rowman & Littlefield, 2005), 119–42.

6. Tom Beaudoin, *Virtual Faith: The Irreverent Spiritual Quest of Generation X* (San Francisco: Jossey-Bass, 1998), 73–95, and Anna Roper, "A Young Person's Perspective on Authority and Sexuality," in *Embracing Sexuality*, ed. Joseph Selling (Aldershot: Ashgate, 2001), 75–88.

7. Roper, "A Young Person's Perspective," 76.

8. See George Lindbeck, *The Nature of Doctrine* (Philadelphia: Westminster Press, 1984), for a theoretical explanation; Stanley Hauerwas and David Burrell,

"From System to Story: An Alternative Pattern for Rationality in Ethics," in *Truthfulness and Tragedy,* ed. Stanley Hauerwas (Notre Dame, Ind.: University of Notre Dame Press, 1977), 15–39, for a classic application to ethics.

9. Joan Timmerman, *The Mardi Gras Syndrome: Rethinking Christian Sexuality* (New York: Crossroad, 1984), xiii.

10. Timmerman, *The Mardi Gras Syndrome,* 70.

11. Monica Ashour, "Women and the Third Millennium," see *www.tobet.org/Women_for_the_Third_Millennium_talk.htm.* As with NFP (Natural Family Planning), numerous lay organizations (with looser or tighter associations with clerical ministers) exist within the church with the explicit agenda of promoting and "evangelizing" the Theology of the Body, such as TOBET and *www.theologyofthebody.net.*

12. Christopher West, *Theology of the Body for Beginners: A Basic Introduction to Pope John Paul II's Sexual Revolution* (West Chester, Pa.: Ascension Press, 2004). In explaining the theology of the body, I am relying very much on this text and the study guide that accompanied West's video series, rather than on West's much longer exegesis or on John Paul II's original texts. Very few people who are participating in the "ecclesial phenomenon" I am describing here are working with these original texts, which are dense and extremely lengthy. So, for the purposes of studying the way in which the Theology of the Body is being received, these more accessible teaching texts better highlight the crucial selling points. I leave it to others to figure out how accurately these basic texts capture John Paul's actual teaching.

13. West, *For Beginners,* 10–11.

14. Of course, as one student also noted, this meant that one "needs to buy in to the tradition, before you get the buy-in to Theology of the Body."

15. On poor formation, see, as an example, the very strong language used by Dean Hoge, et al., *Young Adult Catholics* (Notre Dame, Ind.: University of Notre Dame Press, 2001).

16. See the very lucid and articulate critique along these lines by Luke Timothy Johnson, "A Disembodied Theology of the Body," *Commonweal* 128, no. 2 (January 26, 2001): 11–17. West has developed a lengthy response to Johnson, which counters Johnson carefully on several of his points, but also generally suggests that Johnson has "sold out" the real possibilities and potentialities of sexuality (thus implicitly accusing him of having a too negative view of sex!) because he cannot accept the teaching on contraception. See Christopher West, *www.christopherwest.com/article5.asp.*

17. The sociologist Peter Berger explains the notion of plausibility structures as follows: "We obtain our notions about the world originally from other human beings, and these notions continue to be plausible to us in a very large measure because others continue to affirm them. . . . It is only as the individual remains within this structure that the conception of the world will remain plausible to him." See Peter Berger, "Plausibility Structures," in *Religion: North American Style,* 3rd ed., eds. Thomas E. Dowdy and Patrick H. McNamara (New Brunswick, N.J.: Rutgers University Press, 1997), 20–21. I thank Mark Massa, S.J., for a conversation which put me onto this idea.

18. For example, see Timmerman, *The Mardi Gras Syndrome,* 95.

19. See Timmerman, *The Mardi Gras Syndrome,* 32–33. One of the weakest links in many of the cases from this era is this reliance on such broad historical generalizations about how the tradition has been contaminated by dualism (from whatever source or sources). Recent historiography on early Christian asceticism, led magisterially by Peter Brown's *The Body and Society* (New York: Columbia University Press, 1988), has decisively displayed how early Christian thinking, far from being dualistic, often saw various forms of sexual renunciation as politically liberating and embodying the eschatological hope in the here and now.

20. A thought-provoking teaching tool in this regard is "The Core Variables of Love Economics," *www.solvedating.com/love-core.html.*

21. Colleen Carroll, *The New Faithful* (Chicago: Loyola Press, 2003), 123–36.

22. William Sneck, "Premarital Divorce," *America* 117, no. 15 (November 15, 1997): 27.

23. In their book on dating and spirituality (Donna Freitas and Jason King, *Save the Date* [New York: Crossroad, 2003], 143–47), King and Freitas try to make a positive out of the "breaking up" aspect of dating by arguing, using the metaphor of a shipwreck, that the pain of a breaking-up process can lead us to reassessment and to the discovery of new horizons and "beautiful beaches." But, as one of my student TAs put it, "Yeah, or you can drown and die!" I think it is difficult to support the idea that relationships involving this kind of emotional intensity can be healthily regarded as temporary. Friendships of great intimacy can sometimes end, of course, but this is often enough due to circumstances. An intentional ending is rarely if ever pretty.

24. See Timmerman's final chapter for these distinctions, Timmerman, *The Mardi Gras Syndrome,* 104–9.

25. This move does have some implications that the Theology of the Body ignores. For example, West, when asked the classic "How far is too far?" question, rebuts not by reiterating traditional teaching, but rather by suggesting the question is itself formed by legalism, and rather we should be asking, "Is what I'm doing really love or really for myself?" This response suggests a level of fluidity in what is "real" that was probably not present in traditional moral theology.

26. Charles Taylor, *The Ethics of Authenticity* (Boston: Harvard University Press, 1991), 5.

27. Navarro, "Spreading the Pope's Message of Sexuality"

28. Lauren Winner, *Real Sex: The Naked Truth about Chastity* (Grand Rapids, Mich.: Brazos Press, 2005), 38.

29. Winner, *Real Sex,* 90.

30. Here I should note that this generalization may be more applicable to whites and African-Americans than to other social groups in American society.

31. Freitas and King, *Save the Date,* 36.

32. Barbara Dafoe Whitehead and David Popenoe, "The State of Our Unions: The Social Health of Marriage in America 2001: Who Wants to Marry a Soul Mate? New Survey Findings on Young Adults' Attitudes about Love and Marriage," *www.marriage.rutgers.edu/Publication/Print/PrintSOOU2001.htm.*

33. David Matzko McCarthy, *Sex and Love in the Home* (London: SCM Press, 2001), 52, citing Eva Illouz, *Consuming the Romantic Utopia: Love and the Cultural*

Contradictions of Capitalism (Berkeley: University of California Press, 1997), 153–84.

34. While my interview sample is too small to offer really effective generalizations, I would hypothesize that Theology of the Body generally appeals to two sorts of people: people disaffected by the past emptiness of their sexual experience (often men?) and people with very little experience of relationships (often women?). Both of these groups find in the Theology of the Body a support for their own idealism about love and relationships, about the immense possibilities offered by human relationships.

35. Richard Gaillardetz, *A Daring Promise: A Spirituality of Christian Marriage* (New York: Crossroad, 2002).

36. West, *For Beginners,* 10.

37. I thank Lisa Cahill for making this observation in response to this paper. In my interviews, it is notable that gender complementarity, so vital to Theology of the Body, is nowhere mentioned by my respondents, nor do they focus on some of the contested normative issues.

Chapter 3 / "When they rise from the dead," William Mattison

Thank you to the following friends who kindly read and critiqued earlier versions of this paper: David Cloutier, Julie Rubio, John Berkman, James F. Keenan, S.J., and David Schindler. It is obviously not the case that each endorses everything said here.

1. George Weigel, *Witness to Hope* (New York: Cliff Street Books, 1999), 343.

2. Mireya Navarro, "Spreading the Pope's Message of Sexuality and a Willing Spirit," *New York Times,* June 7, 2007, 1(B).

3. See David Cloutier's contribution to this volume, "Heaven Is a Place on Earth: Analyzing the Popularity of Pope John Paul II's Theology of the Body." See also Naomi Schaefer Riley's "Happy — and Chaste — on the College Campus," *The Chronicle Review, The Chronicle of Higher Education,* July 8, 2005. Riley notes the popularity on college campuses of two recent books on chastity: Wendy Shalit's *A Return to Modesty: Discovering the Lost Virtue* (New York: Free Press, 1999) and Lauren F. Winner's *Real Sex: The Naked Truth about Chastity* (Grand Rapids, Mich.: Brazos Press, 2005). Interest in the theology of the body appears to be part of a larger phenomenon.

4. Some speculation is made at the end of this essay, however, as to how popular appeal may drive some of the features of the theology of the body which are critically examined here.

5. The story of Christ's teaching on marriage in the resurrection in light of the Sadducees' question about the woman with seven husbands is found at Mark 12:18–27, Matthew 22:23–33, and Luke 20:27–40. The particular line in the title of this essay is found at Mark 12:25 and paralleled at Luke 20:35 and Matthew 22:30.

6. Christopher West claims there are 129 addresses. See his *Theology of the Body Explained* (Boston: Pauline Books and Media, 2003), 4. Weigel details the dates and sections of the group of talks in his *Witness to Hope,* 335, and claims there are 130.

7. The theology of the body also includes a fourth set of (sixteen) addresses on *Humanae Vitae.*

8. Throughout this section John Paul harkens back repeatedly to the account of human sin in Genesis 3.

9. For clear, concise summaries of the overall content of the theology of the body, see Weigel, *Witness to Hope,* 334–43, and John Grabowski, foreword to *Theology of the Body: Human Love in the Divine Plan,* by John Paul II (Boston: Pauline Books and Media, 1997), 15–19. See also Mark Latkovic, "Pope John Paul II's 'Theology of the Body' and the significance of Sexual Shame in Light of the Body's 'Nuptial Meaning': Some Implications for Bioethics and Sexual Ethics," *Nova et Vetera* 2 (2004): 305–36. For a vision of nuptiality deeply shaped by John Paul II's thought (published after this essay was submitted), see Angelo Cardinal Scola, *The Nuptial Mystery* (Grand Rapids, Mich.: Wm. B. Eerdmans, 2005).

10. John Paul II, *Theology of the Body,* 66.

11. At times John Paul II uses the term "spousal significance."

12. John Paul II, *Theology of the Body,* 63.

13. John Paul II, *Theology of the Body,* 64.

14. John Paul II, *Theology of the Body,* 66, citing *Gaudium et spes* 24.

15. John Paul II, *Theology of the Body,* 65.

16. John Paul II, *Theology of the Body,* 63.

17. John Paul II, *Theology of the Body,* 245.

18. John Paul II, *Theology of the Body,* 244.

19. John Paul II, *Theology of the Body,* 238.

20. John Paul II, *Theology of the Body,* 263.

21. John Paul II, *Theology of the Body,* 267.

22. John Paul II, *Theology of the Body,* 247, non-Latin emphasis added (cf. 66).

23. John Paul II, *Theology of the Body,* 147.

24. John Paul II, *Theology of the Body,* 247.

25. John Paul II, *Theology of the Body,* 77.

26. John Paul II, *Theology of the Body,* 65, emphasis added (cf. 76).

27. In fact, the tradition has consistently recognized that though there is no marriage in heaven, in the resurrection people are male and female. See St. Augustine, *The City of God* (London: Penguin Books, 1972), 1057–58. See also St. Thomas Aquinas, *Summa Theologiae,* English Dominicans trans. (New York: Benziger, 1948), Supplementum, 81, 3. See also his *Summa Contra Gentiles* (Notre Dame, Ind.: University of Notre Dame Press, 1975), IV.88. John Paul obviously affirms this as well (John Paul II, *Theology of the Body,* 239).

28. John Paul II, *Theology of the Body,* 47.

29. John Paul II, *Theology of the Body,* 46.

30. John Paul II, *Theology of the Body,* 65.

31. John Paul II, *Theology of the Body,* 354.

32. John Paul II, *Theology of the Body,* 305, emphasis added.

33. As noted above, the fourth and final set of the Wednesday audiences is devoted to reflection on *Humanae Vitae* and the regulation of birth. Luke Timothy Johnson calls this a disproportionate concern for regulation of birth in his critical review of the

theology of the body. See his "A Disembodied Theology of the Body," *Commonweal* 128, no. 2 (January 26, 2001): 11–17.

34. West has an in-depth commentary on John Paul's *Theology of the Body* entitled *Theology of the Body Explained.* He also has two more popular presentations of the theology of the body entitled *Good News about Sex and Marriage* (Cincinnati, Ohio: Servant Books, 2000) and *Theology of the Body for Beginners* (West Chester, Pa.: Ascension Press, 2004). For some idea of the popularity of West's work, see his homepage at *www.christopherwest.org.*

35. Thanks to David Cloutier for suggesting this term in our conversations on this topic.

36. West, *Theology of the Body Explained,* 83.

37. West, *Good News about Sex and Marriage,* 21.

38. Perhaps West, and Grabowski as noted in the following lines, both springboard off John Paul's phrase that "the institution of marriage expresses the beginning of the fundamental human community," without seeing this phrase in context of the entire sentence: "According to Genesis 2:24, the institution of marriage expresses the beginning of the fundamental human community which through the 'procreative' power that is proper to it serves to continue the work of creation. 'Be fruitful and multiply' (Gen 1:28)." See John Paul II, *Theology of the Body,* 335.

39. See his foreword to John Paul II, *Theology of the Body,* 17 and 19, respectively. Grabowski's own constructive thought on marriage and sexuality can be found in his *Sex and Virtue: An Introduction to Sexual Ethics* (Washington, D.C.: Catholic University of America Press, 2003). There Grabowski articulates a covenantal view of marriage and sexuality that, while clearly influenced by John Paul's theology of the body, does not afford marriage and sexuality the same ultimacy (32–48).

40. West, *Good News about Sex and Marriage,* 18.

41. West, *Theology of the Body Explained,* 14.

42. See Pope John Paul II, *Letter to Families* (Boston: Pauline Books and Media, 1994), no. 19: "The Church cannot therefore be understood as the Mystical Body of Christ, as the sign of man's Covenant with God in Christ, or as the universal sacrament of salvation, unless we keep in mind the 'great mystery' involved in the creation of man as male and female and the vocation of both to conjugal love, to fatherhood and to motherhood. The 'great mystery,' which is the Church and humanity in Christ, does not exist apart from the 'great mystery' expressed in the 'one flesh' (cf. Genesis 2:24; Ephesians 5:31–32), that is, in the reality of marriage and the family."

43. West, *Good News about Sex and Marriage,* 19.

44. West, *Good News about Sex and Marriage,* 21.

45. The title of a recently released set of audio tapes / CDs by Christopher West further illustrates this point: *God, Sex, and the Meaning of Life* (West Chester, Pa.: Ascension Press, 2004).

46. West, *Good News about Sex and Marriage,* 17.

47. West, *Good News about Sex and Marriage,* 18.

48. West cites this phrase from John Paul and immediately grafts marriage and sexuality onto it: "That [the nuptial meaning] was the sentiment of sexual desire as God created it and as they [Adam and Eve] experienced it: to make a gift of

themselves to each other in the image of God." See West, *Good News about Sex and Marriage,* 23.

49. In one passage in his *Theology of the Body Explained,* West offers a beautiful account of how virtuous marriage and sexuality do *not* constitute the fulfillment of the Christian life: "It is entirely human to yearn for marital love. Yet we must be careful never to 'hang our hats on a hook that cannot bear the weight.' Anyone who looks to marriage as his ultimate fulfillment is setting himself up for serious disillusionment. Realizing that earthly marriage is only a sign of the heavenly marriage to come, and that the union to come is a gift extended to everyone without exception, takes a tremendous burden off people's expectations for ultimate happiness through marriage in this life. Only within this perspective does marriage even take on its authentic purpose and meaning. Only within this perspective will a person who enters marriage be able to avoid suffocating his spouse with his expectations and hopes for ultimate fulfillment. Then and only then can marriage bring the true measure of happiness and joy it is intended to bring. As a married man, I will be the first to extol the joys of married life. But these are only a foretaste, only a foreshadowing of the eternal joys to come" (264).

Had this been the consistent perspective of West's work on marriage and sexuality, this section of the essay would not exist. But as the preponderance of other problematic quotations indicates, that is not the case.

50. See David Cloutier's piece in this volume, "Heaven Is a Place on Earth?"

51. West, *Good News about Sex and Marriage,* 20.

52. West, *Good News about Sex and Marriage,* 19.

53. David McCarthy, *Sex and Love in the Home,* 2nd ed. (London: SCM Press, 2004), 45.

54. McCarthy, *Sex and Love in the Home,* 44.

55. McCarthy, *Sex and Love in the Home,* 47. Here McCarthy claims that some transcendent personalists like Vincent Genovesi even narrow the symbolic meaning of sex further to genital contact or the moment of orgasm.

56. McCarthy, *Sex and Love in the Home,* 44.

57. See Johnson, "A Disembodied Theology of the Body." See also West's reply, available at *www.christopherwest.com/article5.asp* (August 19, 2005).

58. McCarthy, *Sex and Love in the Home,* 47.

59. McCarthy, *Sex and Love in the Home,* 46.

60. West, *Theology of the Body for Beginners,* 10.

61. This insight, without the problematic act-centeredness, is seen in John Paul's claim that "life according to the Spirit is also expressed in the mutual union (cf. Gen 4:1) whereby the spouses becom[e] one flesh. . . . " John Paul II, *Theology of the Body,* 349.

62. McCarthy, *Sex and Love in the Home,* 43.

63. In fact, to continue West's otherwise helpful Eucharistic analogy of two-in-one flesh union, Catholics can affirm the real presence in the Eucharist at Mass without cleaving that particularly special presence from the Church *communio* as Body of Christ, called to live as that Body in its actions beyond the altar. For the analogy of marital union and the Eucharist, see West, *Good News about Sex and Marriage,* 20–21.

64. In this sense David Cloutier's critique in an earlier paper of the theology of the body's lack of eschatology is not accurate. See his "Composing Love Songs for the Kingdom of God? Creation and Eschatology in Catholic Sexual Ethics," *Journal of the Society of Christian Ethics* 24, no. 2 (2004): 71–88. For John Paul, marriage is not just a "practice for this world and the present society, defined by the concrete ends it pursued" (73). Both John Paul and West do see married life (and not just celibacy) as an anticipation of heavenly union with God. However, as seen below, Cloutier's critique stands in that the "eschatology" presented is more a "return to Eden" than a healing of wounded sinful humanity (74).

65. See Cloutier, "Composing Love Songs," 74.

66. Cathleen Kaveny, "What Women Want: Buffy, the Pope, and the New Feminists," *Commonweal* 130, no. 19 (November 7, 2003): 22.

67. For the historical background of this phrase in reference to creation, see Russell Hittinger's *The First Grace: Rediscovering the Natural Law in a Post-Christian World* (Wilmington, Del.: ISI Books, 2003), xi.

68. Christopher West, "Theology of the Body," *Commonweal* 130, no. 22 (December 19, 2003): 24. This brief letter is West's response to Kaveny's critique of him in the November 7, 2003, issue of *Commonweal.*

69. For an insightful expansion on this point using the categories of "wholesomeness" and "holiness," see M. Cathleen Kaveny, "Wholesomeness, Holiness, and Hairspray," *America* 188, no. 7 (March 3, 2003): 15–18.

70. On the works of mercy, see James F. Keenan, S.J., *The Works of Mercy: The Heart of Catholicism* (Lanham, Md.: Rowman and Littlefield, 2004).

71. A focus on the transformative power of grace in these acts surely resonates more with those experienced in Christian marriage than a fixation on sexual intercourse as transformed by grace.

72. Cited in Richard Gaillardetz, "Marital and Ecclesial Commitment," *America* 189, no. 3 (August–November 2003): 9. See also his *A Daring Promise: A Spirituality of Christian Marriage* (New York: Crossroad, 2002).

73. Gaillardetz, "Marital and Ecclesial Commitment," 11.

74. Consider, for example, the claim in one Wednesday audience that it is not lust that engenders sexual spontaneity, but rather self-control that leads to a "deeper and more mature spontaneity" (173). A graced sex life is apparently also the most exciting one!

75. West, "Theology of the Body," 24.

76. West, "Theology of the Body," 24.

77. Sexual sin can be present in varying degrees, of course, and it may be the case that many of West's audience have not, for instance, had lustful sexual relations. For such people the "purity" of original innocence may seem an attainable ideal. Nonetheless, it would be foolish (and prideful) to think anyone in West's audience (or any audience for that matter) without sexual sin, even if it be at the level of interior act.

78. Kaveny, "What Women Want," 22.

79. Kaveny, "What Women Want," 22.

80. There are other problems in the theology of the body that are not as immediately evident from an eschatological perspective, and thus not treated here. For

instance, the theology of the body's vision of marriage and sexuality is impoverished by inadequate attention to family life, including the raising of children and the family's "open" or "public" status as connected to broader communities (including the larger Church community) as "domestic Church." There is a certain irony here, since important contributions to the theology of marriage and sexuality were made by John Paul II and others during his pontificate. For the family as domestic Church, see John Paul II's *Familiaris Consortio* (Boston: Pauline Books and Media, 1981), sections 42–45 and 49–55. See also: Julie Hanlon Rubio, *A Christian Theology of Marriage and Family* (New York: Paulist Press, 2003), 183ff.; McCarthy, *Sex and Love in the Home,* 85–108; and Florence Bourg, *Where Two or Three Are Gathered: Christian Families as Domestic Churches* (Notre Dame, Ind.: University of Notre Dame Press, 2004).

81. See St. Augustine's *Teaching Christianity* (New York: New City Press, 1996), 159–60.

82. See Exodus 11:2 and 12:35–36.

Chapter 4 / Being in Love and Begetting a Child, Christopher Kaczor

1. The procreation and education of children should be understood together, in the sense that merely procreating children without sufficient care to provide for their proper upbringing would be contrary to "responsible parenthood," the vocation of the married couple. In what follows, I speak for the most part of the procreation of children but always, of course, within the context of responsible parenthood, a matter for careful discernment by the couple.

2. For a corrective to certain interpretations of the fall that lay heavier blame on Eve than on Adam, see Scott Hahn, *A Father Who Keeps His Promises: God's Covenant Love in Scripture* (Ann Arbor, Mich.: Servant Publications, 1998), chap. 3.

3. James M. Rhodes, *Eros, Wisdom, and Silence: Plato's Erotic Dialogues* (Columbia and London: University of Missouri Press, 2003), 244, 276.

4. Plato, "Symposium," trans. Michael Joyce, in *The Collected Dialogues,* ed. Edith Hamilton (Princeton: Princeton University Press, 1961).

5. Plato, "Symposium," 191 a–b.

6. Plato, "Symposium," 191 b–d.

7. Leon Kass and Amy Kass, eds., *Wing to Wing, Oar to Oar: Readings on Courting and Marrying* (Notre Dame, Ind.: University of Notre Dame Press, 2000), 215.

8. Stanley Rosen, *Plato's Symposium* (South Bend, Ind.: St. Augustine's Press, 1999), 139.

9. Plato, "Symposium," 192 a.

10. Plato, "Symposium," 192 b.

11. Plato, "Symposium," 191 d–e.

12. Alan Bloom, *Love and Friendship* (New York: Simon and Schuster, 1993), 478.

13. See William F. May's treatment of sex as divine, in his article, "Four Mischievous Theories of Sex," in *Wing to Wing, Oar to Oar*, ed. Kass and Kass.

14. Martha Nussbaum, *The Fragility of Goodness: Luck and Ethics in Greek Tragedy and Philosophy* (New York: Cambridge University Press, 1986), 172, 173.

15. David M. Buss, *The Evolution of Desire: Strategies of Human Mating,* rev. ed. (New York: Basic Books, 2003).

16. Is this perspective a "male" view, since men are said by some to be more attracted visually and quickly and women less visually and less quickly? If one understands "sexual attraction" as the desire for copulation, and if one believes that female and male sexuality manifests inherent differences, the objection is apt. On this view, relatively more men but relatively few women desire sexual intercourse simply on the basis of the physical attractiveness of a potential partner. However, if one understands "sexual attraction" as a positive response simply to another's physical appearance, then there would be virtual unanimity that both men and women make about the attractiveness of persons such as "he's handsome" or "she's quite attractive" after meeting them or merely seeing them suggests no important difference between the sexes. "Sexual attraction" understood as mere aesthetic judgment surely is common to both sexes in terms of immediacy, even if "sexual attraction" understood as desire for sexual intercourse is not common to both sexes with the same immediacy. So *eros* and physical attraction would seem to share in the possibility of arising at "first sight."

17. C. S. Lewis, "Eros," in *Wing to Wing, Oar to Oar,* ed. Kass and Kass, 289.

18. Bloom, *Love and Friendship,* 478.

19. Plato, "Symposium," 192 a–b.

20. See Bloom, *Love and Friendship,* 439, 442–43.

21. Though Platonic dialogues often have an ironic tone, the satirical possibilities are perhaps heightened in this speech by Aristophanes. In his comedy *Clouds,* Aristophanes depicted Socrates as pompous, absent-minded, and accident-prone. In *Clouds,* Socrates was one night "studying the course of the moon and its revolutions and was gazing open-mouthed at the heavens, a lizard crapped upon him from the top of the roof." One could read Aristophanes' speech in the *Symposium* as returning the favor of unflattering portrayal. Might Plato be putting this speech in the mouth of Aristophanes, certainly comical but perhaps also absurd, to illustrate not the truth of views held by Aristophanes but their foolishness? Is the true point of the story the very opposite of what appears at face value — that eros is best between a man and woman, that eros and procreation are not accidentally linked but ordered to one another? The complex relationship between the historical Socrates and the historical Aristophanes, as well as the Aristophanic Socrates and the Platonic Aristophanes, has been given scholarly attention by Leo Strauss, *Socrates and Aristophanes* (New York: Basic Books, 1966), 5, 8; Bloom, *Love and Friendship,* 478; Martha Nussbaum, "Aristophanes and Socrates on Learning Practical Wisdom," in *Aristophanes: Essays in Interpretation,* ed. Jeffrey Henderson (New York: Cambridge University Press, 1980), 43–97; and Rhodes, *Eros, Wisdom,* 242–64.

22. Plato, "Symposium," 192 d–e.

23. Rhodes, *Eros, Wisdom,* 271.

24. Bloom, *Love and Friendship,* 484–85.

25. For a different perspective on love and unity, not leading to dissimilar conclusions, see Thomas Aquinas, *Summa Theologiae,* I-II, 28, 1.

26. William F. May, "Four Mischievous Theories of Sex," 189.

27. Homer, *The Odyssey,* trans. Robert Fitzgerald (New York: Doubleday, 1963), 130.

28. Dante Alighieri, *The Divine Comedy: The Inferno/The Purgatorio/The Paradiso,* trans. John Ciardi (New York: New American Library, 2003), Canto 5.

29. Rosen, *Plato's Symposium,* 145.

30. Rosen, *Plato's Symposium,* 157.

31. Rosen, *Plato's Symposium,* 150.

Chapter 5 / Under Pressure, Cristina L. H. Traina

Earlier versions of portions of this paper were presented at Boston College in February 2004 and at the Common Ground initiative meeting held at Marymount University in Arlington, Virginia, in March 2004.

1. Pope John Paul II, *Veritatis Splendor,* paragraph 18. See also paragraph 19: "every believer is called to be a follower of Christ (cf. Acts 6:1)."

2. The limits of place and time do not include acceptance of unjust treatment. They do include circumstances. If I happen to be born in World War II France or contemporary Afghanistan, war will shape my vocation; if I happen to be born in a country where there is an epidemic, a famine, slavery, or a devastating earthquake, these too will shape my vocation.

3. Moral growth proceeds first from commitment to respect the commandments — "the absolutely essential ground in which the desire for perfection can take root and mature" — and then recognition that one wishes to go further, to take a step that "requires mature human freedom ('If you wish to be perfect') and God's gift of grace ('Come, follow me')" (*Veritatis Splendor* paragraph 17). Yet, "following Christ is thus the essential and primordial foundation of Christian morality: just as the people of Israel followed God who led them through the desert towards the Promised Land (cf. Exodus 13:21), so every disciple must follow Jesus, towards whom he is drawn by the Father himself (cf. John 6:44)" (*Veritatis Splendor* paragraph 19). Developmentally, one must begin with the commandments rather than the desire for radical discipleship, but paradoxically it appears one cannot be Christian without this desire.

4. *Veritatis Splendor* paragraph 18, for example.

5. See Wanda Diefelt, "Beyond Compulsory Motherhood," in *Good Sex: Feminist Perspectives from the World's Religions,* ed. Patricia Beattie Jung, Mary E. Hunt, and Radhika Balakrishnan (New Brunswick, N.J.: Rutgers University Press, 2001), 96–112.

6. On myths about sexual behavior in the twentieth century, see Stephanie Coontz, *The Way We Never Were: American Families and the Nostalgia Trap* (New York: Basic Books, 1992). Whether one agrees with Coontz's social and political agendas or not, her examination of actual sexual behavior is revealing.

7. See *Catechism of the Catholic Church,* paragraphs 362–65. *Familiaris consortio* affirms this claim explicitly and implicitly in paragraphs 11, 16, 19, and 32.

Persona humana (paragraphs 10–11) argues that because the body is the temple of the spirit, embodied sexual acts, far from "peripheral" to soul and heart, are intimately related to one's basic commitment to God.

8. St. Augustine of Hippo, *Concerning the City of God: Against the Pagans*, trans. Henry Bettenson, intro. John O'Meara (New York: Penguin, 1984), I.I.13.

9. St. Thomas Aquinas, *Summa Theologiae*, trans. The Fathers of the English Dominican Province (New York: Benziger Brothers, 1948; reprint, Westminster, Md.: Christian Classics, 1981), II-II q. 142.1.

10. See *Persona humana*, paragraph 1.

11. *Summa Theologiae* II-II q. 142.1.

12. See, among others, Congregation of the Doctrine of the Faith, *Considerations Regarding Proposals to Give Legal Recognition to Unions between Homosexual Persons* (2003), paragraph 3. See also Susan A. Ross, *Extravagant Affections: A Feminist Sacramental Theology* (New York: Continuum, 1998).

13. See *Gratissimam sane,* paragraph 12.

14. *Considerations*, paragraph 3. Catholic Christian teaching has at some times emphasized matrimony as a source of sanctifying grace and at others, the grace of forgiveness for sexual sins of the flesh. Current teaching emphasizes the strengthening of the couple and their individual growth in holiness. See *Familiaris consortio,* paragraphs 13, 56, 68, and *Considerations,* paragraph 2.

15. Suggestive in this way is Monika Hellwig's well-known book *The Eucharist and the Hunger of the World,* 2nd ed. revised and expanded (Lanham and Chicago: Sheed and Ward, 1992).

16. Most desire for physical affection is not reducible to genital desire, although in our culture, in which informal affectionate touch is rare, it is frequently read as sexual and may largely be met through sexual touch. With much of contemporary psychology, I contend that human beings have a great desire for affectionate touch that does not have its "finality" in reproductive coitus. This desire may be classed as a need, for failure to fulfill it leads to or exacerbates developmental problems, depression, stress, failure to thrive, poor sleep, increased levels of pain, and a number of other conditions contrary to biological, social, spiritual, and emotional health. See Cristina L. H. Traina, "Touch on Trial: Power and the Right to Physical Affection," *Journal of the Society of Christian Ethics* 25 (2005): 3–34.

17. In this essay, *sensuality* refers to desire for touch that is not explicitly sexual, and to its satisfaction. *Sacramental* refers to a quality of transcendence and openness to grace but may not involve *sacrament* in the formal sense.

18. For a useful comparison of contemporary secular and Christian traditional understandings of marriage, see Adrian Thatcher, *Marriage after Modernity: Christian Marriage in Postmodern Times* (Sheffield, U.K.: Sheffield Academic Publishers, 1999), chapter 2. The term "secular" is problematic, as there are no clear divisions between the dominant vision — which can be labeled "secular" because it does not refer explicitly to religion — and diverse religious views, which are tinged with the dominant view, coexist with it, and in a political sense shelter under it.

19. Clearly this is one point at which, in strongly patriarchal cultures, a woman's or young boy's "self" might need assertion.

20. See *Gratissimam sane,* paragraph 12. This qualification is necessary, as marriages outside the Church are still true marriages; see, for instance, *Familiaris consortio,* paragraph 13.

21. See The Pontifical Council for the Family, *The Family and Human Rights,* paragraphs 15, 16, 43.

22. *Gratissimam sane*, paragraph 9; *Donum vitae*'s condemnation of the view of children as "products" reinforces the caution against narcissism.

23. See *Persona humana,* paragraph 7 on many of these points. See also *Familiaris consortio,* paragraph 41 on hospitality, and *Gratissimam sane,* paragraphs 13–14 on selfish understandings of pleasure. Procreation is not essential to marriage, or infertile marriages would be invalid.

24. *Humanae vitae*, paragraph 17; see also *Gratissimam sane,* paragraph 13. See Adrian Thatcher's reference to Sally Cline, *Women, Celibacy and Passion* (London: André Deutsch, 1993), 27, in *Marriage after Modernity,* 178.

25. *Summa Theologiae* I-II, q. 94.2.

26. See *Summa Theologiae* II-II qq. 141.3–4.

27. In Thomas, continence, lust, and purity all refer to "venereal pleasures." See *Summa Theologiae* II-II qq. 155–56; 154; 151.4.

28. This section depends heavily on St. Thomas Aquinas, *Summa Theologiae* II.II qq. 141–70, with grateful appreciation for Diana Fritz Cates's clear and concise essay, "The Virtue of Temperance (IIa IIae, qq. 141–70)," in *The Ethics of Aquinas,* ed. Stephen J. Pope (Washington, D.C.: Georgetown University Press, 2002), 321–39.

29. Dan Brown, *The Da Vinci Code* (New York: Doubleday, 2003).

30. "Chastity includes an *apprenticeship in self-mastery* which is a training in human freedom. The alternative is clear: either man governs his passions and finds peace, or he lets himself be dominated by them and becomes unhappy" (*Catechism,* paragraph 2339). "The virtue of chastity comes under the cardinal virtue of *temperance,* which seeks to permeate the passions and appetites of the senses with reason" (*Catechism*, paragraph 2341).

31. Cates, "Virtue of Temperance," 325–27.

32. *Summa Theologiae* II-II q. 142.1 on insensibility.

33. Thomas points out that social and cultural customs often permit "a kiss, caress, or touch" to be carried out "without lustful pleasure" and that these are morally blameless but also apparently morally irrelevant. His only concern is that these actions may be taken for the purpose of lustful pleasure. See *Summa Theologiae* II-II qq. 151.4, 154.4.

34. For a review and theological treatment of the psychological literature, please see Traina, "Touch on Trial."

35. See, for example, *Persona humana,* paragraph 5.

36. *Catechism*, paragraph 2332. See also *Persona humana,* paragraph 1.

37. Karol Wojtyla, *Love and Responsibility,* trans. H. T. Willetts (New York: Farrar, Straus, and Giroux, 1981; first Polish edition, 1960), 109.

38. *Catechism,* paragraphs 2346, 2347. See also *Persona humana,* paragraph 12: "It is important in particular that everyone should have a high esteem for the virtue of chastity, its beauty and its power of attraction. This virtue increases the human

person's dignity and enables him to love truly, disinterestedly, unselfishly and with respect for others."

39. The terminology is still unclear. Vatican documents seem to imply a Freudian expansion of the ideas of chastity and sexuality to include the whole person, embracing an affectivity that is not genital or marital: sexuality and chastity comprehend more than sex. On the other hand, I have been attempting an arguably pre-modern distinction between sexual touch (perhaps meaning heterosexual intercourse, or perhaps we mean orgasm) from sensuality generally: touch is a general category of which sex is the ecstatic and/or potentially procreative subset. Both statements make useful distinctions, but they imply a different use of terminology.

40. *Catechism*, paragraph 2348.

41. *Catechism*, paragraph 2343; see also *Familiaris consortio*, paragraph 34, and *Persona humana*, paragraph 12.

42. *Persona humana* suggests that adolescence is at least a partially excusing condition for masturbation (paragraph 9) and urges similar caution in judging homosexual acts (paragraph 8); paragraph 10 suggests that in cases of sexual sin a person often does not give full consent. In traditional theology, even when virtue is infused through grace, the acts of the virtues must be cultivated gradually. Finally, Thomas notes that intemperance—desire unrestrained by reason—is childish, another indication that temperance is a matter of maturity and training (*Summa Theologiae* II-II, q. 142.2).

43. *Catechism*, paragraph 2343.

44. *Familiaris consortio*, paragraph 85.

45. Wojtyla, *Love and Responsibility*, 215–16.

46. *Catechism*, paragraph 2340.

47. *Catechism*, paragraph 2344, italics removed.

48. See, e.g., *Summa Theologiae* II-II q. 153.2.

49. See, for example, *Humanae vitae*, paragraphs 9, 21; *Familiaris consortio*, paragraph 32; *Gratissimam sane*, paragraph 12. The question is how to preserve the symbolism of a single flesh without committing the heresy of implying a single will.

50. *Familiaris consortio*, paragraph 33.

51. For instance, if a woman's husband is not sufficiently virtuous to forego sex when she may be fertile, her obligations to existing children and to non-contraceptive sexuality may be mutually exclusive. For an arresting example, see Diefelt, "Beyond Compulsory Motherhood."

52. Wojtyla, *Love and Responsibility*, 233–34, 272–76.

53. *Gratissimam sane*, paragraph 12. On gender imbalance in pleasure, see among others Christine E. Gudorf, *Body, Sex, and Pleasure: Reconstructing Christian Sexual Ethics* (Cleveland: The Pilgrim Press, 1994); and Patricia Beattie Jung, "Sanctifying Women's Pleasure," in *Good Sex*, ed. Jung et al., 77–95.

54. See Cristina L. H. Traina, "Papal Ideals, Marital Realities: One View from the Ground," in *Sexual Diversity and Catholicism: Toward the Development of Moral Theology*, ed. Patricia Beattie Jung and Joseph Coray (Collegeville, Minn.: Liturgical Press, 2001), 269–88.

55. This is not a recent observation; see *Summa Theologiae* II-II q. 154.2 and 154.3.3.

56. See, for example, *Gratissimam sane,* paragraph 12. This is implicitly recognized in scholastic writings on sexuality, which often assume that men are the moral actors in rape, fornication, etc.

57. See, for example, *Familiaris consortio,* paragraph 6; *Gratissimam sane,* paragraph 13. For a powerful discussion of some of these forces, see David K. Shipler, *The Working Poor: Invisible in America* (New York: Knopf, 2004).

58. See, for example, *Familiaris consortio,* paragraph 85.

59. Christine E. Gudorf draws some of the same parallels between war and abortion; I am suggesting we apply them to sexuality. See "To Make a Seamless Garment, Use a Single Piece of Cloth," *Cross Currents* 34 (1984): 473–91. See also Mary E. Hunt, "Just Good Sex: Feminist Catholicism and Human Rights," in *Good Sex,* ed. Jung et al., 158–73. Some may disagree with some elements of her list of criteria, but a number should find wide consensus.

60. *Persona humana,* paragraph 9, explicitly cautions against this use of sociology. Certainly unreflective prescriptive use of sociology is irresponsible, but insofar as it helps us discover descriptively what makes for successful unions, it is of great value.

61. *Considerations,* paragraphs 5–8. See also *Gratissimam sane*, paragraphs 13–14, on the dangers of a pleasure-centered sexuality.

62. *Humanae vitae,* paragraph 11.

63. Wojtyla, *Love and Responsibility*, 229.

64. Father Patrick Brennan, sermon, Holy Family Church, Inverness, Ill., February 16, 2003; courtesy of Edward F. Koncel.

65. *Veritatis splendor*, paragraph 91.

66. In John Paul II's writings sexual sins are always sins against persons and against dignity. In addition, all acts of non-marital sex exploit women, even when those women also are at fault in some sense. On the latter, see Wojtyla, *Love and Responsibility*, 221.

Chapter 6 / Celibacy, John O'Malley, S.J.

1. For arguments favoring this opinion, see, e.g., Christian Cochini, *Apostolic Origins of Priestly Celibacy,* trans. Nelly Marans (San Francisco: Ignatius Press, 1990), and Stefan Head, *Celibacy in the Early Church: The Beginnings of a Discipline of Obligatory Continence for Clerics in East and West,* trans. Michael J. Miller (San Francisco: Ignatius Press, 2000).

2. See, e.g., Will Deming, *Paul on Marriage and Celibacy* (Cambridge: Cambridge University Press, 1995).

3. See "Damasus I," in *The Papacy: An Encyclopedia,* ed. Philippe Levillain, 3 vols. (New York: Routledge, 2001), 1:477.

4. See "Gregory I," in Levillain, *Papacy,* 2:639.

5. See "Hormisdas," in Levillain, *Papacy,* 2:736.

6. Johannes Dominicus Mansi, ed., *Sacrorum conciliorum nova et amplissima collectio,* 53 vols. in 60 (Florence: Expensis Antonii Zatta Veneti, 1758–98), 2:1101.

7. Mansi, *Conciliorum collectio,* 2:11.

8. Mansi, *Conciliorum collectio,* 3:192–93.

9. For the role of the popes all the way through the history of the issue, the best treatment is Georg Denzler, *Das Papsttum and der Amtszoelibat,* 2 vols. (Stuttgart: Anton Hiersemann, 1973–76).

10. Mansi, *Conciliorum collectio,* 6:439.

11. J.-P. Migne, *Patrilogiae cursus completus.... Series Latina,* 221 vols. (Paris: Migne, 1844–64), 54:1204: "Unde, et de carnali fiat spirituale coniugium, oportet eos nec dimittere uxores, et quasi non habeant sic habere, quo et salva sit caritas connubiorum et cesset opera nuptiarum."

12. These are the basic arguments given by Pope Damasus in a letter wrongly attributed in the *Patrilogia Latina* to Pope Siricius, Migne, *Patrilogia Latina,* 13: 1184–85.

13. The literature on the subject is immense. Basic, however, are two books: Uta-Renate Blumenthal, *The Investiture Controversy: Church and Monarchy from the Ninth to the Twelfth Century* (Philadelphia: University of Pennsylvania Press, 1988), and H. E. J. Cowdrey, *Pope Gregory VII, 1073–1085* (Oxford: Clarendon Press, 1998).

14. See, e.g., "Why Celibacy? Odo of Cluny and the Development of a New Sexual Morality," in *Medieval Purity and Piety: Essays on Medieval Clerical Celibacy and Religious Reform,* ed. Michael Frassetto (New York: Garland Publishing Company, 1998), 81–115. This volume of essays is the best treatment of the issue for this period.

15. Quoted in Brian Tierney, *The Crisis of Church and State, 1050–1300* (Englewood Cliffs, N.J.: Prentice-Hall, 1964), 32.

16. Peter Damian, "*De celibatu sacerdotum,*" in Migne, *Patrilogia Latina,* 145: 379–88.

17. See, e.g., Anne Barstow, "The Defense of Clerical Marriage in the Eleventh and Early Twelfth Centuries: The Norman Anonymous and His Contemporaries," Ph.D. diss., Columbia University, 1979.

18. Norman Tanner, ed., *Decrees of the Ecumenical Councils,* 2 vols. (Washington, D.C.: Georgetown University Press, 1990), 1:198.

19. See Denzler, *Papsttum,* 2:181–233, and Egidio Ferasin, *Matrimonio e celibato al concilio di Trento* (Rome: Lateranum, 1970). It is interesting to note how little attention is paid to the issue in the standard history of the council, Hubert Jedin, *Geschichte des Konzils von Trient,* 4 vols. in 5 (Freiburg, Germany: Herder, 1949–75).

20. "*Oratio habita ab oratore Illustrissimi Domni Alberti ducis Bavariae,*" in *Concilium Tridentinum,* 13 vols. in 14 (Freiburg, Germany: Herder, 1901–2001), 8:620–26.

21. "*Oratio,*" in *Concilium Tridentinum,* 8:621, my translation.

22. Tanner, *Decrees,* 2:755.

23. Tanner, *Decrees,* 2:755.

24. For Vatican II and its immediate aftermath, see Denzler, *Papsttum,* 2:290–370.

25. See Denzler, *Papsttum,* 2:238.

26. Tanner, *Decrees,* 2:1062.

Chapter 7 / The Perils of Celibacy, John Witte Jr.

1. The case is recounted in Theodore Muther, *Doctor Johann Apell: Ein Beitrag zur Geschichte der deutschen Jurisprudenz* (Köningsberg, Germany: Universitäts-Buch-und Steindruckerei, 1861), 14ff., 72ff. Excerpts from the pleadings and court records are included in *Politische Reichshandel: Das ist allerhand gemeine Acten Regimentssachen und weltlichen Discursen* (Frankfurt am Main, Germany: Johan Bringern, 1614), 785–95, and in Johann Apel, *Defensio Johannis Apelli ad Episcopum Herbipolensem pro svo conivgio* (Wittemberge, Germany, 1523). The quotes that follow in this section are from these two sources.

2. On the classic arguments for clerical celibacy, see discussion and sources in James A. Brundage, *Law, Sex, and Christian Society in Medieval Europe* (Chicago: University of Chicago Press, 1987); Roman Cholij, *Clerical Celibacy in East and West* (Leominster, U.K.: Fowler-Wright Books, 1989); Elizabeth L. Abbott, *A History of Celibacy* (Toronto: HarperCollins, 1999); Will Deming, *Paul on Marriage and Celibacy: The Hellinistic Background of 1 Corinthians 7* (Cambridge and New York: Cambridge University Press, 1995); Michael Frassetto, ed., *Medieval Purity and Piety: Essays on Medieval Clerical Celibacy and Religious Reform* (New York: Garland Publishing, 1998).

3. On the Lutheran position on celibacy and marriage, see the discussion and detailed sources in my *Law and Protestantism: The Legal Teachings of the Lutheran Reformation* (Cambridge and New York: Cambridge University Press, 2002); and *From Sacrament to Contract: Marriage, Religion, and Law in the Western Tradition* (Louisville: Westminster John Knox Press, 1997), 47ff.

4. *Luther's Works,* ed. and trans. Jaroslav Pelikan et al., 55 vols. (Philadelphia: Fortress Press, 1955–68), 54:31.

5. *Luther's Works,* 28:912, 27–31; *Luther's Works,* 45:18–22.

6. *Luther's Works,* 12:98.

7. *Luther's Works,* 45:47.

8. See Witte, *Law and Protestantism,* 87–117.

9. Quoted by Carter Lindberg, "The Future of a Tradition: Luther and the Family," in *All Theology Is Christology: Essays in Honor of David P. Scaer,* ed. Dean O. Wenthe (Fort Wayne, Ind.: Concordia Theological Seminary Press, 2000), 133, 141.

10. See David Blankenhorn, Don S. Browning, Mary Stewart van Leeuwen, eds., *Does Christianity Teach Male Headship? The Equal Regard Marriage and Its Critics* (Grand Rapids, Mich.: Wm. B. Eerdmans, 2004).

Chapter 8 / Monastic Perspectives on Celibacy, Columba Stewart, O.S.B.

1. Peter Brown, *The Body and Society: Men, Women, and Sexual Renunciation in Early Christianity* (New York: Columbia University Press, 1988).

2. Elizabeth Bryson Bongie, trans., *The Life and Regimen of the Blessed and Holy Syncletica* (Toronto: Peregrina Publishing Company, 1996).

3. Aegidius Bartscherer, *Tyrocinium Religiosum: Or School of Religious Perfection,* 3rd ed., trans. Vincent Huber (Peru, Ill.: St. Bede Academy, 1940).

4. On this tradition, see Columba Stewart, "Evagrius Ponticus and the 'Eight Generic Logismoi,' " in *In the Garden of Evil: The Vices and Culture in the Middle Ages,* ed. Richard Newhauser (Toronto: Pontifical Institute of Medieval Studies, 2005), 3–34.

5. See Columba Stewart, chapter 4, "Flesh and Spirit, Continence and Chastity," in *Cassian the Monk* (New York: Oxford University Press, 1998), and Columba Stewart, "John Cassian's Schema of Eight Principal Faults and His Debt to Origen and Evagrius," in *Jean Cassien entre Orient et Occident,* ed. Cristian Badilita (Paris: Beauchesne, 2003), 1–15.

6. See Columba Stewart, "The Desert Fathers on Radical Honesty about the Self," *Sobornost* 12 (1990): 25–39, 131–56; republished in *Vox Benedictina* 8 (1991): 7–53 and *A.I.M. Monastic Bulletin* 63–64 (1997–98).

7. See Michael Casey, *A Guide to Living in the Truth: Saint Benedict's Teaching on Humility* (Liguori, Mo.: Liguori Triumph Books, 2001).

Chapter 9 / Celibacy under the Sign of the Cross, Margaret A. Farley

1. Sandra M. Schneiders, *Religious Life in a New Millennium,* 2 vols. (New York: Paulist Press, 2000–2001), and *New Wineskins: Re-imagining Religious Life Today* (New York: Paulist Press, 1986); Peter Brown, *The Body and Society: Men, Women, and Sexual Renunciation in Early Christianity* (New York: Columbia University Press, 1988); Jo Ann McNamara, *Sisters in Arms: Catholic Nuns through Two Millennia* (Cambridge, Mass.: Harvard University Press, 1996), and *A New Song: Celibate Women in the First Three Christian Centuries* (New York: Haworth Press, 1983).

2. Other useful studies are included in Peter Brooks, ed., *Christian Spirituality* (London: SCM Press Ltd., 1975); Elizabeth Abbott, *A History of Celibacy* (Toronto: HarperCollins, 1999); Elizabeth Castelli, "Virginity and Its Meaning for Women's Sexuality in Early Christianity," *Journal of Feminist Studies in Religion* 2 (Spring 1986): 61–88; Ross S. Kraemer, ed., *Maenads, Martyrs, Matrons, Monastics: A Sourcebook on Women's Religions in the Greco-Roman World* (Philadelphia: Fortress Press, 1988).

3. See also Karl Rahner, "On the Evangelical Counsels," in *Theological Investigations,* vol. 8, trans. David Bourke (New York: Herder and Herder, 1971); Edward Vacek, "Religious Life and the Eclipse of Love for God," in *Review for Religious* 57 (March–April 1998): 118–37. While many other important works are available, these (along with Schneiders) address issues that are of great importance to the position I myself will argue.

4. I am not distinguishing "celibacy" here from its sometime term, "virginity." The two terms can have different connotations, with sometimes differently gendered meanings. I am also not going to distinguish celibacy from "chastity," or from "continence," though there are more important reasons for doing this (not the least of which is that "chastity" has been used traditionally to refer to marital chastity as well as the vow of chastity in the traditions of religious communities). For careful

delineations of the terms, see Sandra M. Schneiders, *Selling All,* vol. 2 of *Religious Life in a New Millennium* (New York: Paulist Press, 2001), 120–24.

5. I do not claim that Brown draws these conclusions, but only that his (and others') studies lead to them.

6. For general background on the history of sexual ethics, see Margaret A. Farley, "Sexual Ethics," *Encyclopedia of Bioethics,* vol. 5, rev. ed., ed. Warren Reich (New York: Simon and Schuster Macmillan, 1995), 2363–75.

7. Key primary texts for Augustine's view of sexuality include: *On the Goodness of Marriage* (401 C.E.); *On Holy Virginity* (401 C.E.); *A Literal Commentary on Genesis* (401–14 C.E.); *On Marriage and Concupiscence* (419–21 C.E.).

8. Rowan A. Greer, *Broken Lights and Mended Lives: Theology and Common Life in the Early Church* (University Park: University of Pennsylvania Press, 1986), esp. 77–100.

9. Brown, *Body and Society,* 191.

10. Augustine, for example, insisted many times that the disobedient or unfaithful virgin was not to be considered as holy as the faithful wife. One's "state of life" did not guarantee one's achievement of its goals.

11. Relevant writings of Martin Luther include: *Two Kinds of Righteousness* (1519); *Sermon on the Estate of Marriage* (1519); *Treatise on Good Works* (1520); *Estate of Marriage* (1522); *How God Rescued an Honorable Nun* (1524); *On Marriage Matters* (1530).

12. Calvin, unlike Luther, maintained the importance of growth in the Christian life, or what he called "sanctification." See John Calvin, *Institutes of the Christian Religion* III.3–10.

13. There is an important story here that is relevant to gendered perceptions of sexuality — the story of the multiplication of rules for enclosure of women celibates (as distinguished from the much fewer rules for the enclosure of men). The presupposition was not that women were more likely to break their vows of celibacy because of their stronger sexual drive, but that men needed to be protected from contact with women so that men could be helped in controlling their sexual desires.

14. It should be noted, in addition, that psychoanalytic theories — however controversial and changing — do not challenge a view of sex as an indomitable drive, but they have yielded the widely accepted belief that this is simply part of human nature. More than this, some theorists no longer see sex as the fundamental basis for all motivation (since it has become more obvious that there can be multiple motivations for sex). The point is that no overly simplified theory of sexuality can serve to bless celibacy (or, for that matter, to condemn it).

15. For an overall view of this development, see Margaret A. Farley, "Family," in *The New Dictionary of Catholic Social Thought,* ed. J. Dwyer (Collegeville, Minn.: Liturgical Press, 1994), 371–81; "The Church and the Family: An Ethical Task," *Horizons* 10 (Spring 1983): 50–71. For specific documentation of these and other texts, see, e.g., *Gaudium et spes* 52; *Apostolicam actuositatem* 11; *Familiaris consortio* 16; etc.

16. For an overview of some of these arguments, see David Hollenbach, *The Right to Procreate and Its Social Limitations: A Systematic Study of Value Conflict in Roman Catholic Ethics* (Ph.D. diss., Yale University, 1975).

17. One should note, however, that church leaders are still quite capable of ranking celibacy over marriage in terms of the "superiority of this charism to that of marriage, by reason of the wholly singular link which it has with the kingdom of God." *Familiaris consortio,* 16. The issue is whether or not this remains a supportable claim.

18. See, above all, Karl Rahner's many essays in this regard and his *Foundations of Christian Faith,* trans. W. V. Dych (New York: The Seabury Press, 1978), esp. Part III.

19. Thomas Aquinas, *Summa Theologiae* II-II.184.3.

20. *Lumen Gentium* 5 paragraphs 39–42, 6 paragraphs 43–47.

21. See Karl Rahner, "On the Evangelical Counsels," in *Theological Investigations,* vol. 8, trans. David Bourke (New York: Herder and Herder, 1971), 142.

22. Georges Bernanos, *Diary of a Country Priest* (New York: The Limited Editions, 1986).

23. See Michel Foucault, *The History of Sexuality,* 3 vols. (French ed., Paris: Editions Gallimard, 1976–94).

24. With widespread practices of genocide, and with new threats of plague-proportion disease, there may emerge different needs regarding population growth. But even with this possibility, celibacy may have a lot to contribute as an alternative way of rearing, if not bearing, children.

25. Rahner, "On the Evangelical Counsels," 148.

26. Martin Buber, *I and Thou* (Edinburgh: T & T Clark, 1959).

Chapter 10 / Homosexuality and the Church, Christopher Wolfe

1. On typical characteristics of young people with gender identity disorder, based on clinical experience, see George Rekers, *Handbook of Child and Adolescent Sexual Problems* (New York: Lexington Books, 1995).

2. Richard Isay, *Being Homosexual: Gay Men and Their Development* (New York: Farrar, Straus, Giroux, 1989).

3. David Wagner, "The Homosexual Movement in Churches, Schools, and Libraries," in *Same-Sex Matters: The Challenge of Homosexuality,* ed. Christopher Wolfe (Dallas: Spence Publishing Co., 2000).

4. See Christopher West, *The Theology of the Body Explained: A Commentary on John Paul II's "Gospel of the Body"* (Boston: Pauline Books and Media, 2003).

5. That teaching is contained especially in Part Three, Section Two, Chapter One, Article 6, I to III (paragraphs 2331–79) of the *Catechism of the Catholic Church.*

6. One example is lesbian activity that is undertaken, not in response to unchosen same-sex attractions, but as a kind of logical conclusion from some forms of radical feminist ideology.

7. See Jeffrey Satinover, "The Biology of Homosexuality: Science or Politics," in *Homosexuality and American Public Life,* ed. Christopher Wolfe (Dallas: Spence Publishing Co., 1999).

8. Satinover, "The Biology of Homosexuality."

9. For examples, see *Homosexuality and American Public Life,* ed. Christopher Wolfe, chapter 2, "The Development of a Homosexual Orientation," by George Rekers; chapter 3, "The Origins and Therapy of Same-Sex Attraction Disorder," by Richard Fitzgibbons (a counselor who began in anger-management, and found that anger disorders were frequently related to relationships with clients' fathers, and often associated with homosexuality); and chapter 4, "The Gay Deception," by Joseph Nicolosi (founder and president of the National Association for Research and Therapy of Homosexuality, with years of clinical experience helping homosexuals work through the underlying causes of their condition). See also Gerald van den Aardweg, a Dutch psychologist and author of *On the Origins and Treatment of Homosexuality* (New York: Praeger, 1985), and Elizabeth Moberly, *Homosexuality: A New Christian Ethics* (Cambridge, U.K.: James Clarke and Co., 1983).

10. Note that I am not saying here that some sort of statistical patterns of regular behavior in "nature" constitute the basis of what the "natural law" is. (It is virtually a part of nature — something that happens with a certain statistical regularity — that sometimes unnatural things happen, such as birth defects and physical deformities.) The "nature" in "natural law" has to do with intrinsic human ends or purposes, and what is necessary to fulfill them.

11. For an instructive discussion of the importance of the fact that human beings are animals, see Patrick Lee, "Human Beings Are Animals," in *Natural Law and Moral Inquiry,* ed. Robert P. George (Washington, D.C.: Georgetown University Press, 1998).

12. On lesbianism (an understudied topic), see Elaine Siegel, *Female Homosexuality: Choice without Volition: A Psychoanalytic Study* (Hillsdale, N.J.: Analytic Press, 1988); Anne Paulk, *Restoring Sexual Identity: Hope for Women Who Struggle with Same-Sex Attraction* (Eugene, Ore.: Harvest House Publishers, 2003); Jane Boyer, "Freed from Lesbianism," in *Same-Sex Matters;* and chapter 10 of John F. Harvey, O.S.F.S., *The Truth about Homosexuality: The Cry of the Faithful* (Fort Collins, Colo.: Ignatius Press, 1996).

13. A useful account of these events can be found in Charles W. Socarides, *Homosexuality: A Freedom Too Far* (Phoenix, Ariz.: Adam Margrave Books, 1995). Socarides also recommends Ronald Bayer, *Homosexuality and American Psychiatry* (Princeton, N.J.: Princeton University Press, 1987).

14. See, for example, the discussion in Cormac Burke, "Does Homosexuality Nullify a Marriage? Canon Law and Recent Developments in Psychology and Psychiatry," in *Same-Sex Attraction: A Parent's Guide,* ed. John F. Harvey and Gerard V. Bradley (South Bend, Ind.: St. Augustine's Press, 2003), especially 34–42.

15. On the commitment of intellectuals to "expressive individualism," see Robert Lerner, Althea K. Nagai, and Stanley Rothman, *American Elites* (New Haven, Conn.: Yale University Press, 1996).

16. One important point to keep in mind is that sexual feelings are not always unambiguous. There are some people who are clearly heterosexual, but may have experienced some same-sex attraction (or even experimented briefly with same-sex activity) at some earlier time in their lives. Some of those who seek to change their sexual orientation through reparative therapy, and have considerable success in doing so — to the point where heterosexual activity in marriage is deeply satisfactory to

them — may never completely shake off occasional homosexual fantasies or temptations. This is a sign, not of "failure," but of the fact that "success" is always an ongoing effort, even when such efforts are amply rewarded.

17. See Harvey, *The Truth about Homosexuality*, especially chapters 4 and 5.

18. The study appears in the *Archives of Sexual Behavior* 32, no. 5 (October 2003): 403–17.

19. For example, Richard Fitzgibbons emphasizes the importance of understanding the "wounds" underlying homosexuality, and also the importance of forgiveness as a way of healing them. See Fitzgibbons, *Homosexuality and American Public Life,* chapter 3.

20. See, for example, Stephen Macedo's utilization of this argument in his defense of homosexual acts in the "Homosexuality and the Conservative Mind," *Georgetown Law Journal* 84, no. 2 (1995): 261–300.

21. For further discussion of this and related issues, see John Finnis, "The Good of Marriage and the Morality of Sexual Relations: Some Philosophical and Historical Observations," and Patrick Lee and Robert George, "What Sex Can Be: Self-Alienation, Illusion, or One-Flesh Union," both in *American Journal of Jurisprudence* 42 (1997).

22. For a survey of health problems resulting from homosexual activity, see Jeffrey Satinover, *Homosexuality and the Politics of Truth* (Grand Rapids, Mich.: Baker Books, 1996), especially chapter 3; the studies cited in footnotes of "The Negative Health Effects of Homosexuality," *Insight* 232 (Washington, D.C.: Family Research Council, 2001); and John R. Diggs Jr., "The Health Risks of Gay Sex," *www.corporateresourcecouncil.org/white_papers/Health_Risks.pdf.* These health problems include mental health problems as well as physical ones (e.g., depression, suicidal tendencies, addictions).

23. The best known, but more controversial, study is Paul Cameron et al., "The Longevity of Homosexuals: Before and After the AIDS Epidemic," *Omega: Journal of Death and Dying* 29 (1994): 249, which suggests a heterosexual male/homosexual male differential life span of three decades. The conclusions of that study received qualified support from another (less controversial) study that estimates life expectancy for gay males is from eighth to twenty years less than for all men. See Robert S. Hogg et al., "Modeling the Impact of HIV Disease on Mortality in Gay and Bisexual Men," *International Journal of Epidemiology* 26 (1997): 657.

24. Alan P. Bell and Martin S. Weinberg, *Homosexualities: A Study of Diversity among Men and Women* (New York: Simon and Schuster, 1978), 336.

Gay advocates sometimes claim that promiscuity (as well as other homosexual conduct or problems) is the result of the absence of marriage as a legitimate option for homosexuals, but that is unfounded speculation. A similar argument regarding higher rates of mental illness among homosexuals (i.e., that this finding was due to stigma and victimization of homosexuals) has been debunked by the studies showing that such rates continue to be higher in gay-friendly societies like the Netherlands. See T. G. Sandfort et al., "Same-sex Sexual Behavior and Psychiatric Disorders: Findings from the Netherlands Mental Health Survey and Incidence Study (NEMESIS)," *Archives of General Psychiatry* 58, no. 1 (2001): 85–91.

Another piece of evidence casting doubt on the claim that gay marriage will eliminate homosexual promiscuity is the willingness of even relatively moderate gay activists, such as Andrew Sullivan, to promote a view of marriage that tolerates extra-marital sexual activity. Indeed, this tolerance is one of the things he suggests heterosexuals can "learn" from homosexuals. See Wolfe, *Same-Sex Matters,* 21–22.

Finally, the description of actually existing gay sexual culture in Gabriel Rotello's *Sexual Ecology* (New York: Dutton, 1997) — despite his call for greater moderation in gay sexual practices — suggests that promiscuity among homosexuals is not just an incidental characteristic of certain homosexuals.

25. John Paul II, *Salvifici Doloris: On the Christian Meaning of Human Suffering* (1984).

Chapter 11 / Following the Still Small Voice, James Alison

1. I do not know how widespread this is as a genuinely Reformed position. However, this is how Trent depicted the Reformed position. My purpose in adducing it here is to show that, whether or not the position has ever been held by heirs of the Reformation, it is certainly not one that can coherently be held by Catholics.

2. The Catholic and the Reformed positions are identical in recognizing the completely free and gratuitous initiative of God who saves. The difference between them is an anthropological one concerning who we are who are being saved and what that salvation looks like as a human process over time.

3. See, for instance, Exodus 22:28 and the different reactions to it at Jeremiah 19:5–6 and Ezekiel 20:25–26.

4. The Congregation for the Doctrine of Faith, *Homosexualitatis Problema* (Vatican City, October 1, 1986), paragraph 3.

5. See, among other places, but here particularly poignantly, Romans 2:1.

6. Mark 13:31.

Chapter 12 / Descriptions and Prescriptions, Stephen J. Pope

1. The distinction between descriptions and prescriptions was made an important part of moral philosophy by R. M. Hare, *Reason and Freedom* (New York: Oxford University Press, 1963).

2. See "Fidelity Crisis," *Boston College Magazine,* April 2003, themes recently developed in *The Courage to Be Catholic: Crisis, Reform and the Future of the Church* (New York: Basic Books, 2003) and his biography of John Paul II, *Witness to Hope* (San Francisco: HarperCollins, 1999).

3. Weigel, *The Courage to Be Catholic.*

4. Canon 277.

5. Author of *Sexual Morality: A Catholic Perspective* (New York: Paulist Press, 1977). Archbishop Hunthausen of Seattle removed the imprimatur from this book at the request of Cardinal Ratzinger.

6. "Church attitudes were also conditioned by demographic changes within the priesthood, which suffered an alarming decline in numbers from 1968 onward. . . . In consequence, clergy and seminarians were a scarce commodity whose careers should not be lightly jeopardized. For that reason, dioceses granted a wider latitude in

accepting ordinands of suspected homosexual disposition, and were reluctant to take severe action against priests with a sexual predilection for minors. Clerical authorities were predisposed to place their hopes in the efficacy of treatment and therapy rather than punitive measures." *Pedophiles and Priests: Anatomy of a Contemporary Crisis* (New York: Oxford University Press, 1996), 92.

7. This is seen, for example, in the recent Vatican symposium on sexual abuse that featured eight internationally renown psychiatric and medical experts on the topic, including Dr. Martin P. Kafka, a professor of psychiatry at Harvard Medical School. See Cindy Wooden, "Dismissing All Abusive Priests Is Ineffective Strategy, Vatican Told," *Catholic News Service,* April 21, 2003.

8. According to Philip Jenkins, the archdiocese of Chicago in the 1960s and 1970s had on average, "two or three cases each year in which priests were accused of sexual misconduct with minors. The rate rose dramatically to seventeen complaints between 1986 and 1988, and to nineteen in the two years 1990–1991" (Jenkins, *Pedophiles and Priests,* 41). The archdiocese of Chicago instituted comprehensive changes in the fall of 1992, including "a pledge to remove forthwith any clergy accused of child abuse in order to prevent any potential harm to future victims... Where charges were substantiated, priests would in effect pay for the offense for the rest of their lives. There would be years of therapy and counseling, and after this: 'We recommend for each priest that has successfully completed the four year aftercare program: restricted ministry, a mandate restricting access to children, supervised residence, participation in a support group, assignment of a monitor or supervisor for life, and if indicated, ongoing therapy'" (Jenkins, *Pedophiles and Priests*, 49). The Chicago archdiocese also installed and gave important oversight responsibilities to an independent Fitness Review Board. See *www.archdiocese-chgo.org/other.shtm.* These norms pertained only to the archdiocese of Chicago. The bishops conference knew that sexual abuse was a problem by the late 1980s, especially after widespread publicity of the Fr. Gilbert Gauthe case, attention to which was brought by the "Doyle-Mouton Report." In 1992 the NCCB proposed five elements to be implemented in response to allegations of sexual abuse: (1) prompt response, (2) in cases of sufficient evidence, relieve the alleged offenders from ministry and refer him for appropriate medical evaluation, (3) comply with civil law regarding reporting of abuse, (4) reach out to victims, and (5) deal as openly as possible with the members of the community. These provisions were voluntary. Timothy Radcliffe, O.P., also attributes the relatively low incidence of sexually abusive clergy in the United Kingdom to the timely implementation by the Archbishop of Westminster of a predominantly lay independent review team charged with examining accusations of clerical sexual abuse.

9. This notion was employed by Augustine in *De Bono Conjugali*, *On the Good of Marriage,* 3: "Marriages have this good also, that carnal or youthful incontinence, although it be faulty, is brought unto an honest use in the begetting of children, in order that out of the evil of lust the marriage union may bring to pass some good. Next, in that the lust of the flesh is repressed, and rages in a way more modestly, being tempered by parental affection. For there is interposed a certain gravity of glowing pleasure, when in that wherein husband and wife cleave to one another, they have in mind that they be father and mother."

10. "If you do away with harlots," Augustine wrote, "the world will be convulsed with lust' " (Augustine, *De Ordine* 2, 4; Thomas Aquinas, *Summa Theologiae* II-II, 10, 11).

11. Witte, "The Perils of Celibacy: Clerical Marriage and the Protestant Reformation" in this volume, 118.

12. Witte, "The Perils of Celibacy," 119.

13. Cited in Michael Kramer, *New York Daily News,* March 24, 2002.

14. John J. Coughlin, O.F.M., "The Clergy Sexual Abuse Crisis and the Spirit of Canon Law" (paper presented at Boston College Law School, April 2003, publication forthcoming).

15. Cardinal Ratzinger proclaimed that, "less than 1 percent of priests are guilty of acts of this type" (i.e., the sexual abuse of minors) but it is unclear upon what studies he bases this generalization. See "Ratzinger sees media vendetta against Church," *Catholic News* (Australia), December 5, 2002. A 1992 study conducted by the Archdiocese of Chicago found that of 2,200 priests who had served in the past forty years, about 40 priests, or 1.8 percent of the total were probably guilty of at least one case of sexual misconduct with minors at some point in their careers and only one was guilty of pedophilia. This means that 98 percent of priests working in the archdiocese were not guilty of this behavior. The rate of pedophilia was of course even smaller. Philip Jenkins estimates that .3 percent of priests are pedophiles, a lower number than one finds among married men. It needs to be noted, however, that generalizations of this kind are speculative and not substantiated by detailed and comprehensive studies of this issue.

16. Augustine, *De Bono Conjugali,* 6. The lives of the saints testify that entering certain kinds of communities and social institutions can promote moral progress. In this sense, marriage certainly can, under the right circumstances and with the proper intentions, help people become better human beings. But viewing marriage (and family) as a "school of virtue" is different from viewing it as the crude and minimalist "remedy for lust." The history of spirituality is quite unbalanced in this regard in that it gives many more examples of this conversion taking place in the lives of those who embrace celibacy — St. Francis and St. Clare, Dorothy Day and Thomas Merton — than in those who enter into married life. The model of chaste celibacy is even applied to married partners, especially Mary and Joseph.

17. Thomas agreed with Luther about the remedial character of marriage" (the word "remedy" appears ten times in just one article, *Summa Theologiae,* III, 65, 1, of the *Supplementum*), but he also thought that it is much more than a mere "remedy." Each of the sacraments corresponds to a virtue, and marriage to the virtue of temperance (*Summa Theologiae Supplementum* III, 65, 1), and each provides a "remedy" against a certain kind of defect caused by sin. Baptism offers a remedy against the absence of spiritual life, the Eucharist for the soul's proneness to sin, etc. Matrimony functions as a remedy both for "concupiscence" in the individual and for the population decline that would otherwise result from the death of its members. So as to make this point particularly clear, Thomas reiterates: "There was need for a special sacrament to be applied as a remedy against venereal concupiscence: first because by this concupiscence, not only the person but also the nature is defiled:

secondly, by reason of its vehemence whereby it clouds the reason" (*Summa Theologiae Supplementum* III, 65, 1 ad 5). Because of the vehemence of sexual experience, special value lies in virginity, which the person is "unseared by the heat of concupiscence" and has an "integrity free of pollution" (*Summa Theologiae* II-II, 152, 1). Thomas held that virginity is superior to "conjugal continence" in part for Scriptural reasons — the example of Christ, the virginity of his mother, and the teaching of Paul in 1 Corinthians 7 — and on the grounds that the soul (the primary concern of the spiritual virgin) is superior to the body (the concern of the married), and the contemplative life, to which virginity is more suited, is superior to the active life.

18. *Gaudium et spes,* 49; see also Paul VI, *Humane vitae,* 8–9.

19. *Gaudium et spes,* 48, in Austin Flannery, O.P., Vatican Collection, vol. 1 (Northport, N.Y.: Costello Pub. Co., 1988), 951.

20. Walter Kasper, *Theology of Christian Marriage* (New York: Crossroad, 1983), 36.

21. This term is used of marriage in *Gaudium et spes,* 48. Marriage is used as a symbolic of the relation between Yahweh and Israel in Hosea 2, Isaiah 54:4–5, and Jeremiah 2:2, 3:20 and between Christ and the Church in Ephesians 5:21–33.

22. Accenting the positive theological significance of marriage also led the Fathers of the Council to emphasize that marriage is not simply a ritual in which two baptized individuals are legally tied to one another, but an act of worship and the union of two faithful Christians. See *Constitution on the Sacred Liturgy,* 59.

23. *The Catechism of the Catholic Church* teaches that the virtue of chastity involves "the successful integration of sexuality within the person and thus the inner unity of the human in his or her bodily and spiritual being. Sexuality . . . becomes personal and truly human when it is integrated into the relationship of one person to another, in the complete and lifelong mutual gift of a man and a woman. The virtue of chastity therefore involves the integrity of the person and the integrality of the gift" (*The Catechism of the Catholic Church,* 2337).

24. *Summa Theologiae* II-II, 155, 1.

25. Meara's emphasis accords with that of the National Federation of Catholic Youth Ministry, which has developed an extensive program entitled "Restoring Trust: A Youth Ministry Response to Sexual Abuse." See *www.nfcym.org/2001/restoring_trust/index.html.*

26. See Naomi M. Meara, "Rebuilding Community: Credibility, Sensitivity, and Hope," in this volume chapter 1, page 10.

Index

Also by Lisa Sowle Cahill

GENETICS, THEOLOGY, AND ETHICS

An Interdisciplinary Conversation

Research on embryos and stem cells, cloning and genetic enhancement dominates public debates about genetics. Many questions remain: Who will have access to potential benefits? How will the profit motive shape research? What can ethical theory contribute to the discussion? In *Genetics, Theology, and Ethics,* Americans, Europeans, and advocates from the developing world enter the conversation from a theological standpoint, offering provocative analyses on these and other major questions. Edited by Lisa Sowle Cahill.

0-8245-2269-9, paperback